D1602875

Michael
Oakeshott
on Religion,
Aesthetics,
and Politics

Eric Voegelin Institute Series in Political Philosophy:
Studies in Religion and Politics

Jesus and the Gospel Movement: Not Afraid to Be Partners, by William Thompson-
Uberuaga

The Religious Foundations of Francis Bacon's Thought, by Stephen A. McKnight

OTHER BOOKS IN THE ERIC VOEGELIN INSTITUTE
SERIES IN POLITICAL PHILOSOPHY SERIES

The American Way of Peace: An Interpretation, by Jan Prybyla

Art and Intellect in the Philosophy of Étienne Gilson, by Francesca Aran Murphy

Augustine and Politics as Longing in the World, by John von Heyking

Eros, Wisdom, and Silence: Plato's Erotic Dialogues, by James M. Rhodes

*Faith and Political Philosophy: The Correspondence between Leo Strauss and Eric
Voegelin, 1934–1964,* edited by Peter Emberley and Barry Cooper

A Government of Laws: Political Theory, Religion, and the American Founding, by Ellis
Sandoz

Hans Jonas: The Integrity of Thinking, by David J. Levy

Lonergan and the Philosophy of Historical Existence, by Thomas J. McPartland

The Narrow Path of Freedom and Other Essays, by Eugene Davidson

New Political Religions, or an Analysis of Modern Terrorism, by Barry Cooper

Robert B. Heilman and Eric Voegelin: A Friendship in Letters, 1944–1984, edited by
Charles R. Embry

*Transcendence and History: The Search for Ultimacy from Ancient Societies to Post-
modernity,* by Glenn Hughes

Voegelin, Schelling, and the Philosophy of Historical Existence, by Jerry Day

Michael Oakeshott on Religion, Aesthetics, and Politics

Elizabeth Campbell Corey

University of Missouri Press
Columbia and London

Library of Congress Cataloging-in-Publication Data

Corey, Elizabeth Campbell, 1972–
  Michael Oakeshott on religion, aesthetics, and politics /
Elizabeth Campbell Corey.
        p.   cm. — (Eric Voegelin Institute series in political
philosophy)
  Summary: "Argues that Oakeshott's views on aesthetics,
religion, and morality, which she places in the Augustinian
tradition, are intimately linked to a creative moral personality
that underlies his political theorizing. Also compares Oakeshott's
Rationalism to Voegelin's concept of Gnosticism and considers
both thinkers' treatment of Hobbes to delineate their philosophical differences"—Provided by publisher.
  Includes bibliographical references (p.   ) and index.
  ISBN-13: 978-0-8262-1640-3 (hard cover : alk. paper)
  1, Oakeshott, Michael Joseph, 1901–   2. Philosophy,
Modern—20th century. 3. Religion. 4. Aesthetics.
5. Political science—Philosophy. I. Title. II. Series.
  B1649.O344C67 2006
  192—dc22
                                            2006002465

∞ ™ This paper meets the requirements of the
American National Standard for Permanence of Paper
for Printed Library Materials, Z39.48, 1984.

Design: foleydesign
Typesetter: Crane Composition, Inc.
Printer and binder: Thomson-Shore, Inc.
Typeface: Bembo

The University of Missouri Press offers its grateful acknowledgment for a generous contribution
from the Eric Voegelin Institute and the Pierre F. and Enid Goodrich Foundation in support of
the publication of this volume.

TO DAVID AND BOB

Contents

Acknowledgments

It is a pleasure to be able to thank all those people without whom this book would not have been written. It was Bob McMahon who first introduced me to Oakeshott when he gave me the newly published essay "Religion and the World" during the summer before my senior year at Oberlin College. Years later we read *On Human Conduct* together, and I learned what it means to study and love a difficult work of philosophy.

I am grateful for the support of the three political theorists at Louisiana State University: my advisor, Ellis Sandoz; Cecil Eubanks; and Jim Stoner. LSU remains a hidden gem for those who desire a true liberal education and immersion in the history of political thought. There is little pretension in Baton Rouge: just abundant time to read, think, and converse. Oakeshott would surely approve. This book has grown out of my PhD dissertation there, which was supported by the Earhart Foundation.

My thanks also go to Timothy Fuller, whom I first met at a Liberty Fund conference for graduate students. I knew of him already, of course, as the editor of *Rationalism in Politics* and *Religion, Politics and the Moral Life*. He generously agreed to advise my work from afar. This, in combination with his insightful essays and articles, has helped to shape my views on Oakeshott's unusual approach to religion and aesthetics. I owe debts to Corey Abel, Eric Kos, and Glenn Worthington for providing me with copies of Oakeshott's early essays and notebooks.

I thank my parents, Bill and Helen Campbell, for their support of my various scholarly endeavors, and for their insistence that during my years at Oberlin I pursue not just music but liberal arts as well. Sometimes parents see things that the most determined teenager is unable to see for herself. And my most important debt is owed to my husband, David Corey, with whom I am happy to be continually *en voyage*.

Abbreviations

EM   *Experience and Its Modes.* Cambridge: Cambridge University Press, 1933.

HCA   *Hobbes on Civil Association.* Oxford: Basil Blackwell, 1975.

MPME   *Morality and Politics in Modern Europe.* Edited by S. R. Letwin. New Haven: Yale University Press, 1993.

OH   *On History and Other Essays.* Oxford: Basil Blackwell, 1983.

OHC   *On Human Conduct.* Oxford: Oxford University Press, 1975.

PFPS   *The Politics of Faith and the Politics of Scepticism.* Edited by Timothy Fuller. New Haven: Yale University Press, 1996.

RP   *Rationalism in Politics and Other Essays.* Edited by Timothy Fuller. Indianapolis: Liberty Press, 1991.

RPML   *Religion, Politics and the Moral Life.* Edited by Timothy Fuller. New Haven: Yale University Press, 1993.

SJ   "Shylock the Jew." *Caian* 30 (1921): 61–67.

SPDCE   *The Social and Political Doctrines of Contemporary Europe.* New York: Cambridge University Press, 1953.

VLL   *The Voice of Liberal Learning.* Edited by Timothy Fuller. New Haven: Yale University Press, 1989.

WIH   *What Is History? and Other Essays.* Edited by Luke O'Sullivan. Exeter: Imprint Academic, 2004.

WP   "Work and Play." *First Things* 54 (1995): 29–33.

*Michael
Oakeshott
on Religion,
Aesthetics,
and Politics*

1
Introduction

I tried research one summer. . . . A friend of mine, a boy from Pittsburgh named Harry Stern, and I read up the literature and presented the problem. . . . But then a peculiar thing happened. I became extraordinarily affected by the summer afternoons in the laboratory. The August sunlight came streaming in the great dusty fanlights and lay in yellow bars across the room. The old building ticked and creaked in the heat. Outside we could hear the cries of summer students playing touch football. In the course of an afternoon the yellow sunlight moved across old group pictures of the biology faculty. I became bewitched by the presence of the building; for minutes at a stretch I sat on the floor and watched the motes rise and fall in the sunlight. I called Harry's attention to the presence but he shrugged and went on with his work. He was absolutely unaffected by the singularities of time and place. His abode was everywhere. It was all the same to him whether he catheterized a pig at four o'clock in the afternoon in New Orleans or at midnight in Transylvania. He was actually like one of those scientists in the movies who don't care about anything but the problem in their heads—now here is a fellow who does have a "flair for research" and will be heard from. Yet I do not envy him. I would not change places with him if he discovered the cause and cure of cancer. For he is no more aware of the mystery which surrounds him than a fish is aware of the water it swims in.

WALKER PERCY, *THE MOVIEGOER*

We are apt to think of a civilization as something solid and external, but at bottom it is a collective dream. . . . And the substance of this dream is a myth, an imaginative interpretation of human existence, the perception (not the solution) of the mystery of human life.

OAKESHOTT, *HOBBES ON CIVIL ASSOCIATION*

For much of his career, Michael Oakeshott (1901–1990) was known as a political philosopher of a distinctly conservative stripe. Identified by journalists as an articulator of Margaret Thatcher's policies in the 1980s, Oakeshott was presumed by many to be yet another defender of Tory policies and of the status quo. The *New York Times* labeled him a "right-wing guru." Still others went so far as to imply that Oakeshott was a "crypto-fascist."[1]

In terms of philosophical labels, Oakeshott has been characterized as one of the last members of the tradition known as British Idealism. Following in the footsteps of F. H. Bradley and Bernard Bosanquet, Oakeshott is recognized for having written in 1933 a difficult and somewhat obscure book of philosophy, *Experience and Its Modes,* in which he set forth the idea that there are discrete "modes" of experience: science, history, and practice.

Still others recognize the Oakeshott of the 1940s and 1950s, author of *Rationalism in Politics* and proponent of "antique and irrelevant" ideas that fail to take account of the crisis of modernity. Some readers have taken Oakeshott's opposition to Rationalism as evidence of his aversion to rational thought, casting him as an opponent of the attempt to gain theoretical clarity about human conduct.[2] But perhaps most surprising of all is the recent appropriation of Oakeshott by postmodernists such as Richard Rorty, who applaud Oakeshott's "nonfoundational" political philosophy and see him as a fellow traveler.

Commentators thus offer multiple characterizations of Oakeshott: conservative, liberal, philosopher, opponent of Rationalism, postmodernist, polemicist, and skeptic. How, if at all, might these views be reconciled? Or, to pose a more fruitful question, which, if any among them, describe the true Oakeshott? Since several pairs of the characterizations above are exact opposites and thus impossible to reconcile, we might begin by noting that commentators writing on Oakeshott often reveal more about *themselves*—about the prejudices they bring to their subject—than about their subject. Nevertheless, Oakeshott's thought is extraordinarily hard to classify. He is conservative, but his conservatism is grounded neither in natural law nor in an appeal to history. He is a

1. Patrick Riley, "In Appreciation: Michael Oakeshott, Philosopher of Individuality," 649 (quoting from the *New York Times*), 664 (quoting Perry Anderson).
2. David Kettler, "The Cheerful Discourses of Michael Oakeshott," 489; Walter Berns, review of *Rationalism in Politics,* 671.

polemicist, critiquing numerous aspects of the modern world, and yet on the whole he is very much a *defender* of modernity from a philosophical standpoint.[3]

It is, I believe, taking the easy way out to argue that there are "multiple" Oakeshotts: early, middle, and late. The early Oakeshott, it could be argued, was concerned with religion, aesthetics, and Idealist philosophy, while in his middle phase he gave up these interests to write contentious analyses of modern political phenomena. Finally, the late Oakeshott returned to pure philosophy, producing his most systematic work in 1975, a series of three long essays on the character of human beings and political association entitled *On Human Conduct*. But this facile division of Oakeshott's life and work into "stages" merely dodges the question of how best to understand a thinker whose work covers subjects as diverse as religion, philosophy, politics, poetry, history, education, and horse racing.[4]

My thesis is that Oakeshott's output does represent (to borrow a phrase from Oakeshott's Idealist vocabulary) "a coherent whole." For as Oakeshott himself observes quite early in his career, "A man's greatest works . . . differ from his lesser works in degree and not in kind: they may be more perfect, but they express the same idea."[5] It is, of course, true that Oakeshott's thought changed and developed, and that what he wrote as a young man of twenty is not what he argued at seventy-five. Nevertheless, there is a certain moral vision, I want to contend, that lies at the core of Oakeshott's thinking. At this stage we must be content to describe it rather briefly as an essentially religious and aesthetic vision of the character of human beings, in which life is understood as something that ought to be enjoyed and cherished in the present moment, so far as it is possible. Oakeshott's writings are a continual protest against the modern call (now some five centuries old) for all activities and relationships to be put in the service of work, progress, and productivity. Oakeshott's exposition on man's "playful" character recalls other thinkers—such as Josef Pieper and Johan Huizinga—who recognize the vital importance of leisure as a means of facilitating contemplation and what might be called the "life of the spirit." Oakeshott most appreciated those activities

3. Efraim Podoksik makes this case in his recent book *In Defence of Modernity: Vision and Philosophy in Michael Oakeshott*.

4. Oakeshott coauthored a book with G. T. Griffith on the subject of horse racing entitled *A Guide to the Classics, or, How to Pick the Derby Winner*.

5. SJ, 62.

that may be engaged in for their own sake with little or no regard for what will follow. Love, friendship, and poetic contemplation are foremost among these. Like George Santayana, Oakeshott sometimes appears to envy the skylark, the acrobatic flyer who is seen spending "his whole strength on something ultimate and utterly useless, a momentary entrancing pleasure which (being useless and ultimate) is very like an act of worship or of sacrifice."[6]

I recognize, of course, that this view—that Oakeshott's moral vision is grounded in religion and aesthetics—will seem foreign to those who have read only his political works. But it has not gone unnoticed among Oakeshott's more sensitive interpreters. Patrick Riley, Timothy Fuller, and Glenn Worthington have all, in recent years, emphasized the degree to which Oakeshott's reflections on religion inform his view of politics and the human experience as a whole. Oakeshott's outlook "is suffused with a religious character that yields no easy doctrinal formulations," observes Fuller, and his interest in salvation "plays an integral role in his civil philosophy," contends Worthington.[7]

The challenge, therefore, is twofold. First, I must identify the precise nature of Oakeshott's nondoctrinal views on religion and aesthetics, initially by observing his intellectual debts (to Augustine, to the British Idealists, and so on) and then by setting out his own position as clearly as possible. Second, with this position in mind—namely, a moral vision that is informed by religion and aesthetics—I will turn to a consideration of its implications for his political philosophy. I take up the relationship between this moral vision and politics in Chapters 7 and 8. First, however, a discussion is in order about Oakeshott's lesser-known interests in religion and aesthetics.

Moral, Religious, and Aesthetic Questions

Oakeshott did not begin his career as a political philosopher. Indeed, a survey of his early output yields the conclusion that the young Oakeshott was not much interested in politics at all. With the exception of one recently published essay from 1924, he seems to have been preoccu-

6. George Santayana, *Soliloquies in England and Later Soliloquies,* 109.
7. Timothy Fuller, "The Work of Michael Oakeshott," 330; Glenn Worthington, "Michael Oakeshott and the City of God," 378.

pied with questions of a very different sort.[8] On the one hand he considered the nature of history and historiography, for history was his primary field of study while an undergraduate at Cambridge. On the other, he was concerned with questions of religion and aesthetics. Oakeshott penned numerous reviews of religious books that appeared in the *Journal of Theological Studies* and the *Cambridge Review* throughout the 1920s and early 1930s. He also wrote several short essays on religion and morality that were published only after his death in a volume entitled *Religion, Politics and the Moral Life.*

The point I wish to make here is a fundamental one: Oakeshott was concerned, first and foremost, with the moral question of what it is to be a human being. "I desired to know," he wrote in 1924, "what I ought to think about our life as human beings in society." And he observed in another early essay that the man who knows himself best holds "a position of great advantage in any attempt at the discovery of the truth about the universe." This was Oakeshott's starting point: he did not jump headlong into studies of constitutions and parliaments, but rather began by considering the character of human experience. This, of course, necessitated a study of social life, which he interpreted broadly to encompass religion, education, family, marriage, and friendship. The basis of all political theory, he maintained in an unpublished notebook on Plato's *Republic,* "must be sought in the individual consciousness. . . . The justification and nature of the State is in the need of man."[9]

Oakeshott insisted that ethical reflection must logically precede the study of politics. "We shall not go far wrong," he observed, "in starting with the individual and tracing the logical rise of the State from the necessities of his nature." And, in a striking anticipation of his later critique of behaviorism (which in 1924 could not really be said yet to exist), he argued that the raw material of political science "is to be found in the lives and experiences of a schoolmaster, a University teacher, a social worker, or a thoughtful man with many friends, rather than in those of a politician or a collector of statistics." All of this supports a relatively straightforward thesis, namely, that politics will necessarily be incomprehensible unless one has a firm grasp of the character of human beings as the "raw material" of politics. As late as 1975 Oakeshott reiterated this

8. "The Cambridge School of Political Science," in *WIH.*
9. Ibid., 4; "An Essay on the Relations of Philosophy, Poetry and Reality," in *WIH,* 68; Notebook 2/2 on Plato's *Republic,* 54.

view, noting in *On Human Conduct* that the character of a state depends on the character of its associates. A state whose associates embrace individuality will be quite different from one in which solidarity and conformity are prized.[10]

Understanding human beings was no easy task for Oakeshott, because he was not one to ascribe a universal "human nature" to the diverse lot of persons he observed around him. For what he found most remarkable about people was their ability to be morally creative and to envision alternatives for their lives that could never be predicted by an outsider— indeed, not even by a well-trained political scientist. Nevertheless, Oakeshott was compelled by the inquiry into what it is to be human, to conduct oneself as a moral agent, and also by the question of what might be said to offer the greatest happiness to human beings.

Oakeshott was thus particularly interested in religion and poetry, which he saw as types of experience that seemed to promise a special kind of fulfillment. Indeed, he went so far as to argue, in one early essay, that religion "completes" morality—that is, in religion all the deficiencies of ordinary morality are overcome. And while he later abandoned this Idealist language of completion, as well as the idea that the dissatisfaction inherent in moral activity can ever be transcended, he remained fascinated by the idea of a kind of experience that temporarily removes human beings from the "everydayness" of ordinary life. Thus as a young man he immersed himself in the literature of Christian mysticism and in the quasi-mystical meditations of such writers as W. R. Inge and Santayana.[11] Much later, in 1959, he identified poetic contemplation as an experience wherein one is able to transcend the limitations of practical life and exist wholly in the present moment.

Throughout this book I shall argue that comprehending Oakeshott's thought as a whole requires understanding his early preoccupation with moral, religious, and aesthetic questions. Indeed, fully appreciating the richness of his political writings depends on at least partially coming to terms with the moral vision that stands behind them, a moral vision that informed his thought on religion and aesthetics. There is much to support this view, not least Oakeshott's own declarations on the subject, such as, "[Political philosophy] must include the study of things which

10. Notebook 2/2 on Plato's *Republic,* 59, 61; see, for instance, *OHC,* 242.
11. "An Essay on the Relations," in *WIH,* 114–15.

give meaning and significance to the *mere* forms of government and the institutions of human society."[12]

There is another way of presenting this same point, one that I take directly from Oakeshott's reflections on Hobbes. In his famous "Introduction to *Leviathan*," Oakeshott observes that although philosophy may begin as the circumscribed consideration of a particular problem, it is by no means exhausted in the examination of particulars. Rather, philosophy must press on toward a reconciliation of the particular with the general, of the particular "text" with its "context." This enterprise assumes that all so-called discrete topics that may be examined philosophically are, in fact, part of a larger world of ideas. Therefore, "our political ideas and what may be called the rest of our ideas are not in fact two independent worlds." Although they may appear to be separate, "the *meaning* lies . . . in a unity in which the separate existence of text and context is resolved."[13]

The application of this metaphor to my work is obvious. If Oakeshott's political thought is the "text," I am concerned with relating text to "context," which is the whole of Oakeshott's thought, although here I am particularly interested in Oakeshott's moral theorizing and its relationship to religion and aesthetics. To neglect context is at least partially to misunderstand Oakeshott—or, indeed, any other serious thinker. Most of the commentators I quoted at the beginning of this introduction have done precisely this. Their interpretations of Oakeshott are partial, incomplete, and sometimes blatantly biased; for they have seen only the tiny island that protrudes above the ocean and do not realize that there is a mountain beneath it.

The Religious Character of Oakeshott's Thought

As I have already noted, the idea of Oakeshott as a religious thinker may seem counterintuitive to some readers, who are accustomed to thinking of him as an atheist or secularist. Oakeshott did not, after all, spend much time considering religion in his major published writings, and (let it be said at the outset) he showed few signs of orthodoxy. But to dismiss

---

12. "The Cambridge School," in *WIH*, 54 (emphasis added).
13. *HCA*, 4.

Oakeshott's thought on religion because he did not fit conventional notions of what it means to be religious is to make a serious mistake. It is
akin to discounting George Santayana's deep interest in the spiritual life
because he had misgivings about Catholicism. In fact, both Oakeshott
and Santayana were intensely interested in the "life of the spirit" and open
to the multiplicity of ways in which spirit might manifest itself. Both,
moreover, observed a close connection between poetry and religion.

In recent years these aspects of Oakeshott's thought have begun to re-
ceive more attention. As Ian Tregenza has observed, Oakeshott's "concern with Rationalism and the corruptions of practical life seem to
derive from an attitude to experience which could be termed religious."
Moreover, many interpretations of Oakeshott's work have fallen short
because they fail to appreciate "the essentially religious nature of his entire project." And Timothy Fuller makes a similar point, noting that there
is "an obvious connection between Oakeshott's religious view and his
analysis of politics." Readers who take the time to examine Oakeshott's
work as a whole, Fuller observes, will likely "see a connection between
his treatment of Christianity as a tradition—and thus not an 'ideology'—
and his rejection of 'rationalism' in politics."[14]

It is true, however, that Oakeshott's religious views are difficult to get
hold of, much less to arrange in categories that appear familiar. The fact
that Oakeshott is characterized (on the one hand) as an atheist or secularist and (on the other) as someone engaged in an "essentially religious"
undertaking bears witness to this difficulty. Part of this is no doubt due
to the fact that certain readers come to Oakeshott's work with a predisposition against unorthodox expressions of religion and even (I have
often observed) a predisposition against Oakeshott himself.

But another part of the difficulty surely relates to Oakeshott's own
reticence in expressing his views on religion. For while the young Oakeshott stepped bravely into the theological controversies current in Cambridge in the 1920s, he seems later to have recognized more fully "the
difficulty of saying anything of value on the most important questions."[15] After his 1933 publication of *Experience and Its Modes,* Oakeshott did not publish anything on the subject until *On Human Conduct* in
1975. And yet, in a letter to Patrick Riley shortly before his death, he

14. Ian Tregenza, *Michael Oakeshott on Hobbes,* 130, 10; Timothy Fuller, introduction to
RPML, 8, 15.
15. Fuller, introduction to *RPML,* 4.

wrote that he had "gone back" to reflection on religion and wished to "extend those brief pages in *On Human Conduct* into an essay . . . on religion, and particularly on the Christian religion." The desire to write such a work came to him as a result of having reread "all that St. Augustine wrote—St. Augustine and Montaigne, the two most remarkable men who have ever lived."[16] It is a great loss to all his readers that he could not undertake it.

Consequently, those who are interested in Oakeshott's views on religion possess no definitive statement but must gather up the hints he dropped and weave them into a coherent whole. Oakeshott discussed religion explicitly in only a handful of places: several early essays published in *Religion, Politics and the Moral Life,* a consideration of religion as part of "practice" in *Experience and Its Modes,* and another short discussion in *On Human Conduct.* However, if these are the only explicit treatments of the subject, it is fair to say that there are many more implicit references to religion. Indeed, I would go so far as to observe, with those I quoted above, that Oakeshott's work is suffused with a religious sensibility. This "sensibility" (to use one of Oakeshott's favorite words) manifests itself as a disposition to enjoy rather than exploit the created world. It appears in Oakeshott's willingness to suspend worry about the future and regret about the past in favor of living—faithfully—in the present. And it is present in his numerous warnings, in the tradition of Hobbes and Augustine, about the danger of excessive pride.

Oakeshott thus expressed his fundamental religious insights in many ways, but nowhere more clearly than in two separate essays entitled "The Tower of Babel." This biblical image captures the essence of human experience, man's tenuous position between beast and god and between pride and sensuality, "the too much and the too little."[17] The story, for Oakeshott, had significant moral and political implications. For the individual, it is a warning against investing oneself in projects that promise worldly salvation. It is a cautionary tale about the dangers of sensuality and materialism. And it is a condemnation of the prideful human propensity to believe that God may be outsmarted. For a society, the tale is a warning about the hazards inherent in the collective pursuit of perfection and an illustration of the irreparable damage that such a pursuit

16. Quoted in Riley, "Philosopher of Individuality," 664.
17. *HCA,* 163.

wreaks on civil society. I consider the implications of this story in greater
detail in Chapter 6.

Intimately related to this idea of the Tower of Babel as an emblem of
Oakeshott's religious ideas is what Fuller has called Oakeshott's "transposed Augustinianism." In *On Human Conduct* Oakeshott observes that
the appropriate image of a modern European state is expressed in the
phrase *civitas peregrina,* often translated as "resident strangers." The members of such a state do not see themselves as comrades engaged in a common, substantive enterprise, but as "wanderers" or "pilgrims" who travel
on diverse paths yet remain allied in their recognition of certain common conditions. Oakeshott takes this phrase directly from Augustine's
City of God, where in book 18 Augustine observes that a member of the
City of God must live in the world's city "as an alien sojourner."[18] The
challenge, for Oakeshott as for Augustine, was to live fully in the world
without becoming worldly—that is, to appreciate the beauty and goodness of creation while avoiding the corruption inherent in pursuing
worldly goods for their own sake.

No one would argue, of course, that Oakeshott took over Augustine's
framework without modification. And yet throughout Oakeshott's work
there runs a rich Augustinian vein, particularly insofar as he repeatedly
emphasizes the necessity of choosing between opposed alternatives: between "religion" and "the world," between "faith" and "skepticism," and
between "habitual" and "reflective" morality, to name only a few of his
dichotomies. Oakeshott did not think that human conduct might be artificially simplified into pairs of opposites, of which one must be chosen
once and for all. The choices necessarily blur into each other. But Oakeshott did believe that there are significantly different orientations available to human beings and that one's choices matter. He observed a
fundamental divide between alternative ways of viewing the human experience. On the one hand, life may be conceived as wholly "practical,"
that is, as an endless endeavor to satisfy desires. On the other, it may be
seen as an adventure, as something to be engaged in for its own sake and
enjoyed. If this does not exactly mirror Augustine's two cities, it is "nevertheless a comparable imagining of the fault lines of our existence."[19]

One additional point is worth mentioning with regard to Oakeshott's

18. Fuller, introduction to *RPML,* 11; Augustine, *City of God,* 761.
19. Timothy Fuller, "The Work of Michael Oakeshott," 330.

Augustinianism, namely, that his objections to certain defective under-standings of modern politics are strikingly similar to Augustine's cam-paign against Pelagius in the years of the early fifth century. Augustine famously chided the Pelagians for pridefully assuming that they could conquer human imperfection and become godlike. In the same way, Oakeshott berated Rationalists for their faulty assumption that human beings can impose perfection and uniformity upon their political arrange-ments. In *The Politics of Faith and the Politics of Scepticism* Oakeshott ex-plicitly stated that the modern politics of "faith" is Pelagian. He was profoundly skeptical of all governments that pursue perfection "as the crow flies."[20]

Oakeshott's Aesthetics

So far I have suggested that Oakeshott's conception of politics rests on a moral vision that is informed by religion and aesthetics. The first part of this vision should now be clear, if only in outline form. The moral life, according to Oakeshott's understanding, consists not in the construction of a Tower of Babel or in the single-minded pursuit of perfection, moral or otherwise. Rather, it is a graceful—indeed, religious—acceptance of human limitations and human possibilities. The principal limitations are man's tendencies toward pride and dissatisfaction, toward viewing the created world merely as material for his designs. The possibilities depend upon a clear-sighted assessment of one's situation and are most likely to be achieved by living in the present, enjoying what one has, and delight-ing in things such as love and friendship. In short, this moral vision re-jects the worldliness inherent in pursuing accomplishment and material goods, and strives to be "in" the world but not "of" it.

However, if it is difficult to interpret Oakeshott's religious views, it is even *more* difficult to tease out the meaning of his reflections on aesthet-ics. References to aesthetics are scattered throughout his corpus, but Oakeshott's definitive statement on the subject is his 1959 essay "The Voice of Poetry in the Conversation of Mankind." There is, in addition, one other early essay in which he addresses the nature of poetry and re-ligion, "An Essay on the Relations of Philosophy, Poetry and Reality,"

---

20. *PFPS,* 23; "The Tower of Babel," in *RP,* 466.

which was published (along with a number of other previously unpublished essays) only in 2004.

But "The Voice of Poetry" is an enigmatic essay, and the question of
why it appears in *Rationalism in Politics* has troubled readers for decades.
One early reviewer was puzzled about why a subject "so apparently eso-
teric in connection with the main theme" should have been made part
of a collection that ostensibly deals with political issues. Add to this the
fact that "The Voice of Poetry" is an exceedingly unusual account of aesthetic experience itself, and one is left with what seems to be a messy
and confusing problem. It is no wonder that few commentators have
been willing to grapple with the difficulties posed by this essay or to relate it to Oakeshott's larger corpus. It is, in the opinion of many readers,
an interesting but strange diversion from his political thought.[21]

I want to contend that this essay is not at all peripheral to his thought.
Far from being a diversion from the serious business of political philosophy, "The Voice of Poetry in the Conversation of Mankind" is vital to
understanding Oakeshott's moral vision, and consequently his political
vision. My argument, much abbreviated, is that aesthetic experience (or
"poetry," which is the same thing) stands as a model for the kind of
moral conduct Oakeshott finds most satisfactory. The best poets and
artists act creatively and spontaneously when they practice their art,
thinking not about the rules of poetic meter or how to blend colors but
only about conveying images. There is a natural "knowing how" that is
inherent to artistic creation, and this is what moral conduct may sometimes approximate. We share in this creativity at those times when we in-
stantly know how to act in a situation, looking neither for approval from
others nor to "principles" for reassurance.

Moreover, insofar as poetry (contemplation) is something that absolutely takes place in the present, looks for no consequences beyond itself, and promises the most complete enjoyment, it *is* fully satisfactory
experience. The images in aesthetic contemplation, contends Oakeshott,
have the appearance "of being both permanent and unique. Contemplation does not use, or use-up or wear-out its images, or induce change in

21. George E. Catlin, review of *Rationalism in Politics and Other Essays*, 259. The best recent treatment of this essay is Glenn Worthington, "The Voice of Poetry in Oakeshott's
Moral Philosophy." Robert Grant also considers Oakeshott's aesthetic theory in his book
Oakeshott. And W. H. Greenleaf addresses the topic in *Oakeshott's Philosophical Politics*. See
also Howard Davis, "Poetry and the Voice of Michael Oakeshott."

them: it rests in them, looking neither backwards nor forwards." Poetry, thus, is a kind of transcendence—a temporary transcendence, indeed, for the experience is fleeting. But it promises the kind of unity that all other experience can only approximate. "The eye of poetry," Oakeshott explains, "penetrates the husks and hangings which to our gaze surround the realities of life, seeking only that central, immanent beauty which is the life of all that the human eye can see or the human mind conceive."[22] Poetry seems to have appropriated all the characteristics of religion that Oakeshott described in his 1929 essay "Religion and the World."

This argument must be approached with caution, for I do not mean to imply that Oakeshott regarded *all* moral conduct as "aesthetic." Indeed, he was careful to separate out poetry as a distinct "mode" of experience, in the same way he separated out science, history, and practice. And a simple conflation of poetry and practice would be a mistake. Nevertheless, Oakeshott admitted that there are "connections" between poetry and moral conduct. He noted that human conduct has a markedly "poetic character" and observed that certain practical activities "intimate" contemplation, providing "a channel of common understanding . . . between the voices of poetry and practice."[23] Without relinquishing their modal independence, poetry and morality (practice) seem to have an important relationship.

If Oakeshott's conception of the moral life takes its bearings from religion and poetry, as I argue it does, then politics must also reflect this understanding. And it should be no surprise that Oakeshott favored a view of political activity in which individual agents are given the greatest possible latitude to act as they see fit. His mature expression of the kind of politics he applauded—civil association—is an understanding of governing in which human beings have the freedom to "enact" themselves as they desire, all the while observing certain agreed-upon conditions (law). This understanding of government is at the opposite pole from one that desires to control all aspects of the lives of its subjects: to construct, in effect, a Tower of Babel or to usher in "the New Jerusalem."[24]

---

22. "The Voice of Poetry in the Conversation of Mankind," in *RP,* 510; "An Essay on the Relations," in *WIH,* 92.
23. "The Tower of Babel," in *RP,* 485; "Voice of Poetry," in *RP,* 537–38.
24. *OHC,* 184.

Relating This Book to the Literature

It will be worthwhile at this point to take a step back from my argument to reflect for a moment on the place of this book in the recent literature on Oakeshott. Prior to the early 1990s, most studies of Oakeshott's work focused primarily on his character as a specifically "political" philosopher. Such is the approach of W. H. Greenleaf's *Oakeshott's Philosophical Politics* as well as Paul Franco's excellent book, *The Political Philosophy of Michael Oakeshott*. These books have become classics, and they are the essential points of departure for the student interested in examining Oakeshott's work in depth.

But in the nearly fifteen years since Oakeshott's death there has been a growing interest in examining his work in a broader context. As I have already noted, Oakeshott's strong interest in political philosophy emerged only in the 1930s and 1940s, when he established himself as a major interpreter of Hobbes. But before these years (and indeed after them as well) Oakeshott wrote many interesting essays that he did not publish. Since Oakeshott's papers are now available at the London School of Economics and Political Science Archives, scholars have begun to use (and to publish) many of his early works, which deal with such things as religion, history, and morality. It is becoming more and more apparent that Oakeshott's reflections on politics, as important as they are, arose not from a simple interest in current affairs, and *certainly* not from a partisan desire to defend a particular British prime minister and his or her policies. On the contrary, Oakeshott's concern with politics was profoundly philosophical. It was grounded in his desire to understand religion, morality, and—indeed—all things human.

One of the best and most exhaustive recent studies is Terry Nardin's 2001 book, entitled simply *The Philosophy of Michael Oakeshott*. Nardin is concerned with the entirety of Oakeshott's thought and presents his study as an attempt to move significantly beyond Oakeshott's concern with politics. The work as a whole aims to "enter broader debates about the character of human thought and action, the scope and limits of the human sciences, and the relationship of these sciences to other kinds of inquiry and understanding."[25] Paul Franco's *Michael Oakeshott: An Introduction,* published in 2004, is another work that places Oakeshott into a larger literary and philosophical context.

25. Terry Nardin, *The Philosophy of Michael Oakeshott,* 4.

Another commentator has written a series of provocative articles about Oakeshott's conception of religion. Glenn Worthington has considered several of Oakeshott's early essays on religion, noting their marked Augustinian flavor as well as their focus on living in the present. His latest article is a thoughtful consideration of "The Voice of Poetry in the Conversation of Mankind," in which he argues that Oakeshott's conception of aesthetics is ambiguous and contradictory but nonetheless vital to understanding his views on morality.[26] I consider his argument in detail in Chapter 5.

By far the most comprehensive new resources on Oakeshott are those being published in a monograph series by the British press Imprint Academic. Since 2003 four substantive volumes have so far been published in this series, each of which assesses Oakeshott's thought from a different perspective. Most helpful among these for my work have been Efraim Podoksik's *In Defence of Modernity* and Ian Tregenza's *Michael Oakeshott on Hobbes.* Podoksik engages in a substantive investigation of Oakeshott's aesthetics, and Tregenza provides a thoughtful consideration of his religious views. In addition, this series has produced a collection of previously unpublished essays from the archives in a volume entitled *What Is History? and Other Essays,* to which I have referred several times already.[27]

There are, of course, others who have long been aware of the wider context of Oakeshott's thought, and these include Kenneth Minogue (who was a colleague of Oakeshott's), Timothy Fuller, Josiah Lee Auspitz, Wendell John Coats Jr., Robert Grant, Glenn Worthington, and Noel O'Sullivan. All these commentators have significantly influenced my views about the breadth and depth of Oakeshott's thought, and I cite many of them throughout the chapters that follow. In a sense, my work might be characterized as following up the hints that they have provided, and bringing into clearer focus the "intimations" about religion and aesthetics that they and I have sensed in Oakeshott's writings. As Oakeshott himself observes, originality "does not lie so much in the promulgation of some absolutely new idea—for that were well nigh impossible—but in a certain independence and individuality of thought which makes old ideas our own."[28]

---

26. Glenn Worthington, "Poetry in Oakeshott's Moral Philosophy," 310. Worthington's articles on religion are "Michael Oakeshott and the City of God," "Oakeshott's Claims of Politics," and "Michael Oakeshott on Life: Waiting with Godot."

27. See Podoksik, *In Defence of Modernity,* 103–20, and Tregenza, *Michael Oakeshott on Hobbes,* chaps. 4–5.

28. "An Essay on the Relations," in *WIH,* 71.

If one can speak of a kind of scholarly momentum, then, such momentum appears to be building toward precisely what I have undertaken in this book. Prior to the early 1990s such a thesis would have been impossible, since the crucial early works were unavailable. Furthermore, although in recent years many scholars have begun to notice the aesthetic and religious elements in Oakeshott, no one has yet systematically considered these elements or related them to Oakeshott's more famous work on politics. The time is ripe for a careful consideration of these aspects of Oakeshott's thought.

However, any detailed examination of a particular thinker runs the risk of artificially separating that thinker from his intellectual context, perhaps (falsely) suggesting that his ideas developed in isolation from others. This, of course, is far from true for Oakeshott, who read widely and deeply in many academic and nonacademic genres. Some of the most important recent works on Oakeshott have attempted to place him into an appropriate intellectual context, although this is no easy task.[29] Nor is this the primary aim of my book, although I do note Oakeshott's strong affinities with certain aspects of Augustinianism and British Idealism. Nevertheless, there is one thinker with whom Oakeshott cries out to be compared, and this thinker is Eric Voegelin.

The reasons that such a comparison has not been undertaken are understandable, for the two thinkers approach political philosophy in markedly different ways. Voegelin explicitly addresses questions of transcendent experience, while Oakeshott is much more reticent in expressing his views on the subject, as I observe throughout this book. Voegelin is described as a "foundationalist" and Oakeshott an "antifoundationalist," Voegelin a "premodern" thinker and Oakeshott the quintessential "modern."[30] Nevertheless, no one, to my knowledge, has noted a particularly important *similarity* between the two thinkers, namely, what appears to be a fundamental equivalence in their thinking between the concepts of gnosticism and Rationalism. Only Ellis Sandoz, in *The Voegelinian Revolution,* has brought to light Oakeshott's review of *The New Science of Politics,* where he praises Voegelin's analysis of gnosticism as "powerful and vivid enough to make agreement or disagreement with even [the book's] main thesis relatively unimportant." And Oakeshott

---

29. I am thinking particularly of Wendell John Coats Jr., *Oakeshott and His Contemporaries,* and Podoksik, *In Defence of Modernity.*

30. Podoksik, *In Defence of Modernity,* 24. See also David Walsh's insightful comments in *The Growth of the Liberal Soul,* 56–65.

goes so far as to observe in his essay "Rationalism in Politics" that the Rationalist's "cast of mind is gnostic."[31] It is therefore worthwhile and enlightening to examine these two concepts—Rationalism and gnosticism—side by side, as I do in Chapter 9, and to consider whether they do in fact describe the same modern political phenomena. Such a comparison promises to illuminate both thinkers in turn.

Plan of the Work

In Chapter 2, I consider Oakeshott's relationship to Augustine and point out some of the fundamental similarities between the two thinkers. Building on the work of other commentators who have noted this affinity, I argue that Oakeshott reformulates the idea of a "choice" between two fundamentally different orientations (Augustine's idea of the two cities). Oakeshott makes this clearest in his 1929 essay "Religion and the World," where he sets out "worldly" and "religious" as two types of moral personality, but such dichotomies appear throughout his corpus in the various ideal types that represent possible alternatives for moral and political activity. I also argue in this chapter that the two thinkers have a fundamentally similar view of the human condition as well as of the character of human freedom.

Chapter 3 explores the idea of living one's life in the present, a theme that appears throughout Oakeshott's writings. It is something that Oakeshott calls "religious" in his early works, but that gradually comes to describe the aesthetic experience, most notably in his 1959 essay "The Voice of Poetry in the Conversation of Mankind." I place this idea within the context of Oakeshott's thought in his book *Experience and Its Modes* (1933), where he examines various ways (modes) of approaching human experience. The two modes I consider are practice and history, and I argue that the idea of "presentness" can be assimilated to neither of these. Nevertheless, something about this experience of living fully and intentionally in the present was of vital importance to Oakeshott. The ability to live without overemphasizing the importance of past or future events is a crucial part of the moral personality that Oakeshott valued, as I explain in Chapter 6.

---

31. Ellis Sandoz, *The Voegelinian Revolution,* 9; Oakeshott's full review appears in *WIH,* 229–33; "Rationalism in Politics," in *RP,* 6.

In Chapter 4, I examine Oakeshott's explicit discussion of religion, drawing on his early essays and book reviews, his treatment of religion in *Experience and Its Modes,* and his short reflection on religion in *On Human Conduct.* I approach these religious writings in two ways. First, I examine their intellectual and historical context. Thus I consider the British Idealist context in which Oakeshott came to maturity, noting particularly his debts to F. H. Bradley and Bernard Bosanquet on the question of religion. Then I describe Oakeshott's immersion during the 1920s and 1930s in the "English Modernist" movement, which emphasized immediate spiritual experience rather than reliance on creeds, dogma, and authority. Second, I address the less intellectual but more practical side of Oakeshott's thoughts on religion and follow him in his exploration of the human needs that religion addresses. He spells these out most clearly in a short treatment in *On Human Conduct.*

Chapter 5 is an investigation of Oakeshott's thought on aesthetics. I trace the development of this subject throughout his corpus, from his earliest essays through his definitive statement on the subject in "The Voice of Poetry in the Conversation of Mankind." I argue that one may observe a consistent development in his aesthetic theorizing and that in this development Oakeshott moves away from considering religion and poetry as fundamentally similar experiences. Instead, poetry (by which Oakeshott means all kinds of artistic activity, as well as contemplation) takes on a radically nonpurposive character in which it may be enjoyed entirely as an end in itself, with no thought for past or future. I argue that some such conception of experience also informs Oakeshott's views on morality.

In Chapter 6, I turn from aesthetics to morality, making the argument that there is a direct link between Oakeshott's reflections on religion and aesthetics, on the one hand, and his views of moral conduct, on the other. Oakeshott implies such a link when he observes that human conduct has a "poetic character." But commentators have been puzzled by such statements, for elsewhere he observes the intensely "practical" nature of moral conduct. In pursuing a string of endless satisfactions there would seem to be little that could be called poetic. But I argue that a certain kind of moral conduct does indeed satisfy the conditions that Oakeshott has elsewhere called religious and aesthetic. This is conduct that is undertaken in the present and as an end in itself. It is a kind of moral activity that looks not to usefulness, but to enjoyment. It is what I term "liberal" or "aesthetic" morality, as opposed to the "servile" morality that Oakeshott criticizes. In this chapter I consider his two Tower of Babel essays as well as his discussion of moral conduct in *On Human Conduct*.

Chapters 7 and 8 treat Oakeshott's political thought in light of the moral vision I have outlined in Chapter 6. In Chapter 7, I consider Oakeshott's critique of the politics of "faith" as well as his arguments against Rationalism. Both "faith" and Rationalism are examples of a faulty conception of morality in which ideals and rules take the place of personal, lived experience. And in Chapter 8, I examine Oakeshott's preferred conception of politics, in turn built on an understanding of morality that is grounded in his religious and aesthetic thought. I thus look at his treatments both of "skeptical politics" and of politics conceived as "civil association."

Chapter 9 is a comparison of Oakeshott and Voegelin. In this chapter I observe the striking similarities between their conceptions of Rationalism and gnosticism, investigating whether or not these may be conceived as fundamentally "equivalent" for the two men. In many ways these two concepts seem to spring from a common experience of the world, and yet Oakeshott and Voegelin approach certain thinkers in markedly different ways. I thus examine their respective treatments of Hobbes as a kind of "case study." I conclude the chapter by pointing out some of the fundamental philosophical differences between Oakeshott and Voegelin, as revealed by their different treatments of Hobbes.

Conclusion

Oakeshott is often seen as a polemicist and critic, as someone who expertly tears apart certain pathologies of modernity. He is criticized on this score for not offering an alternative, for demolishing the pretensions of Rationalism without putting anything else in its place. This criticism, however, is mistaken. Oakeshott's work does exhibit an alternative moral vision that is markedly different from the Rationalism and Pelagianism he observes running rampant in modern societies. His vision, however, is emphatically *not* "susceptible to propositions," because it is a poetic view, a religious view, and how can a poet or mystic explain his experience to someone who has not shared it? Nevertheless, the hints and suggestions that Oakeshott drops along the way are abundant, and it is the burden of the pages that follow to make his moral vision as clear as possible.

2

Oakeshott and Augustine
on the Human Condition

Those who study the work of Michael Oakeshott often observe his debt to important Western philosophers. Oakeshott's place as a British Idealist has been well documented. And Hobbes's influence upon Oakeshott's political ideas is still more widely recognized.[1] Oakeshott himself saw his work as part of a tradition stemming from Pascal and Montaigne, and throughout his corpus he refers often to Spinoza. But where exactly does he acknowledge his debt to Augustine?

To a casual reader the pairing of Oakeshott and Augustine might appear surprising. For Oakeshott wrote virtually nothing that explicitly considers Augustine's thought, nor can Oakeshott be counted as an orthodox Christian in the Augustinian tradition. Moreover, in his book *Experience and Its Modes* (1933) Oakeshott asserts unequivocally that all experience is mediated through the human mind and that there is no dualism between natural and supernatural experience. In his outright rejection of "another world," Oakeshott seems also to have rejected Augustine's doctrine of the two cities. So far, then, there would appear to be little common ground between the two thinkers. Oakeshott was not only a modern thinker, but also a *defender* of modernity.[2] On the other hand, Augustine was an ancient, "religious" thinker whose ideas are at a distant remove from our contemporary political situation.

But this would be a naive reading of both thinkers, for in crucial respects they are remarkably similar. Oakeshott's skepticism about the per-

---

1. See David Boucher, "The Creation of the Past: British Idealism and Michael Oakeshott's Philosophy of History." For the most recent treatments of Oakeshott's views on Hobbes, see Ian Tregenza, *Michael Oakeshott on Hobbes*, and Stephen Gerencser, *The Skeptic's Oakeshott*.

2. Efraim Podoksik makes this case in his recent book *In Defence of Modernity: Vision and Philosophy in Michael Oakeshott*.

fectibility of human beings and his quiet but insistent reminders of human fallibility distinctly echo Augustine's warnings about these same dangers. Oakeshott's arguments against Rationalism likewise recall Augustine's protests against gnosticism and Pelagianism, and indeed against all those who overreach themselves. And the two thinkers also saw politics in much the same way. The establishment of a stable order is a necessary precondition for human fulfillment, but government (or government-directed enterprise) can never provide what is ultimately satisfying for human beings. Placing one's hopes for salvation in worldly activity is *the* fundamental misunderstanding of the human condition.

And while Oakeshott did not write (or at least did not publish) extensive analyses of Augustine, he knew his work intimately and had worked through it in its entirety. In his later years Oakeshott told Patrick Riley that he had recently reread "all that St. Augustine wrote" and now wished to compose his own version of Anselm's *Cur deus homo.* As a young man, Oakeshott observed that Augustine's *Confessions* is perhaps the "finest expression of what God means to the soul to be found in all the literature of religion."[3] Much later, in *On Human Conduct,* he argued that a God who created self-determining, intelligent beings must be "an Augustinian god of majestic imagination" who had the nerve to create a universe "composed of self-employed adventure[r]s of unpredictable fancy," and to announce to human beings "some rules of conduct, and thus to acquire convives capable of 'answering back' in civil tones with whom to pass eternity in conversation." Oakeshott also thought that Augustine was one of only a very few thinkers who "succeeded brilliantly" in expressing the human experience of religion.[4]

As his early, unpublished writings have come to light in recent years it has become increasingly clear that Oakeshott was fundamentally concerned with questions of religion. In a very early work entitled "An Essay on the Relations of Philosophy, Poetry and Reality," Oakeshott acknowledges his immersion in the literature of Christian mysticism. In "Religion and the World," an essay that I shall consider below, he takes a markedly Augustinian approach in examining the character of "religion" and "worldliness." And Oakeshott's early debts to British Idealist religious thinkers—particularly to Bernard Bosanquet and F. H. Bradley—

3. Patrick Riley, "In Appreciation: Michael Oakeshott, Philosopher of Individuality," 664; "An Essay on the Relations of Philosophy, Poetry and Reality," in *WIH,* 68.
4. *OHC,* 324; Timothy Fuller, introduction to *RPML,* 4.

are striking. But most of these influences recede in importance as Oakeshott's thought matures. After the early 1930s we hear little about, for instance, the Idealist view of religion. Yet his sympathy with Augustine
seems only to increase; and revisiting his interest in theology as an old
man, it is to Augustine that Oakeshott turns.

This will come as no surprise to anyone who surveys the entirety of
Oakeshott's work. For throughout his corpus—from "Religion and the
World" in 1929 to *On Human Conduct* in 1975—Oakeshott is concerned
with a fundamental choice that must be made in human life. This choice
might be described as Augustinian, for it is the question of how to orient
oneself in the world. Oakeshott presents this choice in many different
ways over the course of his career. Sometimes, as in "Religion and the
World," it is presented as an explicitly moral decision that an individual
must make. More often, this choice appears in the contrasting ideal types
Oakeshott sets out as ways of thinking about moral and political life:
faith and skepticism, civil and enterprise association, individuality and
collectivism. All these expressions, however, point to the same fundamental division in human experience; all are markedly different and op-
positional ways of understanding oneself and one's place in the world.
One can either put one's hopes in worldly activity, viewing human activity and government as ways of achieving fulfillment, or one can reject
the idea that government or, for that matter, any kind of human achievement can ever offer the fulfillment desired. Oakeshott's own opinion on
the matter is clearly expressed in a verse from Samuel Johnson that he
quotes in an early notebook on Plato's *Republic:*

> How small, of all that human hearts endure,
> The part which laws or kings can cause or cure.[5]

Politics is a distinctly second-order activity for Oakeshott, though this is
not to say that it is unimportant. A properly ordered politics is a necessary prerequisite for the kind of fulfillment that can only be achieved
outside the political realm.

And yet neither Oakeshott nor Augustine suggests that the choice
about orientation is easy or that it may be definitively resolved. Human
beings are embodied creatures who live in a world that offers infinitely

5. Notebook 2/2 on Plato's *Republic,* 51.

diverse possibilities. There is no simple division between spiritual and material, for everyone must live "in the world." But it is possible to live *in* the world without being *of* it. George Santayana, a thinker who certainly appreciated such distinctions, observed that this kind of character "loves the earth, not the world."[6] Such a description aptly captures the spirit of Oakeshott and Augustine, both of whom were inclined to delight in the beauty they saw around them without becoming worldly. Both thinkers, in quite different ways, remained "otherworldly in the world."[7]

Perhaps the most vivid way of expressing this idea is to consider the image of the *civitas peregrina*. Oakeshott borrows this phrase from Augustine as a way of conveying his conception of human beings as "resident strangers"—people who take part in worldly affairs but simultaneously maintain a certain detachment from them. In the final section of *On Human Conduct* Oakeshott makes a case that his preferred understanding of human association (civil association, or *societas*) is a reflection of the *civitas peregrina,* which he describes as an association "of adventurers each responding as best he can to the ordeal of consciousness," and of partners in "a practice of civility the rules of which are not devices for satisfying substantive wants." For while pursuing substantive wants is certainly a vital part of life, it cannot be understood as the entirety of human experience. Oakeshott thus wants to preserve the freedom of human adventurers to recognize and pursue those things that concern more than worldly survival and achievement. Augustine's mature view is remarkably similar, for he recognizes that while withdrawal from the world is impossible (and undesirable), the challenge is to maintain a "firm and balanced perspective on the whole range of loves of which men are capable in their present state." Both thinkers are acutely aware of "the transience of the conventional life of their fellows."[8] The difficulty, however, lies in preserving this perspective while one is thoroughly immersed in ordinary, everyday life.

In his classic work *Christianity and Classical Culture,* Charles Cochrane remarks that Augustine is fundamentally concerned with what he sees as

6. George Santayana, *Soliloquies in England and Later Soliloquies,* 226.

7. I have borrowed this phrase from Peter Brown, who uses it to describe Augustine's attitude toward life in the world. It applies in a different way, but equally appropriately, to Oakeshott. See Brown, *Augustine of Hippo,* 324.

8. *OHC,* 243; Brown, *Augustine of Hippo,* 325, 322.

the central problem of life: the "problem of consciousness." Can human beings find complete happiness in satisfying the kinds of desires they share with brute creation, or do they require something else? These satisfactions are only partial, and thus Augustine's central question is, "in what is consciousness to discover the fullest measure of satisfaction?"[9] This is Oakeshott's question too. And while the two thinkers do not answer it in precisely the same way, they share a basic view of the human condition, a view that leads them to make similar assessments about human character and about politics.

Human beings, they believe, are flawed, prideful, and apt to overestimate our own abilities. We are very often led astray by desires, preferring immediate sensual gratification to those things that promise a more enduring happiness. And yet we need not be ruled by our passions, for we are blessed with the freedom to orient our wills as we see fit. The adventure of human life thus consists precisely in this exercise of will, and we can neither plead ignorance nor shirk responsibility for our actions. Both Oakeshott and Augustine view human life as alternately an adventure and a predicament, in which we are handicapped by desire and shortsightedness but able—at least partially—to overcome these handicaps if we choose well.

Because of this fundamentally similar judgment about human nature, any examination of Oakeshott's religious views would be incomplete without a consideration of his debt—both implicit and explicit—to Augustine. Both thinkers view the prospect of human fulfillment as dependent (at least in part) on a self-understanding gained through introspection and self-examination, and both may be said to have a conception of "two cities." For both Augustine and Oakeshott, answers to the question of what will provide greatest fulfillment are found in the constant and unavoidable tension between religion and the world, between activities as ends and as means, and between the "practical life" and other modes of experience. These tensions issue from what I have identified as the fundamental choice implicit in the work of both thinkers. This choice is most vividly expressed in Augustine's conception of the "two cities," which provides an appropriate starting point for investigating the similarities between the two thinkers. I therefore consider briefly Augustine's familiar formulation of this idea before turning to several Augustinian

9. Charles Cochrane, *Christianity and Classical Culture*, 389.

interpretations of Oakeshott's early essay "Religion and the World." Next, I consider the view of human beings that Augustine and Oakeshott share, focusing on what I have called the "limiting conditions" of human experience: mortality and the frustrations of the search for power after power. And finally, I consider what both believe human beings may nevertheless achieve. Here I consider Augustine's conception of free will and Oakeshott's idea of freedom as he expresses it in the first essay of *On Human Conduct*.

Augustine's Two Cities

Augustine's conception of the cities of God and man is well known. These cities symbolize two different modes of living and two categorically different types of desires. "I classify the human race into two branches," explains Augustine. "[T]he one consists of those who live by human standards, the other of those who live according to God's will. I also call these two classes the two cities, speaking allegorically." Augustine describes the two cities as formed by two kinds of love: "the earthly city was created by self-love (*amor sui*) reaching the point of contempt for God, the Heavenly City by the love of God (*amor Dei*) carried as far as contempt of self."[10]

Those in the city of man view earthly life as the entirety of existence and are attuned primarily to physical pleasures and immanent fulfillment. These citizens focus on personal desires and attribute success to their own wisdom and virtue, pridefully exalting themselves rather than God. A "self-assertive egotism" is the fundamental motivating force for residents of the *civitas terrena,* and it entails an attitude toward the goods of the world that prizes these goods entirely for their own sake, not as symbols of God's love for man or as signs of better things to come.[11] Like a woman who loves the ring but not the giver, the residents of the city of man love earthly goods but not God, their creator.

Members of the city of God, on the other hand, orient themselves according to spiritual virtues and perceive their earthly life as transitory. Those in the heavenly city tend to think of themselves as pilgrims on

10. Augustine, *City of God,* bk. 15, chap. 1, 595, 593.
11. Cochrane, *Christianity and Classical Culture,* 489.

earth and do not strive to accumulate material possessions. Instead, they direct will and energy toward God, "using" but not "enjoying" goods, with the aim of attaining eternal life.[12] They are like travelers who, when stopping at an inn for the night, make use of the cup, plate, and bed but leave them behind without regret. The values of the *civitas Dei* are spiritual values, and the earthly members of this city are those who, with the angels, will live forever with God in eternal peace. One of the decisive differences between the two types of cities lies in their attitudes toward material goods. For while residents of both cities require these things to sustain life, it is only in the *civitas terrena* that desire for such goods overreaches necessity and becomes possessive.

Oakeshott's Two Cities: Worthington

Two commentators have observed that Oakeshott presents his own version of the Augustinian doctrine of the two cities. Glenn Worthington argues that Oakeshott's reformulation of this idea appears most clearly in his contrast between the "worldly" man and the "religious" man in his 1929 essay "Religion and the World."[13] In this essay, Oakeshott sets out "worldly" and "religious" as two ideal types of moral personality. These types parallel Augustine's distinction between the *civitas terrena* and *civitas Dei*. Thus the worldly man is concerned with getting and spending, with practical achievement in the world of affairs, and with "making a contribution" to some greater enterprise or field of study. His life is spent in the pursuit of immanent ideals. Fulfillment is postponed to the future, and he values himself and others solely on the basis of accomplishment.

Oakeshott's religious man, by contrast, does not postpone fulfillment to the future but is fully engaged in each moment. He finds meaning in present activity and lives life as its own end rather than as a means to some future satisfaction. He understands practical endeavors as activities that have a distinct, though limited, value. Activities that *do* stand as ends in themselves—for example, love, friendship, and contemplation—are the religious man's true focus. And although he must take part in worldly

---

12. Herbert A. Deane, *The Political and Social Ideas of St. Augustine,* 43.
13. Glenn Worthington, "Michael Oakeshott and the City of God," 378.

activities to survive, the spirit in which he undertakes such actions clearly distinguishes him from the worldly man.

Worthington describes these two characters as representatives of "two systems of value, which are distinguished from one another in terms of the relation that each posits between the worth of a self (what ought to be) and that self (what is)." In other words, he observes that Oakeshott's moral characters have fundamentally different orientations. Those who are worldly are in a state of constant anxiety, for their focus is always on the future. On the other hand, those who are religious avoid this intrinsic dissatisfaction by refusing to engage in speculation about the future or about how the "world" perceives them. A religious system of value "is realized in a self that takes the measure of itself from within itself" rather than in one that looks to others for approval. Religion values the spirit in which actions are undertaken, not the concrete results of those actions. In considering the religious character of its activities, "a self more surely possesses itself in living its life than in its attendance on worldly affairs."[14]

The two worlds Oakeshott describes in his essay are ultimately incommensurable because they entail radically different ideas about how one ought to live. Nevertheless, each person holds a dual citizenship, according to Oakeshott, for there is a worldly and a religious aspect that may be identified in each and every action. It is here that Oakeshott's reformulation of the two cities becomes somewhat less orthodox. For while both Augustine and Oakeshott recognize that "worldly" and "religious" are inseparable aspects of moral conduct—no action may be wholly one or the other—Oakeshott's interpretation of this dual citizenship is at odds with Augustine's. Worthington summarizes the Augustinian position as follows: "For Augustine, the possibility of dual citizenship arises because the character of the city of man is absolutely different from the city of God. On the one hand, the city of man is a human artifact, and thus, as all human artifice, finite and temporal. On the other, the city of God is a divine artifact consisting in the incomprehensible grace of God and is thus infinite and eternal. . . . Augustine argues in terms of a natural-supernatural, or material-spiritual duality."[15] But Oakeshott, who argues that all experience is mediated through the

14. Ibid., 379, 380, 381.
15. Ibid., 382.

human subject, cannot embrace such a radical dualism. For him, the city
of God is unavoidably a part of human experience.

Oakeshott's Two Cities: Coats

Another commentator has also observed marked similarities between
Oakeshott and Augustine by examining this same essay. Wendell John
Coats Jr. expresses the difference between Oakeshott's two ideal types as
a distinction between "use" and "enjoyment." The disposition of the
worldly man is to view all things according to their actual or potential
utility. Thus friends, for such a person, are people who flatter or perform
favors. The religious man, on the other hand, seeks activities that are ends
in themselves and that may be "enjoyed" in their performance. Friendship, on *this* account, is something to be engaged in purely for its own
sake. Coats points out that those who are religious never attempt "to
make utility an end in itself, always viewing utilities simply as means for
the enjoyment of goods that *can* be enjoyed solely for their own sake."
The only true ends for the religious man, maintains Coats following
Oakeshott, are those things that may be enjoyed in this manner, such as
love, friendship, poetry, and the like. Those who are worldly, on the other
hand, believe that useful things (such as money, houses, and other material goods) are ends in themselves. This "use/enjoyment" distinction is
evident in Oakeshott's essay, and it is also reflected in the pages of Augustine's *City of God:* "Every instance of human perversion . . . consists in
willing to use the objects of enjoyment . . . or in willing to enjoy the
objects of use. . . . So, all good ordering . . . requires that the objects of
joy be enjoyed . . . and those of use be used."[16] In his distinction between use and enjoyment, argues Coats, Oakeshott is recasting an
Augustinian insight.

There are other striking parallels between Oakeshott and Augustine.
Coats highlights both writers' preoccupation with human freedom,
pointing out that both argue against deterministic explanations of
human behavior. For Augustine, this emerges as a critique of "physical"
causes, that is, of the idea that human actions are predetermined or
somehow out of an individual's control. The order of human life is "not

16. Wendell John Coats Jr., *Oakeshott and His Contemporaries*, 32.

the order of 'matter' . . . nor yet is it any mere reproduction of a pattern or idea. . . . For the Christian, time, space, matter and form are all alike . . . gifts." Therefore, these are not causes, but opportunities that give "us our status as individuals in the saeculum."[17] Augustine, Coats observes, is concerned with the *meaning* of decisions and actions for the individual agents who engage in them. It is this meaning, and not the fact that an action might seem to have been determined by some external cause, that gives human action its significance.

Oakeshott, likewise, argues throughout his corpus that each person is responsible for who he becomes. Each of us is "wholly responsible for his own experience; each makes his own choices and conducts his own life on the basis of judgments he makes by reflecting on his own experience of the world."[18] Oakeshott believed that human beings are unavoidably self-determined and that there is no single pattern of conduct to be imposed upon them. Moral conduct requires the ability to make one's choices for oneself, and thus to choose either religion or the world.

Oakeshott's Two Cities: Another Interpretation

In casting Oakeshott's "worldly" and "religious" characters as representatives of Augustine's two cities, Worthington and Coats have identified a vitally important aspect of Oakeshott's thought. As I observed above, Oakeshott is concerned with the notion that there is a choice to be made in human life—that there are markedly different alternatives to be confronted in moral and political life. In his early essay "Religion and the World," one finds this idea presented as a distinction between activities undertaken as ends in themselves and those undertaken for some other purpose. This distinction, following Worthington and Oakeshott, is between religion and the world, or as Coats expresses it, between enjoyment and use. However it is designated, this is essentially a choice about how to live. Shall we orient ourselves by means of temporal or eternal goods? The world, Oakeshott observes in a late essay, "has but one language, soon learned: the language of appetite."[19] Is the human experience exhausted in satisfying appetites of various sorts, or can appetite be

17. Ibid., 29.
18. *MPME,* 53.
19. "A Place of Learning," in *VLL,* 41.

transcended by living a life that may be called religious? This question is crucial for Augustine and Oakeshott alike. It is in "Religion and the World" that the twenty-eight-year-old Oakeshott sets out explicitly his early view of religion, and it is worth examining in greater detail as a way of understanding just how Oakeshott saw the two cities.

It is vital to be clear about what Oakeshott means by the terms *religion* and the *world*. As is often the case when reading Oakeshott, it is easier to say what these things are *not* than what they are. Here, "religion" does not require assent to a set of propositions or to a creed. It is neither dogmatic nor denominational. It does not depend on a dualism between natural and supernatural, nor is it a set of moral laws that must be obeyed. For Oakeshott, religion is essentially a way of thinking about the world and of acting in it. It is, in simplest terms, the conviction that life should be taken as it is, and that to live religiously is to live in the present.

Likewise, the "world" in this essay cannot be identified with the merely material. Oakeshott is emphatically not trying to express a naive view that the "physical" world should be rejected wholesale and that the "spiritual" world is to be embraced. Rather, worldliness here represents *a set of values* that prioritizes achievement and investment rather than enjoyment. To be worldly is to believe in the permanence of the things we see around us and to put our faith in progress and projects. To appreciate this essay properly, all conventional notions of "religion" and the "world" must be left behind.

Oakeshott begins the essay by way of historical illustration, setting out alternative ways in which religion (here, Christianity) has been conceived. The early Christians, he observes, understood themselves to be waiting for the Second Coming of Christ. They had no conception of natural and supernatural, as medieval Christians would later, but instead believed that the Second Coming would take place as an imminent event in human history. Thus the early Christian religious life consisted in waiting for a historical event, and keeping oneself "unspotted from the world" was "easily understood and naturally agreeable."[20]

But when the Second Coming did not immediately materialize, the primitive simplicity of early Christianity changed, and the more complex and abstract idea arose of a dualism between "material" and "spiri-

20. "Religion and the World," in *RPML,* 28.

tual" worlds—between natural and supernatural. The early Christian's expectation of a concrete, historical event was transformed into the medieval Christian's expectation of salvation in another realm altogether. To the medieval Christian, "keeping unspotted from the world" now meant ordering one's life so that one could avoid the sinfulness of pleasures: "This world of interests and activities, they believed would be with them to the end, but they must live in it as aliens."[21]

In these contrasting descriptions of religious consciousness Oakeshott presents two different ideas of what it means for a person to live religiously: the early Christian, who lives in expectation of the imminent return of Christ, and the medieval Christian, who believes that salvation will take place in another realm and depends, at least in part, upon one's conduct during earthly life. Both views depend on a dichotomy between religion, on the one hand, and the world, on the other. Furthermore, for both the early and the medieval Christian there is something about the "world" that is understood to be harmful to one's soul, and that should be rejected by the truly religious. So far, then, *religion* and the *world* mean what one would expect: religion requires a "spiritual" orientation, and worldliness consists in placing too much emphasis on material goods and pleasures.

But here Oakeshott begins to diverge somewhat from the Christian tradition he has been explaining. For while *worldliness* clearly also has a negative connotation for Oakeshott, the *world* does not mean for Oakeshott what it meant for that early or medieval Christian. For the latter, the world—"their body and its senses, their mind and its ideas, knowledge and truth, art and literature, politics, patriotism, pleasure and commerce"—was to be rejected wholesale; or, at the very least, involvement in it ought to be minimized. One's vital energies ought to be directed away from material interests and toward spiritual ones. "To be unspotted from the world," explains Oakeshott, "meant to live, without pleasure, a life so divided between this world and the other world that it required the invention of a whole psychology to persuade men of its possibility."[22] Thus natural interests had to be subordinated to supernatural; and sacrifices in this life could be justified by the promise of rewards in the next.

21. Ibid., 29.
22. Ibid.

This, however, is emphatically not Oakeshott's view of worldliness. The world understood as a prison from which we desire escape, the willing abandonment of all sensual and intellectual pleasures in favor of asceticism—such outright rejections of this world are foreign to Oakeshott's view. What he rejects instead is the worldliness inherent in a particular "scale of values . . . a certain way of thinking" that prioritizes usefulness, success, and external results. Thus the religious person does not reject the natural world, friendship, love, art, and politics per se. Instead, such a person rejects the idea of nature harnessed to never-ending projects for material improvement, friendship pursued only for selfish benefits, art in the service of a political program, and so on. "The other world of religion is no fantastic supernatural world, from which some activities and interests have been excluded," Oakeshott maintains; "it is a spiritual world, in which everything is valued, not as a contribution to some development or evolution, but as it is itself."[23] Thus religion does not prescribe (or proscribe) any activities, nor does it provide a set of moral rules. It does, however, state the manner in which life should be lived. Embracing a religious scale of value means to reject utility in favor of enjoyment and to live fully in the moment.

Oakeshott moreover rejects the common view that the way to overcome worldliness is to put one's faith in ideals. If worldliness consists in placing money, comfort, sensual pleasure, and progress before all else, so this argument goes, then self-sacrifice in the pursuit of some greater good must be its opposite, and therefore closer to religion. Pursuing a cure for cancer, advancing the cause of avant-garde music, working to end poverty—all these are examples of such "greater goods." But this pursuit of ideals does not save us from worldliness, Oakeshott observes. Indeed, it only reinforces the mistaken view that life in this world is permanent and stable. Could any notion of life "be more empty and futile," Oakeshott wonders, than the idea that the value of one's life is measured by one's contribution to "something thought more permanent than itself— a race, a people, an art, a science or a profession?"[24] Not only is this view *no different* than the worldly view, it is worldliness taken to an extreme.

Oakeshott maintained this view throughout his life, and much later, in his consideration of religion in *On Human Conduct,* he argued that "the inherently episodic character of the diurnal adventures of self-disclosure

23. Ibid., 30.
24. Ibid., 32.

which compose a human life may be masked in the greatness of an agent's devotion to his aims and in his singleness of purpose, or it may be somewhat more securely hidden where these can be recognized to concur in the promising pursuit of purposes more enduring than those of a single agent and his immediate associates: the iniquity of oblivion eclipsed by posthumous glory." Nevertheless, Oakeshott continued, "what is thus concealed in the illusion of affairs is not thereby extinguished. Every action is a fugitive transaction between mortal agents, its outcome not merely uncertain but fragile and soon dissipated." The pursuit of an ideal encourages the belief that one is making a contribution to something greater than oneself or building a lasting reputation. Most of the time these endeavors require that satisfaction be postponed to the future and that present happiness be sacrificed for the mere possibility of a supposed greater happiness to come. Here Oakeshott makes an Augustinian point about this view of human experience: "What really distinguishes the worldly man is his belief in the reality and permanence of the present order of things." The worldly man believes that the present order is stable "or that it will merely evolve into another. The earth we tread, the species to which we belong, the history we make, the communities we serve, the sciences or arts to which we contribute seem to him permanent."[25]

But these ideas of permanence and stability are mere illusions. For Oakeshott, the only things of permanent value are our selves and the sensibilities we choose to cultivate over the course of our lives. Once we see that "the richest possessions are valueless apart from our possession of them by insight," the way of the world loses its charm. "The worth of a life is measured, then, by its sensibility, not by its external achievement of the reputation behind which it may have been able to hide its lack of actual insight." Religion, therefore, is the cultivation of a personal sensibility and the will to enjoy rather than constantly to appropriate the goods of the world. It requires the recognition that temporal goods do not last, but that insight and the love of wisdom may be, in a certain sense, permanent. Oakeshott is recasting Augustine's insight that the possession of a good will is something "far more valuable than all earthly kingdoms and pleasures; to lack it is to lack something that only the will itself can give, something that is better than all the goods that are not in our power."[26] It is a modern version of the *civitas Dei*.

25. *OHC*, 84; "Religion and the World," in *RPML*, 30, 31.
26. "Religion and the World," in *RPML*, 33; Augustine, *On Free Choice of the Will*, 21.

Oakeshott does much else in this short essay, but here it is important merely to recapitulate his Augustinian dichotomy between two cities. Worldliness, like Augustine's "city of man," requires belief in the stability and permanence of the present order and a focus on those things—material goods, honor, reputation—that are esteemed by those who live according to the values of the world. Religion, on the other hand, rejects the world's values and chooses different priorities: it focuses on enjoyment rather than exploitation of resources, on the achievement of a personal sensibility, and on the difficult but rewarding process of self-examination.

It is worth noting that these conceptions of *worldliness* and *religion* are akin to a later distinction that Oakeshott makes in an essay entitled "Work and Play."[27] In this short piece he defines work as the activity humans undertake to satisfy an endless stream of wants. Play, on the other hand, is activity that is emancipated from wants. When we engage in play we abandon, for the moment, our search for substantive satisfactions. Instead, what is sought is an experience of enjoyment that looks for no justification outside itself. As worldliness and religion echo the cities of man and God, so work and play, respectively, are the activities of the two cities. The important difference between this essay and Oakeshott's earlier "Religion and the World" is that in "Work and Play," *both* kinds of activity are recognized to be important. While it is in play that one exercises the higher parts of one's nature, work is recognized to be an unavoidable part of the human experience as well. The danger Oakeshott identifies and laments is the modern tendency to recognize *only* the value of work and to ignore the supremely civilizing influence of play. For if life is understood only as the endeavor to satisfy wants, then we are once again back in the *civitas terrena* and subject to its unavoidable frustrations.

Thus far I have attempted to show that Oakeshott's conceptions of "worldliness" and "religion" echo Augustine's dichotomy between the two cities. Both thinkers observe that there are alternative ways of orienting oneself in the world, and both recognize that every human being must make a choice between these orientations. However, this choice demands someone who is capable of making it. It requires a self-determined, rational individual who can suffer or celebrate the consequences of his actions. On the question of the kind of moral personality capable of

27. WP, 29–33.

choosing between religion and worldliness, Oakeshott's and Augustine's accounts of the human predicament coincide strikingly. Both describe a proper orientation of the will as a process of self-discovery that is different for every person. This requires self-examination and a reflective consciousness that comes to know itself by making decisions, by acting on those decisions, and by considering and evaluating the consequences that follow from them. The question of religion for Oakeshott, as Fuller has put it, "is constituted in this task he thought of as self-understanding."[28] True religion cannot exist without reflection, without turning the will in the direction one deems good.

Neither thinker, however, believed that the moral creativity involved in self-determination means the freedom simply to choose a new moral persona arbitrarily or to engage in pure experimentation for its own sake. The choices involved in self-determination arise in the context of certain limiting conditions, namely, the mortal character of human life and the frustrating aspects of the human quest for power after power. These conditions combine to form a certain understanding of the human predicament that Oakeshott and Augustine share, and it is worth outlining this understanding before discussing the question of will explicitly.

The Human Condition: Mortality

Oakeshott and Augustine describe the world in ways that constantly recall the most vivid and immediate limiting condition of human life: mortality. Both thinkers were intensely aware of the inevitability of death, which of course marks the end of every individual's ability to carry out plans and projects. Here is Augustine's famous formulation of the predicament: "[F]rom the moment a man begins to exist in this body which is destined to die, he is involved all the time in a process whose end is death. For this is the end to which the life of continual change is all the time directed, if indeed we can give the name of life to this passage towards death. There is no one, it goes without saying, who is not nearer to death this year than he was last year. . . . the whole of our lifetime is nothing but a race towards death, in which no one is allowed the slightest pause or any slackening of the pace." As a young man, Oakeshott

28. Fuller, introduction to *RPML,* 21.

made a similar observation, asserting in 1933 that mortality is "the central fact of practical existence; death is the central fact of life." Many years later he wrote in the same vein that the human condition entails "the pain of disappointed expectations, the suffering of frustrated purposes, the impositions of hostile circumstances, the sorrows of unwanted partings, burdens, ills, disasters, calamities of all sorts, and death itself, the emblem here of all such sufferings."[29]

The death with which Oakeshott and Augustine were concerned is not just the physical death that each person must expect; it is also the unavoidably mortal nature of all human endeavors. Plans inevitably fail to be completed, hopes are disappointed, and friendships end. And though everyone must be concerned with acquisition to ensure survival, this too inevitably entails loss. For man "pursues one thing after another, and nothing remains permanently with him," insists Augustine. Oakeshott likewise describes not merely physical death, but, as he puts it, "the far more devastating mortality of every element of practical existence, the mortality of pleasures and pains, desires, achievements, emotions and affections." He comments on this conception of life, describing morality as "this endless search for the perfect good; an endless, practical endeavour resulting in momentary personal failures and achievements and in a gradual change of moral ideas and ideals, a change which is perhaps more than mere change, a progress towards a finer sensibility for social life and a deeper knowledge of its necessities. But, nevertheless, a battle with no hope of victory, a battle, in fact, in which a final victory is the only irretrievable defeat."[30] The full implications of this view of mortality will be postponed to Chapters 7 and 8, for such a view has important political consequences. Most importantly, it implies that human beings are profoundly limited, and that politics cannot therefore achieve a state of perfection.

But another important consequence of recognizing the ultimate futility of the practical life is that it may begin to turn us toward religion. Augustine strongly admonishes his readers to think of death in order that they might recognize the things that are most valuable. "You can see men shaking with fear, running away, searching for hiding places, hunting for protection, prostrating themselves, giving whatever they have in order to

29. Augustine, *City of God,* bk. 8, chap. 10, 518; *EM,* 273; *OHC,* 81.
30. Deane, *St. Augustine,* 45; *EM,* 273; "Religion and the Moral Life," in *RPML,* 44.

be granted their lives," he describes, "to extend a little bit longer a tenure that can never be secure." Why not instead attend to those things that could move human beings to "shake off their earthly sleepiness at last"?[31] Why not, as Oakeshott and Augustine would seem to exhort their readers, move toward a religious life and reject the desires and frustrations of worldliness?

A caveat must be made here about the spirit in which Augustine and Oakeshott considered mortality. Neither writer approached the subject of death fearfully, and neither was at all morbid or obsessive. In fact, quite the opposite is true. While the two thinkers were constantly aware of the fact of death, their primary aim was to discover how to live a meaningful life. For both, meaning was found in religion. Moreover, their works exhibit a curious mix of pessimism and optimism: pessimism because they recognized the futility of worldliness, and optimism because so much freedom is left to man to determine how he will live. Like Montaigne, they believed that the worth of one's life consists not in the length of days, "but in the use of time; a man may have lived long, and yet lived but a little. . . . It depends upon your will, and not upon the number of days, to have a sufficient length of life."[32] And thus both thinkers could be optimistic about the potential for a certain kind of human flourishing even as they recognized human fallibility and the ultimate limiting condition, death.

The Human Condition: The Search for Power after Power

If mortality is a central concern in Oakeshott and Augustine, it goes hand in hand with another, equally important aspect of the human condition: the frustration and lack of completeness that people are likely to feel as they go about their daily lives. This is not the frustration that accompanies the failure of any given project; it is rather the creeping sense of dissatisfaction that accompanies all practical endeavors. When one task is complete there is always another waiting. Every victory fades quickly, and the prospect of the next one becomes the focus of attention. Hobbes expresses the problem in a vivid and famous formulation: "I put for a

---

31. *The Political Writings of St. Augustine,* 110, 109.
32. Michel de Montaigne, *Essays,* 309.

general inclination of all mankind, a perpetual and restless desire of power after power, that ceaseth only in death. And the cause of this is not always that a man hopes for a more intensive delight than he has already attained to, or that he cannot be content with a moderate power, but because he cannot assure the power and means to live well, which he hath present, without the acquisition of more."[33] Both Oakeshott and Augustine dwell at length on this conception of life as an endless series of tasks in which one endeavor is merely superseded by another and in which there can be no final or complete satisfaction. In *Experience and Its Modes,* Oakeshott calls this interminable series of undertakings "practical life," and I shall consider his conception of it in some detail in the next chapter. Here, however, it is necessary to set out the fundamental features of this understanding that are shared by both Oakeshott and Augustine. For the sake of clarity I designate this endless series of wants and needs, as Oakeshott does, practical life.

Augustine describes practical life as man's pursuit of one thing after another, as a string of limitless desires: "[W]hereunto soever he attains, what he has attained to is forthwith disesteemed by him. Other things begin to be desired, other fond things are hoped for; and when they come, whatsoever it is that comes to thee, is disesteemed." There seems to be no limit to human desires, and people press past their immediate needs to satisfy wants that are merely imagined. Thus a person's appetites "are so multiplied that he cannot find the one thing needful, a single and unchangeable nature, seeking which he would not err, and attaining which he would cease from grief and pain."[34] If practical action is taken to be the whole of life, then dissatisfaction is the only outcome one can expect.

Oakeshott describes precisely the same situation. Practical experience, he points out in *Experience and Its Modes,* "assumes a world of facts which is not merely susceptible of alteration, but which has change and instability as the *very principle of its existence.*" Thus by definition there can be no permanent satisfaction or final fulfillment. Practical experience presupposes its own incompleteness. "[E]ven if we suppose a condition in which everything was as it should be," Oakeshott argues, "that could never be more than a momentary condition. For every achievement

33. Thomas Hobbes, *Leviathan,* 58.
34. Deane, *St. Augustine,* 45.

brings with it a new view of the criterion, which converts this momentary perfection into imperfection. Indeed, we may find that even the
'ought not' of one moment is the 'ought' of another. Nowhere in practice is there uninterrupted progress or final achievement."[35] Practical life
can thus never offer human beings any kind of permanent fulfillment.
The only stopping point for this endless round of "doing" is death. Thus
what I have termed two limiting conditions of human life—the fact of
mortality and the never-ceasing character of practical life—are intimately related. If human life were to consist wholly in engagement in
practical affairs, then it would seem to be a depressing predicament. But
it is the task of both writers to offer alternatives to this view of life as a
series of limitless wants. In the religious life or in "play," one may temporarily leave behind these wants and engage in activities that may simply be enjoyed.

On Human Freedom

As I have just observed, Oakeshott and Augustine had similar perspec-
tives on the human condition. Both were well aware of mortality and the
inevitable frustrations inherent in practical endeavors. But neither thinker
concluded that these conditions combine to form an entirely gloomy
predicament. Their conceptions of freedom allow human beings a great
deal of latitude to choose the kinds of lives they will live. For both thinkers,
the fundamental choice was between religion and worldliness, and it is in
making this choice, not once and for all but again and again over the
course of a lifetime, that a person declares citizenship in either the *civitas
terrena* or the *civitas Dei*.

   The necessity of choosing between these two alternatives is not one
that falls to every living creature. Neither children nor animals are faced
with this burden, since meaningful choice requires a notion of moral responsibility coupled with the freedom to pursue one's ends. And responsibility and freedom are, in varying degrees, denied to these creatures.
But for others—those who bear full responsibility for their actions—this
kind of activity possesses a certain creative element, since in choosing
one must imagine in advance the effects of one's choice. And in choosing

---

35. *EM,* 263 (emphasis added), 291.

repeatedly one forms a consistent character, as Aristotle reminds us in the *Ethics*. For what is character but the disposition to choose in certain ways and not others? Thus the formation of character through intelligent choosing is a kind of moral creativity.

For Augustine, this moral creativity is grounded in a particular conception of the will. He addresses the issue most directly in *De Libero Arbitrio* (*On Free Choice of the Will*) by considering exactly how the will may be understood as free. Oakeshott, on the other hand, shies away from the term *free will*, preferring instead to designate will as "intelligence in doing." A person may be said to have a free will, according to Oakeshott, "because his response to his situation, like his situation itself, is the outcome of an intelligent engagement."[36] Without an intelligence that can recognize alternatives of better and worse, more and less desirable, actions must be determined simply by organic urges and animal instincts. Human "will" is thus equivalent to human intelligence. Although they use different terms, this concept of "will" or "intelligence" is of supreme importance to both thinkers. Each engages in a sustained argument against the kind of philosophical determinism that would deprive human beings of their ability to choose freely.

Augustine on Freedom of the Will

Augustine expresses his views on the nature of free will throughout his corpus, and a "good" or properly oriented will is required for membership in the *civitas Dei*. But he takes up specific questions about free will most explicitly in *De Libero Arbitrio* (*On Free Choice of the Will*). Here he considers what sorts of things humans may legitimately be held responsible for and whether actions are predetermined by a chain of causes that originates prior to birth.

It will be no surprise to any reader of Augustine that he believed human will is not foreordained by either external or internal factors. A person's (external) political or economic circumstances provide the context in which certain decisions are made, but do not dictate what particular actions he will take. Likewise, someone's (internal) tendencies toward anger or envy do not predict the performance of angry or envi-

36. *OHC*, 39.

ous deeds. If we observe such tendencies in our own characters, this ought merely to remind us, as Aristotle observes, to "watch the errors which have the greatest attraction for us personally." They emphatically do *not* push us into conduct that we cannot control or for which we might forsake responsibility. Augustine thus insists that the will's determinations "are governed . . . by a principle of inner control."[37]

Will, therefore, is not a motor set running inside each person, driving him to follow a predetermined course of action. Nor is it something determined by chemical processes or genetic predispositions. For Augustine, will is the decision maker and motive force behind each action. Just as weight carries an apple to the ground, will carries a person to his chosen moral destination. Unlike the apple, however, the fundamental characteristic of will is its freedom, since its movement is not necessary, but voluntary. Augustine compares the movement of the will to the downward movement of a stone, observing that although the stone "has no power to check its downward movement," the soul "is not moved to abandon higher things and love inferior things unless it *wills* to do so. And so the movement of the stone is natural, but the movement of the soul is voluntary." This is the crux of Augustine's teaching on will: each person has a certain freedom to exercise his will but must also bear the consequences of that exercise. If I use my will "to do something evil," he asks, "whom can I hold responsible but myself?" And if the movement of the will were not voluntary, "a person would not deserve praise for turning to higher things or blame for turning to lower things."[38] Will is thus not simply one cause among many; it is *the* efficient cause of all human action, and it is what allows human beings to express themselves creatively and significantly.

Oakeshott on Human Freedom

Oakeshott avoids the term *free will,* preferring instead, as I have noted, to designate the motive force behind action "intelligence in doing." But his account of what it means for a human being to engage in morally significant activity is remarkably similar to Augustine's, though Oakeshott's

---

37. Aristotle, *Nicomachean Ethics,* 50; Cochrane, *Christianity and Classical Culture,* 447.
38. Augustine, *On Free Choice of the Will,* 72 (emphasis added).

view is a pointed response to twentieth-century determinist arguments. His defense of moral autonomy in *On Human Conduct* arises in the context of his strong objections to the idea that human behavior is somehow predetermined by "processes" or "syndromes" over which one has little control. An agent acts on the basis of an understanding of his own situation, according to Oakeshott, and this understanding "cannot be 'reduced' to a component of a genetic, a biochemical, a psychological or any other process, or to a consequence of any causal condition." And if others share this understanding it is not because they "share common organic tensions" or have "similar genetic characters," but because they have "independently learned to think alike."[39]

Moreover, the reasons (not causes) lying behind any action are inextricably linked to this free exercise of intelligence. Each person is at liberty to consider what action he should take, as well to examine and evaluate the motives and intentions that guide that action. Freedom, therefore, appears not just in action but in deliberation, because the "starting-place of doing is a state of reflective consciousness, namely, the agent's own understanding of his situation."[40] Motives, therefore, play a major part in determining the moral significance of human action.

Every action, of course, may be undertaken for a variety of motives. A person may obey a law out of fear of punishment or because he finds that law inherently right. Someone may do a good deed for another person because he wants to be seen doing it or simply because he empathizes with that person's need. There is a greater unity of content (what is done) with form (how it is done) in the latter cases of each pair, for in these the action is undertaken for its own sake rather than for an ulterior purpose. Becoming morally self-aware consists in the closest possible approximation to a unity of form and content, in order that every action is done, so far as possible, for its own sake. Hence, as Wendell John Coats Jr. points out, "poetry or aesthetic experience, or activity that intermittently achieves a unity of content and form . . . is the clearest expression of what is implied in all experience." Of course, not every action can be undertaken in a complete unity of content and form, wholly for its own sake, and Oakeshott recognized this. For much— indeed the majority—of conduct *inter homines* is driven by the desire for

39. *OHC,* 38.
40. Ibid., 37.

certain responses from other people. Yet for Oakeshott this idea of "unified" conduct remained an ideal that stood in opposition to the increasingly utilitarian character of activity in the modern world. The nature of
experience, according to Coats, "is itself creative."[41]

We can conclude that both Oakeshott and Augustine were defenders
of the idea of human freedom against those who would deny or minimize it. Expressions of free will or "intelligence in doing" are not the
creation of a self *ex nihilo*—no mere self-indulgence or pure moral experimentation. On the contrary, this moral creativity takes place among
other people and within inherited traditions; and in neither Oakeshott
nor Augustine is the importance of the individual perspective "ever rad-
icalized into some sort of anarchistic, blindly willful individuality." Nevertheless, it requires someone willing to engage in the most rigorous kind
of continuous self-examination, something that cannot be resolved
"once and for all nor set aside." There is indeed a marked similarity of
spirit between Oakeshott and Augustine. Both believed that the candid
self-examination that leads to action is an "intelligent engagement,
linked with learned and understood belief." William James described
Augustine as "the 'first modern man'; the picture of a concrete human
being in whose presence the barriers of time and space drop away to reveal him as one in all respects akin to ourselves; a being so far unique in
history, yet clothed with the common graces and disgraces of mankind."[42] And Oakeshott was certainly modern, a thinker who was fundamentally concerned with questions of self-understanding and conduct.

Conclusion

One commentator has amusingly described Oakeshott as "Augustine
come again to confound both positivists and reductivists."[43] We can now
appreciate why this is an apt description of him, since we have seen that
his defense of freedom rejects all attempts to reduce human conduct to
organic urges or economic determinism. Moreover, the two thinkers share
a view of the human condition in which the pursuit of unlimited human

41. Coats, *Oakeshott and His Contemporaries,* 35, 34.
42. Ibid., 31; Fuller, introduction to *RPML,* 21; *OHC,* 41; William James, quoted in
Cochrane, *Christianity and Classical Culture,* 387.
43. Coats, *Oakeshott and His Contemporaries,* 28.

perfection is both vain and impossible; for human beings are hemmed in by their mortality and by their endless desires.

I cannot close, however, without taking note of one important difference between Oakeshott and Augustine. For although the argument of this chapter has been that the two thinkers are similar in quite significant ways, they also differ on one crucial point—namely, on the idea of a world to come. Oakeshott consciously limited his theorizing to the human world he saw around him, claiming an inability to philosophize about anything that might lie beyond human experience. And yet in a certain sense his rejection of another realm takes away precisely what makes Augustine's outlook intelligible. Augustine's view entails a graceful acceptance of human limitations, limitations that may yet be *remedied* in a life to come. But without such a source of hope, what reason do human beings have to be optimistic at all, given that we cannot perfect ourselves on earth and then cannot necessarily expect any kind of fulfillment after death?

The question this raises is whether there *is* some equivalent of the Christian idea of transcendent fulfillment in Oakeshott's thought. Sometimes he seems to hint at such a condition, most notably when he observes that poetry offers a certain kind of permanence and "rest." Indeed, at such times his language is remarkably Augustinian, even mystical. And yet there is a very wide gap between the fleeting transcendence offered by aesthetic experience and a world-transcendent God who actively cares about human beings. I do not know whether Oakeshott retained some kind of faith even as he moved away from his early orthodox views.

Still, however, the elements common to both thinkers remain striking. Most important of all is the idea that one must choose an orientation toward the world. This is the familiar idea of two cities—Augustine's city of God and city of man and Oakeshott's religious and worldly ways of living. The choice is one that must be made again and again over the course of a lifetime, not once and for all. Both thinkers believed that these continuous choices, springing from a properly oriented will, constitute the most important part of what it means to be human. It is not what we are seen to do, they would argue, but the *way* we do things that matters—our motives tell whether our wills are good or not. For Augustine, the good will loves what is stable and eternal; it understands that temporal goods are not bad in themselves, but may lead to error when they are loved in place of eternal goods. The good will prefers those things that can be held securely to those that can slip away. "Now no one is secure in enjoying goods that can be lost against his will," argues Augustine, but "no one can lose truth and wisdom against his will, for no one can be separated from the place where they are. What we called separation from truth and wisdom is really just a perverse will that loves inferior things, and no one wills something unwillingly."[44]

Oakeshott's "religious man" likewise embraces the things that appear most stable and lasting—not, as the world would have it, material goods and worldly success, but rather "the achievement of a personal sensibility" and "the realization of a self."[45] Such phrases reflect Oakeshott's notion that moral character—the most permanent and lasting human achievement in this temporal world—arises only as a result of self-examination and reflection on one's motives and actions. As he concludes toward the end of "Religion and the World," it is "only in the world's view that a man is better off for being known to be what he is; for religion it is enough to be it."[46] When, on the contrary, a person chooses to love goods that are not lasting, Oakeshott recounts Augustine's dictum that he "understands neither what he seeks nor what he is who seeks it."[47]

44. Augustine, *On Free Choice of the Will*, 57.

45. "Religion and the World," in *RPML*, 35, 32.

46. Ibid., 37.

47. *OHC*, 84. This quote comes from Augustine's *Harmony of the Evangelists*. The full quote is as follows: "At present it will tarry in the faith of believers, but hereafter it will be possible to contemplate it face to face, when He, our Life, shall appear, and when we shall appear with Him in glory. But if any one supposes that with man, living, as he still does, in this mortal life, it may be possible for a person to dispel and clear off every obscurity induced by corporeal and carnal fancies, and to attain to the serenest light of changeless truth, and to cleave constantly and unswervingly to that with a mind thoroughly estranged from the course of this present life, *that man understands neither what he asks, nor who he is that put such a supposition*" (bk. 4, chap. 10 [emphasis added]).

3

Future, Past, and Present

Let each one examine his thoughts, and he will find them all occupied with the past and the future. We scarcely ever think of the present; and if we think of it, it is only to take light from it to arrange the future. The present is never our end. The past and the present are our means; the future alone is our end. So we never live, but we hope to live; and, as we are always preparing to be happy, it is inevitable we should never be so.

PASCAL, *PENSÉES*

What would it be like to live fully in the present? Although Oakeshott addresses this question directly in only a few places, it lies just beneath the surface of his writings about politics, poetry, and the moral life. It is implicit in his descriptions of both "practice" and "history," as I shall show below, and it is central to his thought about poetry and religion, as I argue in Chapters 4 and 5. At the conclusion of the previous chapter I observed that Oakeshott, like Augustine, was fundamentally concerned with the quest for self-understanding, which requires a proper orientation toward life in the world. There is, indeed, a choice to be made between religion and worldliness. And this choice requires not only a proper perspective on achievement, success, and material goods, but also a certain view of time in which life is lived, as far as possible, neither in the future, nor the past, but the present.

Living in the present is every bit as difficult as keeping a proper perspective on worldly success and material prosperity. For it requires that we neither place our hopes in our future selves nor live on the accumulated capital of past achievements. It certainly goes against everything we hear around us, since looking to the future is a cardinal virtue for politicians, financial planners, and insurance salesmen. And there can be no doubt that we must, to a certain extent, plan for what may lie ahead. But Oakeshott emphasizes that living *wholly* for the future is vain. It encourages a certain sort of dissatisfaction because it allows one to imagine that present ills may be remedied "in the future." It also encourages a kind of postponement of life. Oakeshott offers a vivid illustration of such tendencies in "Religion and the World," when he describes this kind of character as follows: "The safe way is pursued, prudence is made a virtue, and, for the sake of an hypothetical old man, who may bear his name thirty years hence, the young man hoards his energies and restrains his activities."[1]

The idea of living in the present is precisely what the world of practice denies. In the world of practical endeavor one is constantly engaged in conceiving and satisfying desires of all sorts, and there is little room for the enjoyment of what one has. There is, it would seem, no time at all for the present, which must always be used as a way of getting to a desired future. And yet the future, as it too becomes present, can never be properly enjoyed since it is sacrificed to yet another desired future. This transforms humanity into Sisyphus, and life becomes "the pointless trundling of a useless stone."[2] Oakeshott wants to reject this depressing, utilitarian vision, and to recapture the idea of a meaningful life lived in the present. The activities that he finds most significant—love, friendship, and poetic contemplation—are those that lend themselves to such an understanding.

In the pages that follow I discuss briefly Oakeshott's overarching argument in his book *Experience and Its Modes,* his first major philosophical work, published in 1933. I then explain what Oakeshott means when he discusses the modes of practice (future) and history (past). Finally, I address the issue of "presentness," examining what it is, how Oakeshott expresses the concept, and why it is vital to understanding his thought as a whole.

Experience and Its Modes

Experience and Its Modes provides a foundation for Oakeshott's later work, but it is also the culmination of his early intellectual development, and his debt to the British Idealist tradition is evident throughout the book. In this work Oakeshott sets out the primary categories of human experience, which he terms "modes" or "arrests" in experience. These modes should *not* be understood as "parts" of experience; that is, Oakeshott

1. "Religion and the World," in *RPML,* 31.
2. Ibid., 32.

does not say that there is a certain type of experience that may be understood as *exclusively* practical or *exclusively* scientific. Rather, these modes represent ways of looking at the whole of experience, but in each mode the whole is seen from a limited perspective. Practice views the whole of experience from the point of view of what sorts of personal satisfactions it can provide. Science views the world in terms of its quantifiable character. And history orients itself *sub specie praeteritum,* that is, according to a conception of the past. More will be said about these modes shortly, but here it must be emphasized simply that Oakeshott's intention is not to carve up experience into artificial segments, but instead to understand how each mode is limited, from the point of view of the whole.

Oakeshott's understanding of modality is that different modes do not compose a hierarchy, but simply coexist with one another.[3] The idea that the world may be understood in different "modes" is a view expressed by thinkers prior to Oakeshott, notably R. G. Collingwood, whose 1924 work, *Speculum Mentis,* expounds a thesis that is similar in form to Oakeshott's, though it differs in important ways. Most notably, Collingwood argues (as Oakeshott emphatically does not) that a hierarchy or "progression" may be distinguished among the five modes of art, religion, science, history, and philosophy. Oakeshott's major task, on the other hand, is to investigate three of the most distinctive modes of experience—history, science, and practice—and to show that none of these modes can stand on its own as an entirely satisfactory way of understanding experience. The present chapter focuses on Oakeshott's descriptions of two modes in particular—history and practice—and attempts to show how both of them provide a contrast to Oakeshott's idea of a life experienced in the present, or "presentness," as I shall term it for the sake of convenience.

Oakeshott's aim in this early work is to give a reasoned account of human experience and of the ways in which human beings understand their experience. In the Idealist tradition, he would understand this in its fullest sense to be something that encompasses the *entirety* of possible experience or, as he terms it, the "concrete whole." As Oakeshott explains near the beginning of *Experience and Its Modes,* the concrete whole "is

3. Excellent discussions of Oakeshott and modality may be found in Paul Franco, *The Political Philosophy of Michael Oakeshott,* chap. 2, and *Michael Oakeshott: An Introduction,* chap. 2; Terry Nardin, *The Philosophy of Michael Oakeshott,* chap. 1; and W. H. Greenleaf, *Oakeshott's Philosophical Politics,* chap. 1.

not another, separate world, wholly different in character from any abstract world. It is the complete world which every abstract world implies and from which it derives its significance."[4] In fact, nearly all of human experience is, in Oakeshott's account, "abstract" or deficient. It almost always represents an "arrest" in the totality of experience, and in these arrests one chooses to pursue particular interests and occupations while ignoring others. These arrests are the modes, and the most important are history, science, and practice. Each is a coherent—but limited—world of ideas, for by definition each mode excludes the others and none is capable of refuting another.

The only way to attempt to grasp the whole of experience is through philosophy, and for Oakeshott, viewing the world in any particular mode is to have surrendered the impulse to think philosophically. Philosophy, after all, aims at the concrete whole and must press past arrests in experience in order to understand these arrests in themselves and in their relation to the totality of experience. Readers of Oakeshott's work will be well acquainted with his idea of philosophy as a parasitic activity that arises merely to explain goings-on in the world. As I have already noted, the act of philosophizing is not to be confused with "having a philosophy of life" (which would imply general maxims of conduct), nor should philosophy be charged with providing a guide for action. On the contrary: according to Oakeshott, philosophy merely explains action. It is "without any direct bearing upon the practical conduct of life, and . . . it has certainly never offered its true followers anything which could be mistaken for a gospel." Philosophy, according to Oakeshott, can never step into the realm of practice or tell a person what to do. For prescribing action entails the abandonment of philosophy. And yet, he argues, philosophy offers the most complete form of experience. For in refusing to be satisfied with anything short of the whole, it supersedes all arbitrary arrests (modes) in experience and chooses instead to determine "the relative validity of any world of experience." Philosophy is never bound by partisan interests, and it does not surrender to the demands of any mode. In Oakeshott's famous formulation, philosophy is "experience without reservation or arrest, experience which is critical throughout, unhindered and undistracted by what is subsidiary, partial or abstract."[5]

4. *EM,* 80.
5. Ibid., 1, 2, 3.

And yet Oakeshott insists that the philosopher can never be solely a philosopher, for no human being can renounce the pressing demands of other modes of experience. Although the philosopher may be an exile from the practical world, this should not "be taken to mean that he not only is but ought to be a fool in practical affairs. It is *philosophy itself* which must be free from the abstractions of living; and no man is merely a philosopher."[6] No one can avoid the practical mode; and therefore it is more appropriate to call philosophy a mood than a way of life. It is, no doubt, a mood for which many people have no inclination, but it is the only way to supersede the demands of the various arrests and view experience in its entirety. More will be said in the following chapters about Oakeshott's conception of philosophy, and particularly about his view of political philosophy. Here, however, it is crucial simply to recognize that for Oakeshott philosophy stands outside and above the modes of experience. It does not enter into the practical realm by prescribing action, nor does it constitute a distinct mode.

Philosophy, then, is the most complete form of experience; it is "experience become critical of itself, experience sought and followed entirely for its own sake."[7] It is the concrete whole and the logical ground out of which all modes take their bearings. It follows that if experience is understood to be a whole, then viewing this whole through any given mode will necessarily distort it. A scientist, for instance, who views the world *sub specie quantitatis* may be blind to the artist's or the poet's world; and those who understand nothing but practical concerns will usually be impatient with the historian or scientist. Thus the perennial question of college students: what does the study of history or philosophy have to do with anything I *need* to know? In Oakeshott's view, the correct answer would have to be, strictly speaking, that these studies have nothing at all to do with practical life. They are simply ways of explaining the world, and explanation can be understood as a good in itself. Such is the view expressed in Oakeshott's essay "Work and Play" and in all his essays on education. To sum up, the various modes are "arrests" in experience, and these arrests are vital if action is to take place. But no mode can legitimately claim to contain all of experience. If it does, it makes a hubristic mistake.

6. Ibid., 310 (emphasis added).
7. Ibid., 82.

If the discussion of modality in *Experience and Its Modes* is couched in the somewhat abstract language of philosophical Idealism, Oakeshott nevertheless returns to the modes of experience many times throughout his corpus. In a later work, *On History,* he defines *mode* somewhat more clearly as "an autonomous manner of understanding, specifiable in terms of exact conditions, which is logically incapable of denying or confirming the conclusions of any other mode of understanding, or indeed of making any relevant utterance in respect of it." And in "The Voice of Poetry in the Conversation of Mankind" he describes modes as diverse ways of imagining. But since modes represent abstract and deficient worlds of experience, one might be pardoned for wondering why they should be considered at all. Why not simply view experience as a whole, as the philosopher attempts to do? Oakeshott's answer is that modes are important because they represent significant and well-defined forms of human thought and conduct. History, science, and practice are, for Oakeshott, "the main arrests or modifications in experience, the main abstract worlds of ideas." Each is "sufficiently well-organized and developed . . . to present material for analysis."[8] Thus modes are not arbitrary creations of Oakeshott's imagination, but rather major intellectual and moral traditions worthy of examination in their own right.

Furthermore, since even philosophers cannot sustain the philosophical mood at all times, human beings find themselves passing most of their existence in one of these modes. Understanding human conduct requires coming to terms with the way people actually think and live. And most of life takes place, of course, in the mode of practice. Oakeshott includes morality, poetry, religion, and politics in this mode.[9] Indeed, his most famous work, his political philosophy, concerns a human activity (politics) that is eminently practical. But he is also concerned with what he considers the primary "explanatory" modes: science and history—particularly history, as is attested by his numerous later essays on the subject. Even history, however, is liable to be appropriated by the practical mode, and Oakeshott spends considerable energy showing that it is, in principle, independent from practice.

8. *OH,* 3; *EM,* 84.

9. Oakeshott famously "changed his mind" about the character of poetry. While in *EM* he placed it as part of practice, in "The Voice of Poetry in the Conversation of Mankind" it is no longer part of the practical mode, but seems to constitute a mode of its own. A full examination of this change is the subject of Chapter 5.

The argument of the present chapter, however, goes further than merely to claim that Oakeshott was concerned with the three major modes of science, history, and practice, as is already evident. There is a type of experience that lies between the cracks of these modes, and this experience consists in "presentness." It is not something that Oakeshott ever examined systematically, but hints of it appear in nearly every aspect of his work and it emerges in stark opposition to the demands of practice. I examine this idea in greater detail at the end of this chapter, but its outline may be stated briefly as follows. "Presentness," as I have termed it, is experience that looks neither forward nor backward for justification, but exists—and "delights"—wholly in the present moment. It is absolutely nonutilitarian, and as an end in itself needs to produce nothing. It is certainly a rare experience in the lives of most people, but it was of great value for Oakeshott.[10] Its character cannot, however, be fully appreciated until the character of its antithesis—practice—has been clearly described. Thus we must examine what Oakeshott meant when he spoke of the practical life.

PRACTICE

Although the world of practice is a limited one, it was of great importance to Oakeshott both for what it offers and for what it cannot offer. It is in the practical realm that one conceives and satisfies desires, undertakes projects, and enters into relationships of utility and pleasure. Indeed, political activity—though not political philosophy—takes place in the practical realm. And so it would seem that practice is a supremely important realm of human activity. But is it the whole of experience? Oakeshott's answer, of course, is no, but to understand this answer we must first examine carefully what he means by practice. This is a tall order; for, although practice is one of Oakeshott's most central concepts, it appears throughout his corpus in many different guises.[11] Yet certain common elements emerge from the various descriptions. I shall first identify these common elements more generally and then consider Oakeshott's most extended discussion of the practical life as it appears in *Experience and Its Modes.*

10. Wendell John Coats Jr. discusses this experience in the final chapter of his book *Oakeshott and His Contemporaries.* He calls it the "poetic character" of human experience.
11. For an extensive discussion of the place of practice in Oakeshott's thought, see Andrew Sullivan's PhD dissertation, "Intimations Pursued: The Voice of Practice in the Conversation of Michael Oakeshott."

In simplest terms, practice may be understood as the life of action. And in his understanding and criticism of the character of the active life, Oakeshott shares much with both the Christian contemplative tradition and eastern Taoism. Also, one cannot help but think of Pascal's reflections on the vanity of human endeavor. Nothing, Pascal declares, "is so insufferable to man as to be completely at rest, without passions, without business, without diversion." Man then feels his "nothingness, his forlornness, his insufficiency, his dependence, his weakness, his emptiness." Likewise, Chuang Tzu, a Taoist sage whom Oakeshott often quotes, observes that those "who are caught in the machinery of power take no joy except in activity and change—the whirring of the machine! Whenever an occasion for action presents itself, they are compelled to act; they cannot help themselves. They are inexorably moved, like the machine of which they are a part. Prisoners in the world of objects, they have no choice but to submit to the demands of matter! They are pressed down and crushed by external forces, fashion, the market, events, public opinion. Never in a whole lifetime do they recover their right mind! The active life! What a pity!"[12] And while Oakeshott does not go as far as this—in his view the active life is not wholly a pity—he clearly sees its limitations and wants to transcend them.

Practical life, for Oakeshott, is the life of interests, desire, and aversion. It is concerned not merely with personal advancement and physical survival but also with friendships and alliances, the nurture of children, and all moral activity. Practical life is the world of cause and effect. Perhaps most importantly, there is no action in practice that does not have implications for the future, even if those implications are small or nearly insignificant. This life takes place in the present but it *always* looks to a future, nearer or more distant. "With every want we evoke a future," Oakeshott maintains, "and in every action we seek a future condition of things, uncertain of achievement and sure only of its transience. In short, this present of practical engagement is not merely intermittently related to the future; it is itself a present-future. The objects which compose it are recognized in terms of the future they foretell or of their eligibility to satisfy our wants. In this universe of discourse we live always in a future." Thus practice may be described as both the "practical present" (for it is the present understood as the place where one works *toward* future satisfaction) and as a "present-future." Practice can never be self-sufficient or

---

12. Blaise Pascal, *Pensées*, 38; Thomas Merton, *The Way of Chuang Tzu*, 142.

undertaken as an end in itself because by nature it must look forward. It is a world in which things are fixed and have determinate weights and prices—"a world of fact, not poetic image, in which what we have spent on one thing we cannot spend on another."[13] It is not a world that welcomes contemplation or purposeless activity.

Practice is instead a mode of experience where individuals pursue happiness "by seeking the satisfaction of desires which spring from one another inexhaustibly. We enter into relationships of interest and of emotion, of competition, partnership, guardianship, love, friendship, jealousy and hatred," observes Oakeshott. In practical activity we "make agreements with one another; we have expectations about one another's conduct; we approve, we are indifferent and we disapprove."[14] This view of practice appears again and again throughout Oakeshott's writings, and he is at pains to refute those (like Heidegger) who award unconditionality to *praxis*—a move that, to Oakeshott, is both "arbitrary and obscure."[15] In his understanding of the incompleteness of the moral life, Oakeshott owes much to such writers as Augustine, Hobbes, Montaigne, and Pascal, all of whom he admired. But there is more to Oakeshott's view of practice than merely the interminability of endeavors. In *Experience and Its Modes* Oakeshott sets out several additional characteristics of the practical mode.

The conception of the self, Oakeshott observes, "is at once the most important and most characteristic of all the conceptions which go to make up the world of practical ideas."[16] Since practice is concerned with imagining and satisfying wants, it requires a desiring self who seeks those satisfactions. This is not, of course, to say that such a self is necessarily *merely* self-interested (since any self may also desire things for others), but it is to emphasize what is essential about the self: its desires and aversions. In no other mode does the self play such a central role. For although history and science require selves to engage in historical and scientific activity, neither history nor science cares in principle *which* self undertakes this activity. In practice, however, the self stands front and center.[17] The activities of desiring and willing are essential parts of the practical self, far

13. *OH*, 15, 13, 15; "On Being Conservative," in *RP*, 436.
14. "On Being Conservative," in *RP*, 425.
15. *OH*, 24–25.
16. *EM*, 269.
17. The philosophy of F. H. Bradley clearly lies behind this discussion of self. See especially "The Reality of Self" in *Appearance and Reality* and "Selfishness and Self-Sacrifice" in *Ethical Studies*.

more than in any other mode of experience. Indeed, desire and will are intimately linked, for in desiring something one wills that it come about. And will, when exercised in the pursuit or avoidance of something, is activity. The self in practical activity, then, desires certain outcomes and wills them to completion. Practice is "the conduct of life," observes Oakeshott, and practical experience is "the world *sub specie voluntatis.*"[18] The practical self, its activity, and its will are logically inseparable.

The self in the practical realm is also radically separate from other selves. Its freedom from the constraints of others "belongs to it by definition" and is a significant part of what it means to possess moral autonomy. For whenever "an attempt is made to break down the separateness and uniqueness of the practical self, wherever its 'freedom' is denied and wherever it is replaced by an idea of the self based upon some other principle of individuality than separateness and distinction," maintains Oakeshott, "the seeds of disintegration have been sown in the practical world."[19] The world of practice, of human conduct, simply cannot exist in the absence of individuals who have the freedom and inclination to satisfy their desires as they see fit. Oakeshott does recognize that there are "moods" in which a self may desire to be temporarily rid of its individuality, or to enter into communion with others; but to desire this is to move away from practice and toward another realm of experience. It is clear that Oakeshott's view of practice requires a separate, individual self.

Practice also presupposes a particular sense of time. When practical activity is undertaken it is always in order to modify some future state of affairs. The essence of practice is to make actual a "to be" that is "not yet," and practical action "involves a discrepancy between 'what is' and what we desire shall be."[20] There is no practical action that does not involve some sense of dissatisfaction with a given situation. For even if one feels that one's situation is "good," one almost always recognizes that this goodness cannot endure without efforts to maintain it. At the heart of practice there is a fundamental dissatisfaction that is impossible to overcome.

Oakeshott is not, of course, the first to recognize this dissatisfaction. This conception of practice appears in Hobbes's *Leviathan,* where felicity is understood to be the continual gratification of desires. Adam Smith,

18. *EM,* 258, 269.
19. Ibid., 270, 271.
20. Ibid., 257. Here, too, Oakeshott recalls Bradley's discussion of the moral life in "Concluding Remarks," *Ethical Studies.*

too, provides a particularly vivid description in *The Wealth of Nations,* where he observes that the human desire to better one's condition is "a desire which, though generally calm and dispassionate, comes with us from the womb, and never leaves us till we go into the grave. In the whole interval which separates those two moments," he continues, "there is scarce perhaps a single instant in which any man is so perfectly and completely satisfied with his situation, as to be without any wish of alteration or improvement, of any kind."[21] This, then, is the essence of practical life: it "[throws] reality into the future, into something new and to be made." Each instance of reconciliation between present and future causes another to arise, and no reconciliation can ever be final. "Nowhere in practice is there uninterrupted progress or final achievement."[22] The essence of practice is dissatisfaction, because in this realm human beings must always hope to gain in the future what they do not have in the present.

Since practice always aims to reconcile the two worlds of "what is" and "what shall be," it consists in constant activity. Practice is the world "conceived under the category of change," and what cannot be transformed by action does not fall within its realm. Practice is the world of human conduct. Only humans are capable of imagining future states of affairs; and it is a particularly human characteristic to be dissatisfied with one's present situation and to act in order that it might be better. Thus practice is also an unstable world. Unlike science, which is characterized by quantitative facts that are stable and unchanging, "facts" in practice exist in order to be changed through activity. Indeed, as Oakeshott observes, "what is not transient is, for that reason, not real for practical experience." And yet he is careful to point out that there are limits to the changes that can be achieved. For instance, one could never transform the character of practice itself; there is no practical action that could somehow make practice other than what it is. "Wherever there is action there is presupposed a world which action may modify, but which it can never wholly and in principle transform."[23] Thus one may work to achieve a life in which the demands of practical life are minimized, but these demands, so long as one is alive, can never be eliminated. In this context it is worthwhile to recall the "leaky jar" discussion in the *Gorgias,* where Callicles tells Socrates that he thinks happiness consists in "expe-

21. Adam Smith, *Inquiry into the Nature and Causes of the Wealth of Nations,* 341.
22. *EM,* 305, 291.
23. Ibid., 257, 303, 306, 261.

riencing all the other appetites and being able to satisfy them and living happily in the enjoyment of them."[24] Socrates, of course, is not persuaded by this. Neither is Oakeshott.

That the practical world can never be wholly transformed is one of Oakeshott's most fundamental insights into the nature of morality and politics. I address this point later in the book, for I believe it is *the* fundamental insight—a religious and aesthetic insight—that lies at the heart of Oakeshott's political theory. Like Augustine, Oakeshott sees a limited scope for politics because he believes there can be no absolute transformation of present ills into a utopian future. And yet the nature of practice (the continuousness of needs) requires constant attention to such concerns—in short, the maintenance of institutions and relationships or, as Oakeshott puts it, "attending to arrangements." Consequently, Oakeshott spends a tremendous amount of energy analyzing politics, even as he finds politics a rather mundane subject in the great scheme of things. He is, for instance, emphatic about the relative *unimportance* of politics in an essay from 1939 entitled "The Claims of Politics." And although Oakeshott tempers his disparaging view of politics later in his career, he remains convinced that politics can never offer the kind of fulfillment available in other kinds of human activity.

There is one more essential characteristic of the world of practice: if practice is human activity, it also consists in the termination of that activity in death. The world of practice is unavoidably a "mortal world." And mortality here is taken to indicate not only human mortality (though this is perhaps its most vivid manifestation), but also the mortality of all human projects and designs. "Mortality," declares Oakeshott, "is the presiding category in practical experience."[25] Ultimately, the only outcome of practical endeavor is a final failure, the failure to stay alive and to continue the endless activity of practice. This fact alone is enough to suggest that if practice were conceived as the whole of experience, life would be profoundly unsatisfying.

How, then, should the character of this practical realm be approached? Is it something to be celebrated by observing that the possibilities of practice are, in their sphere, virtually endless? Or should it be lamented, since nothing in this realm can ever be fixed or final, and because

---

24. Plato *Gorgias* 494c.
25. *EM,* 258, 273.

practice has an unavoidably mortal character? Oakeshott would seem to answer both questions in the affirmative, for there is in human nature both a desire constantly to change one's circumstances as well as a longing for permanence or completion. But if there can be no real permanence in practice, and if most of human experience takes place in the practical realm, how can one ever achieve anything lasting? The answer to this question, as we shall see, lies in a certain type of *present* experience—one that escapes some of the constraints of the practical life and approaches certain activities as ends in themselves.

To recapitulate what has been observed so far about the character of practice, practice requires a "self" understood to be active. This self engages in projects for the purpose of changing or maintaining a given state of affairs; and the world in which these activities take place is understood to be capable of alteration, which is undertaken to bring together the two worlds of "what is" and "what ought to be." And the discrepancy between present and future is reconciled time and again, as various circumstances arise in an individual's life.

But why, given its inherent unsatisfactoriness, did Oakeshott find practice so important? First, he recognized that of all the arrests in experience, practice is by far the dominant one. While few individuals become historians or scientists, all of us take part in practice by pursuing things we desire. No one can avoid this realm, and thus it largely constitutes what it means to be a human being. Even quietists, Oakeshott argues, do not escape the practical realm; for quietism itself is a particular response to practical concerns. Second, Oakeshott realized that many tangible goods come about in the realm of practice, for as he observes, it is rational to "go on changing one's butcher until one gets the meat one likes, to go on educating one's agent until he does what is required of him."[26] Such utilitarian relationships are unmistakably part of life, and they provide numerous benefits. And it must be admitted that real rewards accompany practical activity. Who does not feel a sense of satisfaction at the successful completion of a difficult project? Third, the realm of practice is the realm of human, moral conduct; and thus it is also the realm of politics. Morality, politics, and religion all derive their character from the fact that they are practical (here, *practical* understood in its most expansive sense). Thus, if he was to theorize political activity accurately, Oakeshott saw that he must understand the context in which it arises.

26. "On Being Conservative," in *RP,* 416.

Nevertheless, this practical aspect also sets limits to the activities of politics and morality. As I noted above, practical activity may alter but not transform; and no amount of practical striving can ever lead to permanent satisfaction. Oakeshott thus had no patience for a "politics of perfection" or for schemes that claim to solve human problems once and for all. Oakeshott's is a fundamentally spiritual way of looking at the world. This spirituality I refer to is not, of course, the spirituality of orthodox religion, though Oakeshott was steeped in the Christian tradition. Rather, Oakeshott's fundamental spiritual insight is his recognition of the transitory nature of human life and thus the unimportance of so much that is valued by the world. The central concern of the religious imagination, for Oakeshott, is the perception of life as unavoidably evanescent and mutable.

Finally, Oakeshott was concerned with practice because he saw the limitations that are inherent in it. Despite the undeniable importance of practical experience, practice cannot be understood to exhaust human experience. Indeed, in the conclusion of *Experience and Its Modes* Oakeshott explicitly emphasizes the deficiency of practice and attempts to show why practice cannot maintain itself as the whole of experience. Furthermore, if Oakeshott's work is considered as a whole, one cannot help but be struck by the sense that practical considerations—important, though they be—are to one side of another interest of Oakeshott's, and this concerns things that are *not* part of practice. This is especially evident in his early work, but it is apparent throughout his career, and particularly in his later essay "The Voice of Poetry in the Conversation of Mankind." In short, Oakeshott's view is this: that practice is unavoidably dominant in human life, for we cannot help but be concerned with our survival and happiness in a mortal world. But the dominance of practice does not prove its superiority, for there are activities that supersede practice and promise a sense of completeness that practice cannot. Thus, what I have termed the "two sides" of practice are its apparent adequacy (since most of human life takes place here) and its *actual* inadequacy (because Oakeshott did not believe that certain valuable activities are subsumed in the practical). Indeed, most people, as Oakeshott observes, are confined within practical experience "as if in a prison."[27] The alternative to practice lies in Oakeshott's conception of "presentness."

What are these things that stand opposite practice? They are activities

27. *EM*, 249.

pursued for no extrinsic purpose, "ends in themselves," things that possess self-sufficiency and a kind of permanence. It is difficult to say with
assurance what activities definitively fall into this group, although love,
friendship, and liberal learning are Oakeshott's most unambiguous examples. Poetry appears as part of practice in *Experience and Its Modes,* but
in Oakeshott's mature thought it constitutes a mode of its own and is
something supremely "present." Thus it, too, takes its place as a nonpractical activity. Philosophy is somewhat more difficult to classify, but not
because Oakeshott changes his mind about its character. The difficulty
with respect to philosophy is a result of Oakeshott's conception of the
nature of philosophy. For on the one hand philosophy is supremely impractical, in that it seems to have no bearing on everyday conduct at all.
But on the other hand, philosophy seems to be interminable—not in the
same sense that practical activity is *temporally* interminable, but because
there is no point at which philosophy can be said to cease. Philosophical
thinking always points beyond the "going-on" it is considering to the
postulates that lie beneath it, and such thinking has no end-point. Thus it
is difficult to know whether it could offer the sort of "presentness" that I
have been describing.

Oakeshott hints at a general category of experience that might escape
the constraints of practice in a striking passage in *Experience and Its Modes.*
The passage occurs in the context of a discussion of the "self" in which
he explains, as has been discussed above, that a concept of the individual
and separate self is necessary for practical activity. But Oakeshott admits
that this concept is not "without its difficulties" and that "[i]t cannot be
denied that there are moods and actions in the conduct of life which
seem to point in a different direction." This different direction, here only
hinted at, consists in a momentary escape from the prison of individual
and separate endeavors required by practical life. The escape consists in a
temporary abandonment of the self. "The attempt oneself, to find oneself in another, to preserve oneself by abandoning oneself, to become
oneself by surrendering oneself," Oakeshott remarks, "appears to imply a
conception of the self somewhat different from that which belongs to
ordinary practical activity." In such moods the self's separateness is "qualified." Oakeshott observes that there exists an experience of self not contained by the *merely* individual, practical self. Such a conception takes
one "outside the world of practical experience." And it is not the philosopher who persuades us of this experience, he observes, but the

"lover, who momentarily convinces us that [the separate self] is an illusion."[28] Thus the individual self, so necessary for practice, is revealed as an abstraction that does not exhaust what it means to be a human being. Oakeshott hints, in this passage, at another realm of experience that is not history, science, or philosophy.

There would seem to be two possible interpretations of what Oakeshott means by moving "outside the world of practical experience." On the one hand, he might be suggesting that the world of practical experience could be superseded by a type of experience in which the self is temporarily "lost," that is, an experience in which the concerns of the practical self temporarily recede. There is evidence to support this view in "The Voice of Poetry." On the other hand, he may be referring to the type of experience he discusses in "The Nature and Meaning of Sociality," where the separateness of the self is overcome by joining oneself to a larger whole. Both of these are intriguing possibilities, and both support the view that Oakeshott recognizes a nonpractical, nonphilosophical "other" kind of experience that might be called, in a sense, "transcendent."

But Oakeshott is quick to return to practical life, and concludes his short digression by observing that "[t]here is no point in the conduct of life at which the assumption that the self is what is separate and self-determined, that the self is the will, can with impunity be abandoned."[29] Indeed, to give up one's self is to abandon the human realm altogether, and this cannot be done. The conduct of life is *human* conduct; it is the moral realm of practice. It is clear, however, that Oakeshott recognizes the human desire to step outside practice—even if only temporarily— and to rid oneself, for a time, of the burden of conduct and self-consciousness. To do so is to renounce practice, at least for the moment. *This* unavoidably temporary and fleeting experience is one that Oakeshott finds vitally important.

So far, then, we have seen that Oakeshott designates practice as the dominant mode in human activity, and it is a forward-looking mode that requires a self, an active will, engaged in the search for future or "present-future" satisfactions. But there is another mode of experience that Oakeshott sees as distinct from practice—at least *potentially* distinct—and worthy of detailed examination. This mode is history, and though it would

---

28. Ibid., 271, 272.
29. Ibid., 273.

appear to deal with the past *simpliciter*, it too often finds itself dominated by practice. A large part of Oakeshott's task in his writings about the character of history is to distinguish exactly what is meant by the concept of "past." Thus it is worth considering the character of history as Oakeshott describes it in *Experience and Its Modes* as well as in other sources.[30]

HISTORY

History's most important postulate is its concern with the idea of the "past." But just what kind of past is this? Oakeshott attempts to define a specifically "historical" past, a past that cannot merely be assimilated to the practical present. His task here is one of definition, but also of protection: he aims to defend history, that is, a particularly pure understanding of history, against its most common misunderstandings and misappropriations. Practice, because it is so immediately pressing, tends to invade the territory of other modes and to insinuate itself into areas of experience where it does not belong. It certainly does this in the case of history— "history is only important for what it can tell us about the here and now," practice argues—and Oakeshott expends much effort defending history from this encroachment.[31]

The crux of his argument may be stated as follows. History, understood essentially, is a mode of experience whose postulates are categorically different from those of practice. History does *not* exist to "illuminate the present" or to "provide lessons" for practical conduct. While practice is the realm of action and morality where all decisions have consequences for an imagined future, history is concerned with the past for its own sake. It is not, Oakeshott emphasizes, an objective series of events; nor is it isolated particles of data that can be collected by any trained practitioner. Rather, history is a construction of the past, by a person

30. His most important discussions of history appear in *EM, OH,* and "The Activity of Being an Historian," in *RP.*
31. Oakeshott's views on history have only recently been studied in depth. The most exhaustive consideration of his thought on this subject is without a doubt Luke O'Sullivan's *Oakeshott on History.* This study builds on the work of David Boucher, who has also considered Oakeshott's views of history in a series of books and articles: "The Creation of the Past: British Idealism and Michael Oakeshott's Philosophy of History," "Human Conduct, History and Social Science in the Works of R. G. Collingwood and Michael Oakeshott," and *Texts in Context: Revisionist Methods for Studying the History of Ideas.*

known as a historian, based on the evidence that survives from past events. The specific "historical past" has never *actually* existed anywhere; it is an inference on the part of the historian and functions as a technical term in Oakeshott's discussion. This sketch will be fleshed out more fully in the paragraphs to follow, for it is, no doubt, an unusual and somewhat difficult conception of history. However, an accurate understanding of what Oakeshott means requires a careful inquiry into the terms he uses, for he is quite specific about the potential meanings of the word *past*.

Oakeshott observes that there are two different meanings of the term *past*. The first is what he calls the "practical past," and it is the counterpart of the practical present. As we recall, the practical present is normally concerned with the future consequences of present actions, but there are times when it may look to the past to glean lessons from it. When it does so, it looks to a specifically *practical* past, one valued solely for its "usefulness" as a guide in present, practical affairs. Here is how Oakeshott describes this practical past:

> Wherever the past is merely that which preceded the present, that from which the present has grown, wherever the significance of the past lies in the fact that it has been influential in deciding the present and future fortunes of man, wherever the present is sought in the past, and wherever the past is regarded as merely a refuge from the present—the past involved is a practical, and not an historical past. . . . [It] will be found, in general, to serve either of two masters—politics or religion.

Wherever the past is thought of as a library of emblems to be retrieved for current purposes, it cannot be anything but practical. Indeed, Oakeshott even questions whether this "practical past" is significantly past at all, for it does its work as part of the practical present. It is the "present contents of a vast storehouse into which time continuously empties the lives, the utterances, the achievements and the sufferings of mankind."[32] In short—and Oakeshott is quite emphatic about this—the practical past is utilitarian in character. It is studied to provide examples and warnings, things to do or to avoid in order to bring about particular results. Alternatively, it may serve the practical present by demonstrating (so-called) immutable laws of causality that claim to predict future events. It should be no surprise that Oakeshott believed that the past understood solely in

32. *EM,* 103; *OH,* 18–20, 43.

its practical aspect is a *misunderstanding*. And so he provides an alternative vision.

This alternative vision is the "historical past," in which there is no place for moral or causal judgments. Here the past is understood not as a harbinger of the future, but as "a complicated world, without unity of feeling or clear outline: in it events have no over-all pattern or purpose, lead nowhere, point to no favoured condition of the world and support no practical conclusions. It is a world composed wholly of contingencies." Strictly speaking, the historical past never actually existed, because each action that is now past took place in *its* present, and so was subject to all the contingencies that go with action in a practical present. Oakeshott elaborates on this point in "The Activity of Being an Historian," where he writes the following: "[I]n an important sense, an 'historical' event is something that never happened and an 'historical' action something never performed. . . . the idiom of happening is always that of practice." The job of the historian is thus "to create by a process of translation; to understand past conduct and happening in a manner in which they were never understood at the time; to translate action and event from their practical idiom into an historical idiom."[33] This is a resolutely non-teleological conception of the past. Historical events are understood neither as the culmination of prior forces nor as predictors of what is to come.

The historical past cannot be understood simply as the recovery of what went before, because Oakeshott argues that there is no "objective course of events" to be retrieved. This, of course, is part of Oakeshott's view, expressed in *Experience and Its Modes,* that there is no experience that can be said to be "pre-thought." The world, in other words, does not exist as a series of objective facts waiting to be discovered, but is, always and everywhere, *someone's* interpretation. The historical past—in the specific sense that Oakeshott uses this term—depends on the activity of the historian, whose business it is to "create and to construct" history out of the evidence that remains to him. However, this does not mean the historian can create or construct a merely arbitrary past. He must create and construct *according to what the evidence obliges him to believe.* And, it should be remembered that the historian is barred from finding general laws in history or from speculating about "causes." A historian might (though he should not, according to Oakeshott) say that certain actions "caused"

33. "The Activity of Being an Historian," in *RP,* 182, 179–80, 80.

other actions; but strictly speaking there can be no cause in history, because history—as it takes place—is merely present action and its contingent consequences among individuals. The historian's task is to set before us "the events (in so far as they can be ascertained) which mediate one circumstance to another." History is concerned with occasions, not causes.[34]

This is what is essential in Oakeshott's understanding of the "historical past": it cannot be used to demonstrate immutable laws of causality, nor can it provide lessons for the present. In the historical past events are "understood in respect of their independence of subsequent events or present circumstances or desires, and are understood as having no necessary and sufficient conditions."[35] Oakeshott is clear that history cannot be assimilated to the models either of science or of practice but is an inquiry in its own right. In the several places he discusses the character of history, his task is to liberate it from the dominance of these other modes and to elucidate its character as something to be valued in itself. Most importantly, the past cannot be understood merely as something useful for present practical life.

So far, then, we have seen that Oakeshott considers two distinct modes, and thus two distinct conceptions of time. Practice is the mode of the "present-future," while history is the mode that concerns itself with past events. Yet although these two modes are *categorically distinct,* they are not always so starkly separated in the lives of human beings, largely because practice tends to dominate all other modes. Practice is indeed the most pressing of all types of experience, since neglecting the practical yields real, often painful consequences. But its dominance does not prove its inherent superiority. Indeed, as I argue in the next chapter (following Oakeshott and Bradley), practice shows itself to be strikingly *unsatisfactory* in that it contains an inherent contradiction. The contradiction is between the "is" and the "ought," which cannot be abolished without abolishing the very nature of practice itself.

PRESENTNESS

An alternative way of understanding oneself and one's actions is what I call "presentness," that is, in acting in such a way that practical concerns about the future recede from view, at least for a time. Presentness and

34. Ibid., 172, 182.
35. *OH,* 174.

practice must therefore be mutually exclusive. However, in the historical mode there exists an intimation of presentness, even though history is ostensibly concerned with the past. As we have seen, history may either be *used* (as it is when it is merely the counterpart of the practical present) or it may be undertaken for its own sake. When the historian approaches the past in the latter mind-set, history becomes a self-sufficient endeavor that has inherent rewards, not practical ones. It is then "an interest in past events for their own sake, or in respect of their independence of subsequent or present events."[36] In this kind of historical inquiry the very *activity* of being a historian (collecting documents, making inferences from those documents, and so on) comes forward as the most important part of history. The essence of history is then understood *not* to consist of the practical lessons that may be distilled from a historian's work, but rather in the "doing" or "writing" of history. Being a historian is here understood as an end in itself.

It is, however, as Oakeshott admits, extraordinarily difficult to maintain the mind-set of the true historian and to avoid slipping back into the language of practice. Moreover, the character of historical activity as an end in itself is available only to the historian *qua* historian. When the historian walks out of his study he is immediately back in the world of practice. Nevertheless, there are intimations of presentness in Oakeshott's particular understanding of history, much as there are in his understanding of liberal learning, despite the fact that in both history and university education there are strong inducements toward placing these activities in the service of practice. History is thus deemed important when it prevents us from "making the same mistakes again," and university education finds its justification as the means to a successful career. Oakeshott, of course, rejects all such purposes for history and education, designating these activities as most valuable when they are engaged in for themselves by those few who understand the value of such endeavor.

Nevertheless, it does seem that the purest form of "presentness" lies elsewhere, in a kind of experience that can, at times, wholly escape practice. As the most dominant of all the modes, practice usually insists on taking first place in human experience. It is in the practical realm, after all, where issues of life and death, desire, aversion, and morality must be addressed. But practice is explicitly future-looking. And, since it is always action for the sake of something else, it is an irreconcilable disunity of

---

36. "The Activity of Being an Historian," in *RP,* 170.

form and content.[37] That human life overwhelmingly takes place in the practical realm is undeniable, but that this is the *only* way life may be understood is not at all clear.

Oakeshott often writes about the incompleteness and dissatisfaction entailed in the practical life, and he offers an alternative way of thinking about the world. He addresses the idea of presentness explicitly in two essays, "Religion and the World" and "On Being Conservative," which I shall discuss shortly. First, however, it is essential to set out in greater detail precisely what Oakeshott seems to mean when he describes these "present" experiences.[38]

In the preceding pages I have frequently used the phrase *end in itself* as a way of distinguishing a certain type of human activity. The idea lies at the heart of the conception of life that Oakeshott found so important. It means, as we have already seen above, acting in such a way as to reject the assumption that everything must be "for" something else, and therefore to reject the worldliness that comes with constantly pursuing far-off ends. To engage in activities as ends in themselves is to have moved away (at least temporarily) from the framework of means and ends. In this rejection Oakeshott has much in common with Walter Pater, whom he read extensively in his youth.[39] Both Pater and Oakeshott rejected the utilitarian conception of life (Oakeshott's "practical realm") and valued instead a more personal, insightful, and ultimately more creative way of viewing human conduct. Pater observes that for most of us "the conception of means and ends covers the whole of life, and is the exclusive type or figure under which we represent our lives to ourselves. Such a figure, reducing all things to machinery . . . is too like a mere picture or description of men's lives as we actually find them, to be the basis of the higher ethics. It covers the meanness of men's lives . . . but not the intangible perfection of those whose ideal is rather in *being* than in *doing*—not those *manners* which are, in the deepest as in the simplest sense, *morals.*"[40] Practice, of course, is constant "doing," but presentness offers a chance

37. See Coats, *Oakeshott and His Contemporaries,* 104–5.
38. Coats calls this the "poetic character" of human activity and remarks that to act in this manner is "to insist on the inseparability of the form and content . . . to insist that there is no goal or end of an activity in advance of the activity" (*Oakeshott and His Contemporaries,* 105). Glenn Worthington also calls this kind of activity poetic in his article "The Voice of Poetry in Oakeshott's Moral Philosophy."
39. According to Timothy Fuller, Oakeshott was recognized for outstanding scholarship while an undergraduate at Cambridge, and he chose as his prize Pater's complete works.
40. Walter Pater, *Appreciations,* 61.

simply to "be." What is valued is not worldly success, but the achievement of a sensibility, of personal insight, sincerity, candor, and, ultimately, self-understanding.

Indeed, if the concept of activities as "ends in themselves" is one essential component of presentness, then the cultivation of self-understanding is the other. The word *self-understanding* has suffered much abuse, since it has often been used to describe a radically individualistic, relativist, subjective "finding oneself" that is not what Oakeshott and Pater mean by the term. *Self-understanding* for them means learning—often with difficulty—to find one's place in the world, to recognize those things worth pursuing and to reject those that are not. It also means cultivating a personal sensibility that will prove the most enduring of all possible achievements.[41]

This self-understanding also entails a rejection, or at least an attenuation, of the practical self. Self-understanding, if it be more than merely superficial, must penetrate beneath this practical self whose only concerns are desires and aversions, means and ends. Self-understanding is not merely understanding what kind of food one likes best or one's favorite place to vacation. Oakeshott explains his idea of self-understanding most clearly in his essays on education, where he argues that human learning "is concerned with perceptions, ideas, beliefs, emotions, sensibilities, recognitions, discriminations, theorems and with all that goes to constitute a human condition." The end of life "is not action but contemplation . . . a certain disposition of the mind," expounds Pater in a similar vein, and for this to be so the demands of practice must be put off—at least intermittently.[42]

There is, indeed, a freedom that comes with letting go of practice. As Oakeshott once commented, "[I]t is a blessed relief to gaze in a shop window and see nothing we want." This kind of self—the self whose practical concerns may with profit sometimes be ignored—enjoys the possibility of a freedom greater than any offered by practice. This self understands that there is everything to be gained by the "purposeless" impassioned contemplation of which Pater speaks. "Life is the end of life" is a maxim that best describes this intentional living in the present; and it consists in cultivation and refinement of one's intellect and emotions through a

41. See "Religion and the World," in *RPML*, 34.
42. *VLL*, 22; Walter Pater, *Marius the Epicurean*, 117. This cultivation of self-understanding through liberal education is the subject of Oakeshott's essays in *The Voice of Liberal Learning*.

special sort of education. This education is not "the conveyance of an abstract body of truths or principles . . . but the conveyance of an art—an art in some degree peculiar to each individual character."[43]

The idea of "presentness" that I have been describing is thus a way of orienting oneself in the world. It is the endeavor to approach activities as ends in themselves, to reject the idea that life must be solely a matter of means and ends, and it is a release from the relentless desires and aversions of practical life. I suppose there is a case to be made that even the most "practical" and utilitarian activities can be approached as ends in themselves. Certain activities (friendship, love, conversation) tend to lend themselves to this understanding more than others (investing in the stock market or grocery shopping). To live in the present is to cultivate a certain kind of character, to strive to gain insight, to downplay the importance of practice, and thus to become the kind of individual Oakeshott describes in "Religion and the World."

In "Religion and the World" Oakeshott writes explicitly about the importance of living in the present. To avoid the constant frustrations of practice, he argues, one must endeavor to live a life that is truly contemporary. Living solely for the future is "vain," he observes. In this essay Oakeshott equates "presentness" with religion, and thus to live religiously is to live fully in each moment, letting go of past and future. "The goal of life is not, for us, distant," he contends, "it is always here and now in the achievement of a personal sensibility." Ambition, he posits, or the practical life, "and the world's greed for visible results, in which each stage is a mere approach to the goal, would be superseded by a [religious] life which carried in each of its moments its whole meaning and value."[44] Living such a life is the only way to overcome the limitations of practice.

Oakeshott describes a sort of freedom that comes with living in the present. This freedom consists in choosing to focus on one's self and character rather than on career or contribution, in rejecting the glory of "worldly" achievement in favor of finding meaning in the actual conscious living of one's own life. It is an ideal, to be sure, and not one that can—or should—ever wholly supersede life in the practical realm. But it is an ideal often overshadowed in a world that prioritizes achievement, success, and purposeful enterprise. In the "extemporary life" set forth in this ideal, "nothing is of final worth except present insight, a grasp of the

43. "On Being Conservative," in *RP,* 424; see Pater, *Appreciations,* 60; Pater, *Marius the Epicurean,* 118.
44. "Religion and the World," in *RPML,* 35, 32.

thing itself." Thus "presentness," in "Religion and the World," may be understood as the religious life that supersedes the incompleteness of practice. Once again, Pater is helpful here, as he comments on the importance of living in the present:

> [T]owards such a full or complete life, a life of various yet select sensation, the most direct and effective auxiliary must be, in a word, Insight. Liberty of soul, freedom from all partial and misrepresentative doctrine which does but relieve one element in our experience at the cost of another, freedom from all embarrassment alike of regret for the past and of calculation on the future: this would be but preliminary to the real business of education—insight, insight through culture, into all that the present moment holds in trust for us, as we stand so briefly in its presence.

True value, then, is found not in the results of an action, but in a unity of manner and motive in action itself.[45] Thus what emerges from both Oakeshott and Pater is a very particular philosophy of life, and it is what I have called "presentness," or a unity of form and content. This is the alternative to life understood on the model of a machine, where all actions are inputs calculated to result in certain future outputs.

Oakeshott also makes an explicit case for "present-living" in his essay "On Being Conservative." Here he sets out a rather unusual version of conservatism, a kind that values an intentional life in the *present*. In contrast to the common view that conservatives reverence the past and yearn for a return to some mythical golden age, Oakeshott believes that the essence of conservatism is to enjoy what one has. There is no "mere idolizing of what is past and gone. What is esteemed is the present." This kind of conservatism shows itself wherever such present enjoyment is pursued "and not a profit, a reward, a prize or a result in addition to the experience itself." It centers upon a "propensity to use and to enjoy what is available rather than to wish for or to look for something else; to delight in what is present rather than what was or what may be." Moreover, this disposition is "appropriate in a large and significant field of human activity."[46] Here, as in "Religion and the World," the most valuable things are those that may be approached as ends in themselves.

---

45. Ibid., 37; Pater, *Marius the Epicurean*, 117; Pater, *Appreciations*, 62. This idea foreshadows Oakeshott's later conception of morality as "self-enactment."
46. "On Being Conservative," in *RP*, 408, 415.

Oakeshott admits that this view of things is not likely to be embraced by the world at large, for it runs directly counter to the world's values. It is, as he says, an understanding fit only for "poets and women." But Oakeshott was quite fond of poets and women. And this is an understanding he holds very dear, one he never loses sight of even as his theorizing takes him right into the midst of the supremely practical concern: politics. For Oakeshott recognizes of the practical life (or "work," as he puts it in one essay), that the creature of wants who lives within this conception is condemned "to a life in which every achievement is also a frustration." There is something lacking in the happiness that is available in practical achievement, and the creature of wants "is a creature of unavoidable anxieties. If he is temporarily successful he may forget these anxieties; but he is in the position of a man who has mortgaged his future in a huge hire-purchase debt." There is no way out of this situation per se, but there is a way to mitigate the frustration that comes with it—though this requires a radical shift in understanding. No practical activity will suffice to relieve the inadequacy of practice; the problem of salvation is, as has been pointed out, always constituted in self-understanding. In an unpublished notebook, Oakeshott goes so far as to observe that achievement is the "diabolical" element in human life precisely because it reduces all human experience to investment and explicitly denies the value of poetic or what I have termed "present" experience. "The symbol of our vulgarization of human life," Oakeshott laments, "is our near exclusive concern with achievement . . . [but] Christianity is the religion of non-achievement."[47]

This chapter has argued that "presentness" is a way of describing an experience that was important to Oakeshott. Although this kind of experience does not constitute a mode of its own, it emerges in opposition to the demands of practice (which is oriented toward the future) and history (which is concerned with the past). Oakeshott's conception of this experience shares much with the thought of Walter Pater, who emphasizes the cultivation of personal insight as a more lasting achievement than any promised by practical activity. Indeed, Oakeshott even calls this achievement "religious." It would seem, then, that religion could offer an escape from the practical realm and a way of living fully in the present.

47. "Religion and the World," in *RPML,* 33; WP, 31; Timothy Fuller, introduction to *RPML,* 3; quoted in Ian Tregenza, *Michael Oakeshott on Hobbes,* 147–48.

However, this would be a mistaken conclusion. For although Oake-shott equates presentness with religion in "Religion and the World," the remainder of his essays about religion argue a quite different point. Indeed, in every other mention of religion throughout his corpus, Oake-shott is quite clear about its explicitly *practical* nature. So although we have identified a particular type of experience—what I have termed "presentness"—the question of how that experience relates to religion remains open. There are good reasons for thinking that truly "present" experience may lie in a wholly different kind of experience—the realm of poetry and aesthetics. The following chapter, however, investigates Oakeshott's treatment of religion, asking and answering the question of how religion and practical life relate, and how "presentness" might or might not fit into this scheme. The question of "presentness" in Oake-shott's aesthetic theory is yet another consideration, which I will address in Chapter 5.

4

Oakeshott's Religious Thought

As I showed in the previous chapter, Oakeshott appears to be trying to identify a type of experience that is truly "present." He demonstrates that most experience tends to be overtaken by the demands of practice, but he also gives hints that certain activities are more thoroughly protected from these encroachments. Oakeshott suggests that religion is capable of satisfying the desire for presentness in his essay "Religion and the World," in which he presents an Augustinian choice between two ways of living. One of these consists in an unsatisfactory worldliness, while the other offers fulfillment through religious, noninstrumental conduct. Religion appears in this essay as a type of experience that escapes the contingencies of practice, as something that consists in the present "achievement of a personal sensibility."[1] Religion thus seems to be something that is truly an end in itself.

However, despite this essay's suggestiveness, Oakeshott ultimately found that religion did not offer the kind of "presentness" for which he was searching. For when "Religion and the World" is read alongside Oakeshott's other early essays on religion, such as "Religion and the Moral Life" and "The Importance of the Historical Element in Christianity," one discovers that religion *cannot* be an absolute escape from contingency. In these essays Oakeshott repeatedly emphasizes that religion is something requiring a moral personality—a self—and thus it is thoroughly practical. It therefore does not offer release from the constraints of time and contingency, but rather a certain type of fulfillment for the moral personality. Religion understood in this way is not a mystical loss of self. On the contrary, it is something that requires that the self be found in its most complete and adequate form.

1. "Religion and the World," in *RPML*, 35.

To anticipate the conclusion of this chapter, Oakeshott concluded that religion and practice are intimately related. Religion is, in one formulation, the "completion" of practice—the whole in which the abstractions of practical life are resolved. It offers a kind of satisfaction that cannot otherwise be achieved in the ordinary moral life, and it is the most fulfilling type of practical activity. Religion is a kind of unity within personality that manifests itself in a corresponding unity of conduct. Activities are undertaken because they satisfy a clear-sighted understanding of what is ultimately satisfactory.

Religion and the moral life are therefore not radically severed, but part of the same continuum of experience. Conducting oneself religiously does not imply stepping "out of time" into some sort of mystical present. Nor is it a type of activity in which one's moral personality recedes. And yet even as religion is thoroughly practical, it also partakes of "presentness" to a certain degree, in that true religious faith encourages an attenuation of anxiety about the future. The person of faith is probably able to enjoy and delight in what lies before him, rather than being wistful for the past or anxious about the future. Nevertheless, Oakeshott finds that the most complete form of "presentness" is possible not in religion, but in aesthetic experience, as the next chapter attempts to show.

To understand exactly how Oakeshott comes to this view of religion we must examine more closely the places in which he explicitly considers it. These consist of the several early essays mentioned above as well as his short treatments of religion in *Experience and Its Modes* and *On Human Conduct*. I consider these as a whole, as together expressing different facets of Oakeshott's religious ideas. It is true that after the 1930s Oakeshott hardly ever considered religion in print (the one notable exception being his all-too-short treatment in *On Human Conduct*), but his strong early interest in religion should not be underestimated. Indeed, I believe it provides the moral basis for his later political writings.[2] I therefore examine his religious views under three headings.

First, I discuss Oakeshott's understanding of the connection between morality and religion. This requires an examination of his conception of the moral life, focusing particularly on the British Idealist context in which he composed his early essays. Second, he insists on the personal,

2. Ian Tregenza supports this view when he observes that Oakeshott's "concern with Rationalism and the corruptions of practical life seem to derive from an attitude to experience which could be termed religious" (*Michael Oakeshott on Hobbes*, 130).

unmediated nature of authentic religious experience against the view that religion stands or falls on the basis of historical investigation. A proper understanding of religion (and here Oakeshott means Christianity) requires a focus not on the historical foundations of religion but on direct spiritual experience. Oakeshott was thus involved in the debates during the 1920s among English Modernists regarding the meaning of history in the Christian experience. The general outlines of this debate provide essential context for his essay "The Importance of the Historical Element in Christianity."

The third section of this chapter, however, takes a somewhat different turn. In this section I consider a very straightforward question: what are the ordinary human needs that religion promises to satisfy? This is simply to follow Oakeshott's lead, for as Fuller has observed, Oakeshott "personally sympathized, in religious matters, with the simple, direct and immediate against the sophisticated, detached and intellectual."[3] While his religious views may have taken shape in the rarefied atmosphere of philosophical Idealism and religious Modernism, Oakeshott is careful not to confuse a philosophical account of the religious experience with religion *as it actually exists* for human beings. As he repeatedly emphasizes, religion is eminently practical. As such, it promises to make life more meaningful for ordinary people.

These three categories—the moral life and British idealism, the experiential nature of true religion in the debates over Modernism, and the practical needs religion addresses—do not exhaust the possible approaches to Oakeshott's religious views, but they do provide a way of understanding some of the major issues in these often-overlooked early writings. Moreover, taking these views together and setting out a clear view of Oakeshott's thoughts on religion is vital in differentiating religion from another kind of experience that appears consistently throughout Oakeshott's corpus. This "other" kind of experience is one in which the moral element recedes and the self—the moral personality essential to practice—temporarily disappears. Although Oakeshott does not identify it as such, this type of experience is something almost mystical.[4] It is the moral personality's desire to escape morality for a while, to transcend itself and its desires and to contemplate rather than to will. This escape, of

3. Timothy Fuller, introduction to *RPML*, 14.
4. Oakeshott is explicit about his interest in mysticism in an early essay entitled "An Essay on the Relations of Philosophy, Poetry and Reality," in *WIH*, 67–116.

course, is only temporary, for there can be no permanent retreat from the demands of practice. Nevertheless, this "mystical" element of Oakeshott's thought has not been sufficiently noted; and I believe it is a crucial part of his description of certain types of experience. In the present chapter it is enough to note that this type of experience exists but is not, strictly speaking, what Oakeshott understands as religion. The mystical character of a certain kind of experience appears more clearly when Oakeshott turns to theorizing aesthetics.

Oakeshott and British Idealism

Although today Oakeshott is best known as a political philosopher, in certain circles he is still identified primarily as a thinker in the British Idealist tradition. In his early writings, Oakeshott acknowledges his debt to Idealist thinkers such as F. H. Bradley and Bernard Bosanquet, with whom he has much in common. This debt has been well documented by scholars.[5] For present purposes, it is most important to focus on one particular facet of this tradition, namely, the Idealist conception of morality and the way in which morality intersects religion.

The Idealists have a distinctive notion of what it means to live morally. For them, morality does not consist in obeying a set of rules imposed from outside, but may instead be identified as a process of "self-realization." In self-realization we "make real" the intimations and intuitions we have about ourselves by speaking and acting in ways that display individual character. Everything one does is part of the process of self-realization, for each action is an attempt to discover one's native aptitudes and talents and to put them into practice. At the core of self-realization is the idea that a self is "always in the making."[6] Self-realization is not something that can be achieved once and for all, but an unceasing process of making decisions and taking actions that reflect an agent's self-understanding. Some such idea surely lies behind Oakeshott's later conceptions of self-enactment and self-disclosure, both of which are vital parts of an agent's task of making real the insights one has about oneself.[7]

5. See David Boucher and Andrew Vincent, *British Idealism and Political Theory,* and David Boucher, "The Idealism of Michael Oakeshott."
6. A. J. M. Milne, *The Social Philosophy of British Idealism,* 29.
7. See *OHC,* 70–78.

However, the intensely personal nature of self-realization need not entail either an isolated self or a process of self-realization that is *merely* subjective. Human beings, after all, live among others, and self-realization largely depends on communities. Indeed, the very idea of morality depends upon a community in which people interact and have the potential either to help or to harm one another. No individual is wholly isolated, and it is a misunderstanding to speak of persons simply as if they were discrete units that could be added together to compose a state. In "My Station and Its Duties," one of the most famous formulations of this idea, F. H. Bradley points out that no such "individuals" exist. A person "is what he is because he is a born and educated social being, and a member of an individual social organism. . . . if you make an abstraction of all this . . . what you have left is not an Englishman, nor a man, but some I know not what residuum, which never has existed by itself, and does not so exist. If we suppose the world of relations, in which he was born and bred, never to have been, then we suppose the very essence of him not to be." Self-realization, then, takes place in a community of others who are also concerned to realize themselves. The individual and community are two parts of a whole, and neither can exist without the other. The individual's quest for self-realization is, of course, vitally important, "but it is no more than the inside; it is one factor in the whole, and must not be separated from the other factor." The mistake of conceiving morality in wholly individualistic terms is that it overlooks this other part and separates "what can not be separated."[8] Thus there are two vital aspects of this Idealist view of self-realization. One is the inner-directed attempt to realize oneself through actions that express a certain self-understanding. The other is the effort to integrate such activity into the community of others in which one lives. The moral life, then, presupposes an individual who is at once responsible for his actions and formed by his society.

Morality is not, however, a process in which an agent may easily and without effort satisfy his desires. It is an endless process of becoming, a quest always to be better. In moral activity an agent perceives the "ought" that must become an "is" through his effort. Since moral decisions are part and parcel of every single day in every human life, there is no point at which one may be finished with morality. Life, insofar as it is the life

8. F. H. Bradley, *Ethical Studies,* 166, 177.

of human beings, is moral. To resume the discussion of the previous chapter, morality is part of the "practical life" in which ideas and actions have consequences. The burden of choosing morally (of choosing well *or* badly) cannot be avoided.

The moral life is not only interminable; it is also incomplete and un-satisfactory. It entails an inherent self-contradiction, since morality asks human beings to realize "that which can never be realized," that is, per-fect moral goodness. If this were realized, morality would "efface itself as such. . . . Where there is no imperfection there is no ought, where there is no ought there is no morality, where there is no self-contradiction there is no ought. The ought is a self-contradiction." As Bernard Bo-sanquet observes, mere morality says, "'You *ought to be* equal to the situ-ation.' The good is imperative on you here and now and you are to make it real in and by your will. . . . Out of every moral success the further 'ought' springs up to condemn you once more." There can be no point at which a human being might say "I am content," because he could *al-ways* be better. This endless sense of "ought" is a central part of morality, indeed it is inherent in morality, for there remains, according to Bradley, "a perpetual contradiction in myself, no less than in the world, between the 'is to be' and the 'is,' a contradiction that cannot be got rid of with-out getting rid of morality."[9]

Morality, on this account, is a preeminently frustrating endeavor. Oake-shott discusses this in his section on practical experience in *Experience and Its Modes,* pointing out the fleeting nature of the sense of completion that sometimes comes in moral life. "[E]ven if we suppose a condition in which everything was as it should be, that could never be more than a momentary condition," he maintains. This is because each achievement "brings with it a new view of the criterion, which converts this mo-mentary perfection into imperfection. Indeed we may find that even the 'ought not' of one moment is the 'ought' of another."[10] In Idealist terms, this conception of morality is "abstract." It cannot, by itself, satisfy the human desire for some sort of permanent good.

This, then, is Oakeshott's Idealist view of morality: it is an endless quest for satisfaction that promises no termination point. There are, of course, satisfactions to be had in the moral life, but they always point to

9. Ibid., 234; Bernard Bosanquet, *What Religion Is,* 10–11; Bradley, *Ethical Studies,* 175.
10. *EM,* 291.

others that lie ahead. One wonders what part religion plays in this conception of morality. Is religion simply a more imperative set of "oughts" that must be obeyed at greater cost? Is it the imposition of "eternal laws" or "eternal truths" that transcend the shifting human ones? It may come as no surprise that these alternatives are not how Oakeshott, Bradley, or Bosanquet view the religious life. Religion does not come from outside the moral world—it is not the radical entrance of the divine into temporality, but is instead the ultimate completion of the moral world. Completion comes about when we join something greater than ourselves. This "something greater" need not *necessarily* be religion (it might be, for example, the love of country involved in patriotism), but it is not yet religion until it is the fullest and most satisfying experience possible. Bosanquet describes the experience as follows:

> We are saved from isolation; we are saved by giving ourselves to something which we cannot help holding supreme. . . . Every man, we must hope and believe, has somewhere an allegiance that binds him, some disloyalty which he would rather die than commit. And if you know what this is, then you know where his religion lies. . . . Nobody is anything except as he joins himself to something. . . . you cannot be a whole unless you join a whole. This, I believe, *is* religion.[11]

Religion thus offers a kind of satisfaction that *mere* morality cannot provide.

In Idealist terms, religion is the concrete whole of which mere morality is an abstraction. It promises a stopping point, a place where the endless "oughts" become, at last, an "is." As Bradley puts it, "[W]hat in morality only is to be, in religion somehow and somewhere really is." The importance for practice of this religious viewpoint "is that what is to be done is approached, not with the knowledge of a doubtful success, but with the fore-felt certainty of already accomplished victory." I give up my particular will, in other words, to become a part of the divine will. This is accomplished through faith. "You must resolve to give up your will, as the mere will of this or that man," expounds Bradley, "and you must put your whole self, your entire will, into the will of the divine." According to Oakeshott, the religious consciousness requires a belief "in

---

11. Bosanquet, *What Religion Is,* 6, 12.

an object other than myself; an object, moreover, which is real." And thus in religion the goodness for which we vainly strive may be transformed into an already-received goodness that requires "losing ourselves in God."[12] It demands the renunciation of personal will and the realization that the goodness we seek cannot be achieved solely by human effort.

This brief sketch of the relationship between morality and religion cannot do justice to the richness and complexity of the Idealist tradition in which Oakeshott came to philosophical maturity. Nevertheless, it serves as the background for Oakeshott's early thought on religion, and since religion is the primary question of this chapter, this sketch of Idealism shall have to suffice for the present. It should, however, make clearer Oakeshott's argument in his 1927 essay entitled "Religion and the Moral Life," which otherwise appears as a somewhat cryptic summary of unfamiliar arguments. In this essay Oakeshott attempts to establish the connections between morality and religion "not merely practically, but theoretically and as a whole."[13] He examines three theories of the relationship between religion and morality.

The first possibility Oakeshott considers is that religion and morality are simply equivalent. His examination of this view is over almost before it begins, since he simply dismisses it as a positivist "travesty of human experience expressed by means of an abuse of language."[14] The second possibility, however, appears more plausible: religion is the sanction for morality. Since human beings are unable to find a universal basis for moral law in nature, according to this argument, the "higher sanction" of a divinely revealed moral law must serve as the foundation for morality. But Oakeshott ultimately finds this position untenable and refutes it by defending the proposition that morality is itself the *condition* of religion. In other words, religion does not come down as a judge to mete out rewards and punishments to human beings, but instead requires that we be moral already if we are to be religious. One cannot be religious without moral autonomy.

To put the point differently, if the moral law were an absolutely binding command imposed by God, then how could we choose to be moral? An irresistible command precludes free activity. If a religion "reveals the moral law as something requiring mere obedience, then that religion is

12. Bradley, *Ethical Studies,* 334, 325; "Religion and the Moral Life," in *RPML,* 42.
13. "Religion and the Moral Life," in *RPML,* 39.
14. Ibid., 40.

false," concludes Oakeshott. Actions are not moral or immoral unless they reflect an agent's insight into the conditions that serve as the basis for his choosing. In this particular line of reasoning Oakeshott relies heavily on John Oman's *Grace and Personality,* which is a sustained argument for moral autonomy as the crucial component of authentic religious experience. Such autonomy appears "in the essential quality of our experience, that it is self-conscious; in the essential quality of our aims, that they are self-directed; in the essential quality of our acts, that they are self-determined," Oman observes. At the same time, both Oman and Oakeshott are concerned that autonomy not be taken too far. If it is true that religion is meaningless without moral independence, it is also true that "morality ceases to be truly ethical when religious dependence is rejected . . . [and] morality, without religion, lacks a wide heaven to breathe in."[15] Thus, like both Bradley and Oakeshott, Oman observes a vital connection between religion and morality.

Oakeshott's third suggestion in "Religion and the Moral Life" is the one he finds most adequate as a description of the relationship between religion and morality: that religion is the "completion of morality." This is, in essence, a restatement of Bradley's argument that religion is the concrete whole of which morality is only a part. It is worth quoting in full Oakeshott's view:

> Morality is this endless search for the perfect good; an endless, practical endeavour resulting in momentary personal failures and achievements and in a gradual change of moral ideas and ideals, a change which is perhaps more than mere change, a progress towards a finer sensibility for social life and a deeper knowledge of its necessities. But, nevertheless, a battle with no hope of victory, a battle, in fact, in which a final victory is the only irretrievable defeat. And what is it that urges us on to these moral innovations, that gives insight, energy and power to invent and to refine in the moral life, where achievement is convention, and convention only a seed which, except it be cast into the ground, cannot live? What is it that, without attempting to supply a sanction, shows the whole from which this endless "ought to be" is an abstraction? This, I think, is what we call religion; the motive power, the growing point and the completed whole of merely moral ideals.[16]

15. Ibid., 43; John Oman, *Grace and Personality,* 42, 62.
16. "Religion and the Moral Life," in *RPML,* 44–45. For the parable of the "seed" that Oakeshott alludes to in this quote, see Matthew 13:23–31 and John 12:24.

Oakeshott builds on the groundwork he has laid in making the case for morality as the condition of religious belief. He points out that just as autonomy by itself is not sufficient for moral activity—"free action is not moral unless it is also wise"—so moral activity is not complete without the "ideality" of religion.[17] Although personal autonomy and moral activity are essential parts of human experience, they require something more before life may be said to be fully satisfactory. This "something more" is religion.

The major conclusion that may be drawn from this essay is that morality and religion are closely related and appear to exist as points on a continuum of experience. Religion is not some kind of mystical self-forgetting, but a preeminently practical experience that addresses the "self" of moral conduct. It is the fulfillment of all the deficiencies of practice. To fill out this account of this practical character of religion, however, we must turn again to *Experience and Its Modes*. There Oakeshott observes that religion "belongs to the conduct of life: it is the alteration of practical existence so as to agree with an idea." It cares nothing "for what lies beyond the world of practice; if it looks to 'another' world, it is for the purpose of determining what shall be our conduct in 'this' world."[18] Even the quietist argument that religion is a retirement from life is not a refutation of religion's practical character, but a confirmation of it. For retirement from the hustle and bustle of life is no less practical than engagement in it. It is merely a different practical response.

Oakeshott reiterates his observations about the practical character of religion in a number of other works as well: "[R]eligion deals with environment in a practical and not a theoretical manner, 'by way of feeling and value,'" he argues in a review; "Religion is, after all, nothing if not practical," for "our felt [practical] wants are the starting points of religion, and these thoughts of religion must compel action." Religion and the religious consciousness are "essentially practical. . . . Our felt wants are, of necessity, the starting point of our religion," Oakeshott observes in a 1928 essay entitled "The Importance of the Historical Element in Christianity." The "thoughts of religion must also be feelings in that they must possess the force and liveliness, which we connect with feeling, to strike the mind and compel not merely acquiescence but action."[19] In

17. "Religion and the Moral Life," in *RPML*, 44, 45.
18. *EM*, 294.
19. Review of *Science, Religion, and Reality*, by J. Needham, 319; review of *The Christian Religion and Its Competitors To-day*, by A. C. Bouquet, 440; "The Importance of the Historical Element in Christianity," in *RPML*, 71.

acting religiously, the self can never be "lost," because this moral self is precisely what religion addresses.

Yet religion demands more of a person than does ordinary practical experience. Religious activities are undertaken with a greater degree of intensity. It is, indeed, a "rare and peculiar genius which enables a man to see clearly what belongs to his life and to follow it without reserve, unhindered by the restraint of prudence or the impediment of doubt," notes Oakeshott. And yet this is precisely what religion demands: an unhindered devotion to one's purpose and a lack of doubt about its appropriateness. Religion is therefore not just another *form* of practical experience; it is "practical experience at its fullest, and is the consummation of all attempts to change or maintain our practical existence." Thus religion is not, strictly speaking, "part" of practice—not simply some motive that might affect one's moral conduct. I observed above that religion addresses itself to the practical self, and perhaps this would seem to imply that religion is part of practice. But strictly speaking, this cannot be because it would imply that practice could contain religion. In actuality, religion is itself the larger whole in which morality—and all the rest of practice—inheres. As Oakeshott observes, religion is the completion of morality "as the concrete whole is the completion of all the abstractions analysis may discover in it."[20] Religion is conduct raised to a high degree of self-awareness, to a unity of motive and action, form and content.

So far I have discussed the Idealist context that lies behind Oakeshott's essay "Religion and the Moral Life" and have observed that religion addresses the practical—the highest, but nevertheless practical—needs of mankind. There is, however, one other point in this essay that bears mentioning, and it is Oakeshott's use of the word *insight*. In his 1929 essay "Religion and the World" he uses the word to describe the essence of living religiously when he argues that "nothing is of final worth except present insight, a grasp of the thing itself." And in the essay we have just been considering he also discusses insight at several points: "to a moral personality nothing is of value except through personal insight," and "knowledge of anything is not true knowledge unless it is personal insight."[21] Of course, insight is not the only criterion of experience or knowledge, and Oakeshott recognizes this. But it is a condition of truly understanding or experiencing anything as one's own. Why should this

---

20. *EM,* 295, 294; "Religion and the Moral Life," in *RPML,* 42.
21. "Religion and the World," in *RPML,* 37; "Religion and the Moral Life," in *RPML,* 43, 44.

be worth noting? First, the idea of insight is central to Oakeshott's view of human beings as morally autonomous, responsible actors, a view he held throughout his life. Autonomy and moral decision-making cannot exist without the component of insight—an insight that consists of understanding oneself and the actions one proposes to take. Indeed, self-enactment (a form of moral activity that Oakeshott discusses in *On Human Conduct*) depends on such an understanding. Insight is essential to living a moral and, therefore, a religious life.

Furthermore, this emphasis on insight prefigures an issue that Oakeshott considers at length later in his career. Insight is an essential part of what it means to act within the bounds of law and to accept authority. As he observes in another early essay, entitled "The Authority of the State," authority—one might as easily substitute religion here—does not consist in the commands given by someone or something utterly external, but in our willing acceptance of the ground of that authority. In other words, neither law nor religious precepts are *in themselves* authoritative for us until we grasp them by insight—by understanding them for ourselves. "An authority," Oakeshott observes, "is not a person or institution whose experience we decide to accept and make use of where our own appears deficient, for such an 'authority' is secondary and compels not by its own but by a borrowed power; a real authority is the whole ground upon which our acceptance or rejection of anything is based. To have a belief it must be ours, and even if it were derived from some external source, that which actually compels us to hold it is the ground on which it has been accepted, that is, the whole world of ideas into which it has been fitted and in the light of which it has been understood and appropriated."[22] Insight is what provides meaning in the moral life. It is not the *only* criterion of meaning (insight may be liable to correction or it may simply be mistaken), but without it one cannot truly act either religiously or morally. It is an essential part of the direct, experiential nature of religion that Oakeshott finds so important. But it is also, as later chapters will show, a crucial part of what it means to act politically. Thus an argument can be made that Oakeshott's religious understanding lies behind his view of the moral persona required to engage in politics—what he will call the morality of the individual, as I discuss in Chapter 7.

22. "The Authority of the State," in *RPML,* 79.

British Modernism

Another side of what I have called Oakeshott's emphasis on the personal, insightful, immediate nature of religion consists in a proper understanding of Christianity. During the 1920s and 1930s Oakeshott was immersed in a contemporary movement in British religious life then at its peak, known as the "Modernist" movement. An extended treatment of this phenomenon lies beyond the scope of the present work, but the basic outlines of English Modernism are worth setting out, for it was a crucial part of Oakeshott's early intellectual formation. There are echoes of it in all his religious writings, and particularly in his essay "The Importance of the Historical Element in Christianity."

English Modernism may be described as an intellectual movement that aimed at liberalizing or "modernizing" Christianity. It was an attempt to meet the challenges posed to Christianity by recent historical and scientific scholarship that questioned the biblical accounts of creation and the idea of miracles. Modernists, by their own account, wanted not to tear down religion, but instead to build up a kind of faith that could weather "the threatening storms of scientific and historic criticism, and . . . find for [religion] some more trustworthy basis than mere authority, the respect for which has greatly decayed under modern conditions." Modernists concentrated on finding an absolute ground for religion that consisted in conduct, emotion, and even philosophy—in sum, they wanted a truly "spiritual" religion. Religious beliefs, argued Percy Gardner, a leading Modernist and author of *Modernism in the English Church* (1926), "can only be justified when they are based on realities and experience, and can only lead to success and happiness when they are suited to their environment, psychological, intellectual and spiritual."[23] Thus the Modernists saw immediate, personal experience as vital to true religion. They understood that received doctrine, creeds, and the institutional church might actually be hindrances to thinking and acting religiously.

The central problem that Modernism faced was preserving an essence of Christianity in the face of modern criticism of all types, primarily scientific and historic. Late-nineteenth- and early-twentieth-century

23. Alan M. G. Stephenson, *The Rise and Decline of English Modernism,* 66; Percy Gardner, *Modernism in the English Church,* 9.

historical criticism tended to cast doubt on the existence of miracles and thus to threaten the entire foundation of traditional Christian belief. And yet the Modernists were in a difficult position. On the one hand they saw the church as overly authoritarian, relying too much on dogmatic formulations of belief and placing too little emphasis on the actual religious experiences of living persons. "The majority of thoughtful churchgoers," Gardner noted, "feel that the statements embodied in creeds and articles of belief are full of difficulty, partly because they are very hard to understand . . . and partly because . . . they seem archaic and quite out of relation to the facts of the religious life."[24] On the other hand, there were those in Britain who, in the face of modern intellectual movements—or perhaps simply as a result of the modern loosening of morals—had rejected religion altogether and become "worldly." The Modernists wished to position themselves between these two extremes, neither rejecting religion outright nor accepting traditional religion as it had been passed down to them. They found it necessary to chart a different course altogether.

This different course manifested itself in a focus on "spirit" as the internal driving force of religious consciousness. If modern historical or scientific scholarship threatened the biblical account of creation, the Modernists wished to respond to that challenge by redefining Christianity to effectively eliminate the threat. According to the Modernists, the truth of religion did not depend upon proving the veracity of historical events, and thus religion might stand alongside even the theory of evolution. W. R. Inge, a prominent Modernist, described the new conception as follows:

> As soon as we realize that the religion of the Spirit stands on its own feet; that . . . we are in communion with a living Christ; we shall be under no temptation to place ourselves again under the yoke of bondage for the sake of the illusory security which the religions of authority still offer. And above all, we shall be ready to accept without reserve the revelations which have come to us in recent times through natural science. We do not always realize how profoundly the scientific temper has altered our standards of evidence, of probability, even of veracity, nor how much remains to be done before the stumbling-blocks which traditional theology has placed or left in our path are removed. To the religion of the spirit these

24. Gardner, *Modernism in the English Church,* 8.

obstacles are of small account. They have nothing to do with our knowledge of God through Christ, nor with our duty to our fellowmen.[25]

Inge described here a type of religious experience that can stand unthreatened by the challenges of history and science. It requires only a vivid, immediately felt communion with "the Spirit."

This argument for a religion of "spirit" does not rest solely, if indeed at all, upon a historical foundation. As such it is in line with Oakeshott's modal separation of history and practice, since the truth of religion, in his account, does not depend for its legitimacy on the discoveries of history or science. Religion is "essentially a matter of present and actual belief about the world," observes Oakeshott. And although there exists a past that "influences and perhaps controls" present belief, this past "cannot itself be made a foundation or a ground of present belief." To fuse the claims of science or history with those of religion is to commit, in one of Oakeshott's oft-repeated phrases, an *ignoratio elenchi* (the fallacy of irrelevance). Nevertheless, this occurs all the time—particularly when history is invoked as a sanction or support for a particular religious view. "When we wish to give to our beliefs the force and liveliness which belong to them," Oakeshott maintains, "we find in the *language of history* a ready means for expressing our desires."[26] But this is a misuse of history.

It is at least worth noting that in many respects Oakeshott's alliance with the Modernist movement was quite uncharacteristic of him. For Modernism was a reformist, rationalist approach to the religious life. Consider, for instance, Gardner's critique of institutional Christianity. It is, he declared, "so much out of harmony with scientific and intellectual progress that it even seems to the majority of highly educated men in Roman Catholic countries to be almost unworthy of attention."[27] In promoting the removal of creeds and dogma from religious life, the Modernists argued against tradition and for a self-consciously intellectual approach to religion. They appeared to be reinventing Christianity in their own image; and this was precisely the sort of project that the more mature Oakeshott found so dangerous. What appealed to Oakeshott in Modernism, however, was its emphasis on direct, vital, "present"

25. W. R. Inge, *The Platonic Tradition in English Religious Thought*, 32.
26. Review of *The Historical Element in Religion*, by Clement C. J. Webb, 97; *EM*, 105.
27. Gardner, *Modernism in the English Church*, 172.

spiritual experience. An emphasis on the lived experience of religion remains constant throughout his various explorations of the subject.

"The Importance of the Historical Element in Christianity" is Oakeshott's most explicit contribution to the debates about Modernism. In
this essay, which was prepared for the 1928 Conference of Modern
Churchmen, Oakeshott takes on two views of historical Christianity
that he thinks are mistaken. First, he considers the idea that there exists
something called "original Christianity" and that it is the only authentic
Christianity. Anything that deviates from *this* Christianity, it is asserted, is
not Christian. Oakeshott refutes this view by pointing out that we can
have no such knowledge of an "original Christianity" because the New
Testament (not to mention all subsequent Christian history) "is a record
of change and development," and at what point did that change and development cease to be original?[28] In a book review from about the same
time, Oakeshott argues against a similar view of "originality" that finds
the identity of Christianity to be "Jesus' religion." Oakeshott asks in what
"Jesus' religion" would consist. Would it be only what Jesus said, or would
it also include the events that followed from his death? In other words,
how could we successfully (and universally) limit the concept of original
Christianity? Oakeshott argues that we can do so only by interpreting
events through our own judgment. There can thus be no absolute criterion for what "original Christianity" might look like.

The second view Oakeshott refutes is that there is somehow an "unchanging core or center" of Christianity that has persisted since its beginning. Those who hold this view, Oakeshott remarks dryly, "may be
invited to show us this unchanging central substance." He objects that
the attempt to identify a "core" of beliefs is to create an abstraction—
something that has never actually existed—"a wretched fraction of . . .
our experiences." Christianity is a religion that is manifest in living persons. It is incorrect to speak of it as something fixed once and for all, as
something "static, made, and not even in a process of being understood."[29] For Oakeshott, writing in the context of British Idealism and
Modernism, Christianity is just the opposite of static: it is dynamic and
changing. The central task for a Christian, in Oakeshott's view, is to arrive at one's own understanding of what Christianity means. It is not an

28. "The Importance of the Historical Element," in *RPML,* 65.
29. Ibid., 66; review of *Can We Then Believe?* by Charles Gore, *Essays Catholic and Critical,* by E. G. Selwyn, and *The Inescapable Christ,* by W. R. Bowie, 315.

abstract doctrine, far less a set of theological propositions. To identify it as such is to miss the entire experiential context in which Christianity has meaning. An identity that consists in such an abstraction (what would remain of Christianity after all the "nonessential" differences in tradition and belief have been whittled away) is no identity at all.

But Oakeshott is left with a problem. If the historical element in Christianity is not "original Christianity" or a "core set of beliefs," then what is it? Before he sets out his own view Oakeshott asserts that both these views are grounded in a basic misunderstanding of the concept of identity. Identity, he argues, is not mere "sameness." To say, for instance, that one's house is the same today as it was yesterday (even though one has done nothing at all to change it) is merely to say that A equals A and is a tautology. The significance of identity lies in its ability to endure through *changes.* In other words, there must be some aspect of a phenomenon that has a qualitative sameness even while other aspects of it are transformed. This issue of identity is a more pressing issue in Christianity than in most other religions. For in these other religions, Oakeshott observes, "there has often been little change of surrounding civilization and little internal development; Christianity, however, has suffered both extensively."[30] It is Oakeshott's task in this essay to find some answer to the question of what part historical understanding plays in Christianity, and in exactly what the "identity" of Christianity may be found.

Oakeshott provides the following answer. Identity, he argues, "so far from excluding differences, is meaningless in their absence, just as difference or change depend on something whose identity is not destroyed by that change." As noted above, to say that something is exactly the same is not yet to say anything about identity. If identity is to be a meaningful concept at all, then it requires that some sort of change take place even as something else simultaneously stays the same. In the case of Christianity, observes Oakeshott, "there is no fixed original datum for us to adhere to," for the reasons outlined above. But if, as is the case with Christianity, "there has been change and development [then] there must also be an identity, for without an identity there can be no change." Some have solved this dilemma by postulating an "original Christianity," while others claim that there exists an essential core of Christian beliefs. Nevertheless,

30. Review of *The Making of the Christian Mind,* by G. G. Atkins, 204.

the requirement that some part of a substance be unchanging does not lead Oakeshott back to either of these positions. Instead, he makes the radical—and indeed, somewhat troubling—assertion that "the characteristic of being Christian may properly be claimed by any doctrine, idea or practice which, no matter whence it came, has been or can be drawn into the general body of the Christian tradition without altogether disturbing its unity or breaking down its consistency." Anything that does not cause an "absolute break" in the development of the Christian tradition may potentially be integrated into the tradition. This is a more fluid understanding of Christianity than either "original Christianity" or one involving "an unchanging core of Christian beliefs." And, in keeping with Modernism, it allows the discoveries of science and history to be integrated into the Christian tradition. For one of Modernism's central tenets is its willingness "to recognize that all new knowledge, of whatever kind, has relevance" for religion.[31]

There are, of course, problems with this definition. As Timothy Fuller has pointed out, Oakeshott's idea of what exactly would constitute an "absolute break" is left ambiguous. It is not at all clear that Oakeshott thinks there could be any such break in history that would disrupt the continuity of the Christian tradition, for Christianity has survived many crises that seemed to portend its complete disintegration. But this, of course, opens the door to what might be seen as a more gradual corruption of Christianity. It is worth considering, in this context, the recent controversy over the ordination of a homosexual bishop in the American Episcopal Church. As a group, Episcopalians are divided on the question of whether this ordination constitutes an "absolute break" or whether it is simply a natural evolution. This example, however, points directly to the problems in Oakeshott's definition. How can such a fluid understanding of Christianity preserve its distinctiveness at all? Some thinkers have attempted to solve these problems by articulating a set of minimally required beliefs. Hobbes, of course, does this when he asserts that everything necessary to salvation is contained "in two virtues: *faith in Christ,* and *obedience to laws.*"[32] But Oakeshott is unwilling to take this way out.

Setting aside, for the present, the difficulties with his view, what is

---

31. "The Importance of the Historical Element," in *RPML,* 67; review of *The Making of the Christian Mind,* 207; "The Importance of the Historical Element," in *RPML,* 67; Stephenson, *Rise and Decline,* 79.

32. Timothy Fuller, introduction to *RPML,* 17; Thomas Hobbes, *Leviathan,* 398.

Oakeshott trying to accomplish in taking on this question of the historical element in Christianity? He is primarily trying to remind his audience of the necessity of having a personal, immediate experience of Christianity. This immediacy is too easily lost when emphasis is placed on history, doctrine, and dogma. Religion, we recall, is practical for Oakeshott; and so it must be subject to a "pragmatic test"—that is, do our religious beliefs have an effect on our present conduct? Once again, Oakeshott reminds us of his argument for "presentness" when he observes that what religion demands "is not a consciousness of the necessity and individuality of past events, but a consciousness of the individuality of present experience. . . . And because religion is nothing if not contemporary, the historical element of our religion must be interpreted so as to give it a permanent and not a merely temporary meaning." An overemphasis on history blinds us to the fact that Christianity is a living religion. To be authentic it must spring from the convictions of contemporary believers. Religion is "a matter of present and actual belief about the world," and though the past is important it cannot be made the ground for this present belief. The only ground for present belief consists in entering into a religious life "because we know that [religion's] scale of values and its way of thinking satisfy us more than any other."[33]

In a book review written at about the same time, Oakeshott remarks that "although there is certainly a past which influences, and perhaps controls, present belief, it cannot itself be made a foundation or a ground of present belief." The only true ground of belief is one that consists in a person's full, inward acceptance of Christianity. In an early essay Oakeshott observes that Christianity "is true [and] real to those only who find it already within their heart, to those only to whom its message 'breathes such sense as their sense breeds with it.' As a religion it is true without our acceptance, it has an ultimate truth quite apart from any human consciousness—but to us, if we do not find it already within ourselves, we shall attach it to our stock of 'reasoned beliefs' in vain."[34] Oakeshott thus argues forcefully against the idea that Christianity is a set of external precepts that possess binding authority. For him, beliefs are authoritative only because of what they mean to each human being.

---

33. "The Importance of the Historical Element," in *RPML*, 72; review of *The Historical Element in Religion*, 97; "Religion and the World," in *RPML*, 30.

34. Review of *The Historical Element in Religion*, 97; "An Essay on the Relations," in *WIH*, 89–90.

The Character of Religion

So far we have observed that religion is thoroughly practical—the "completion" of moral life—and that Oakeshott's early views about religion arose in the context of Modernist debates over the character of Christianity. However, when Oakeshott turned from such philosophical considerations toward the actual needs that religion addresses, he found these to be remarkably straightforward. If his discussions of Idealism and Modernism are difficult and somewhat academic, his view of religion itself is quite simple. This makes perfect sense, for Oakeshott thought that religion, as practiced by ordinary people, is not at all complicated. As Timothy Fuller points out, Oakeshott sympathized "in religious matters, with the simple, direct and immediate against the sophisticated, detached and intellectual."[35] Religion is one of the simplest and most elementary human needs, if also the most important.

In Oakeshott's view, religion can be equated with neither philosophy nor theology, nor does it require in its devotees any inclination for these activities. Religion offers, instead, comfort, solace, and consolation for the difficulties of the moral life. It gives meaning to activities that might otherwise seem endless and mundane. In short, it is "practical," as observed above, although its "practicality here has no ordinary sense. It is the intimation of the completion of the endless tasks of daily life and the consolation for their interminability."[36] Oakeshott explicitly addresses this practical nature of religion in two places. One is in *Experience and Its Modes,* where he describes the sort of practical conduct that would qualify as "religious," and the other is in *On Human Conduct,* where he enumerates the concrete, practical needs religion fulfills.

In *Experience and Its Modes,* Oakeshott describes religious experience as the consummation of practice. Practice becomes religion when it is least reserved, least hindered by extraneous interests, least confused by what it does not need, and most nearly at one with itself. The best way to illustrate these characteristics is by looking again at "Religion and the World," where Oakeshott explains the type of moral character that is also religious. In such a person conduct closely approximates a unity of form and content. As we recall, in that essay Oakeshott describes religious

---

35. Timothy Fuller, introduction to *RPML,* 14.
36. Ibid., 19.

conduct as that which takes place so far as possible in the present, conduct that is full of insight, and which most fully allows the "realization of a self." In short, to engage in the religious life is to act with self-awareness, demonstrating an understanding not only of one's motives but of the *right* motives. To act "religiously" so that one may be seen doing it is not truly religious. Religious conduct (an idea echoed in Oakeshott's later term *self-enactment*) may, and often does, take place without an audience. To act religiously is to act authentically, so that activities and motives are in complete accord. Whenever "the seriousness with which we embrace [the] enterprise of achieving a coherent world of practical ideas reaches a certain strength and intensity," Oakeshott contends, "whenever it begins to dominate and take possession of us, practice has become religion." Kind acts are done for kindness' sake, not for the praise of others; work is done as an end in itself, not for fame or glory. In short, living religiously means to conduct oneself in accordance with what one says: "what is important for religion has always been the profession which is contained in the actual conduct of life."[37]

Oakeshott addresses the practical nature of religion once again in *On Human Conduct,* written more than forty years after *Experience and Its Modes.* In a tantalizingly short treatment, Oakeshott describes religion as the motive of all motives and observes that the primary function of religion is to offer "reconciliation" to the dissonances of the human condition.[38] In this essay Oakeshott abandons the Idealist language he employed in his early discussions of religion, and instead focuses on the concrete reasons for the existence of religion. These consist of three separate but related categories.

First, religion may be a solace for misfortune. Every human life involves suffering, and religion offers some measure of relief from this experience. This relief may be merely a somewhat "prosaic consolation," or it may promise the sufferers future happiness; but it springs from the human need to be comforted. Religion is thus meant to address "the pain of disappointed expectations, the suffering of frustrated purposes, the impositions of hostile circumstances, the sorrows of unwanted partings, burdens, ills, disasters, calamities of all sorts, and death itself, the emblem here of all such sufferings."[39]

37. *EM,* 292; "Religion and the World," in *RPML,* 32; *EM,* 295, 292.
38. *OHC,* 85.
39. Ibid., 81.

But consolation for misfortune is only one of religion's tasks. Oakeshott observes that religion also offers a way of dealing with human sin. Since the problem of sin can never be eradicated from earthly life, religion offers a way of making sin (and the guilt that issues from it) less damaging to the soul. A religious faith "is both a belief that this [severance from God through sin] cannot be unconditionally irreparable and an image of this reconciliation here or hereafter." Sin, of course, is an offense against God and thus "the relationship it threatens or severs is paramount."[40] Yet religion, in various ways—absolution, atonement, confession—provides a way of lessening sin's fatality.

It is, however, Oakeshott's final reason for finding religion so important that lies at the center of his entire view. Religion provides consolation for the futility of human life and reconciliation to nothingness. "All is evanescent," concludes Oakeshott, and no amount of practical activity per se can qualify this. Those who attempt to avoid this truth by constantly immersing themselves in projects and "business" of various kinds merely deceive themselves. "Where conduct is the choice and pursuit of substantive conditions of things every achievement is evanescent," Oakeshott observes, "and (as Augustine says) he who thinks otherwise 'understands neither what he seeks nor what he is who seeks it'. And no projected future can be any different from the present in this respect." Although there are moods in which certain kinds of conduct seem to escape this verdict, they do not; they are merely qualified. Self-enactment, says Oakeshott, offers "the echo of an imperishable achievement," but it is not imperishable.[41]

Here we have reached what is surely Oakeshott's central religious insight: that human life and its satisfactions are unavoidably transient. There are times when this transience may seem to be overcome, but our world is unavoidably a mortal world. "Every action is a fugitive transaction between mortal agents, its outcome not merely uncertain but fragile and soon dissipated," observes Oakeshott. This is where religion's task is most difficult: to convince people of the futility of all they normally value—reputation, achievement, and material goods—and then to console them in the face of that futility. It is interesting to note that this view is essentially the same as one Oakeshott put forth more than forty years earlier in a book review, where he wrote what seems to be a description of re-

40. Ibid., 83.
41. Ibid., 83–85.

ligion: "[I]t is a kind of reconciliation to mortality, a feeling of permanence in transience, either reached after frustration and pain or seized intuitively in youth."[42]

This is a clear-sighted assessment of the universal human condition; for it recognizes at once man's importance to himself and his unimportance to the world around him. It also highlights the central religious task for all human beings: to reconcile themselves to the fleetingness of the things they normally consider constant and to find something that is *actually* permanent and lasting. Oakeshott observes that religious faith provides something like this, and it is worth quoting this passage in full:

> Religious faith is the evocation of a sentiment (the love, the glory, or the honour of God, for example, or even a humble *caritas*), to be added to all others as the motive of all motives in terms of which the fugitive adventure[r]s of human conduct, without being released from their mortal and their moral conditions, are graced with an intimation of immortality: the sharpness of death and the deadliness of doing overcome, and the transitory sweetness of a mortal affection, the tumult of a grief and the passing beauty of a May morning recognized neither as merely evanescent adventures nor as emblems of better things to come, but as *aventures,* themselves encounters with eternity.

This is, of course, not an orthodox Christian's answer to the issue of what to do about the transitory nature of human life. And yet it is both a recognition of the human condition and an intimation of reconciliation. Religion may, on the one hand, sink to the "prose" of a merely anticipated release from present ills. Or it may, on the other, rise to "a serene acquiescence in mortality and a graceful acceptance of the *rerum mortalia,*" in which the "poetic" qualities of its images, rites, observances, and offerings convey a sense of immortality.[43]

Conclusion

I began this chapter by observing that in his essay "Religion and the World" Oakeshott identifies religion with perfect presentness. The religious

42. Ibid., 84; review of *Adventures of Ideas,* by A. N. Whitehead, 75.
43. *OHC,* 85–86.

person lives a life that is truly "contemporary," focusing on neither the past nor the future. Such a person rejects the quest for fame and fortune, preferring instead to cultivate a personal sensibility that cannot be taken away. There is something not only religious but poetic about living life in such a manner; for such a life requires, above all, "insight."[44] Like the poet, who must have an intuitive sense for his art, the religious person has an intuitive sense of what is satisfactory for his life. The emphasis on present, lived experience is also evident in Oakeshott's consideration of the historical element in Christianity, where he argues that what matters for the Christian is a "living faith" as well as "the power to stand on the point of the present," rather than a search for the historical Jesus or some original form of Christianity.[45]

And yet, as I have also observed, even as he begins by focusing on the immediacy and presentness of religion, Oakeshott also recognizes more and more the undeniably practical character of religious belief. As he clarifies his view of practice, following the Idealism of Bradley and Bosanquet, he emphasizes the insuperable lack of unity that exists between the "is" and the "ought." Practical life can offer no final satisfactions, for it is never finished. Religion, therefore, as the "completion" of practice can offer only "intimations" of immortality, as Oakeshott observes in *On Human Conduct*. If there is a kind of presentness to be found, we must look elsewhere, as Oakeshott appears to do in his thought about aesthetics.

This chapter has attempted to show that Oakeshott was, as a young man, fundamentally concerned with religious questions. Why, then, does he appear to "abandon" this interest in the 1930s, returning to it only in a few pages in *On Human Conduct*? This is an interesting and important question. Part of it certainly has to do with what I have already observed, namely, that as he matured he realized the difficulty of speaking on what he perceived as the "most important questions." Oakeshott's hesitance to declare his views on religion might therefore indicate a kind of intellectual humility, perhaps a kind of nondogmatic agnosticism about the Christian tradition he had inherited. Maurice Cowling, one of Oakeshott's most astute commentators, speculates that his silence on religion results from the fact that "religion had become

---

44. Oakeshott is almost certainly borrowing this concept from Walter Pater. See, for instance, his *Marius the Epicurean,* chap. 8.
45. "The Importance of the Historical Element," in *RPML,* 69.

everything men do."[46] That is, Oakeshott may have seen his contemporaries embracing all of life—particularly politics and morality—with the single-mindedness and fervor that he thought should be reserved for religion. This, of course, goes against Oakeshott's own philosophical and moral temperament and is likely to become exactly the sort of "Rationalism" he found objectionable. But whatever the reasons for Oakeshott's turn away from explicit consideration of religion, religious ideas and categories continued to structure his thought about morality and politics throughout the remainder of his career. In Chapters 6, 7, and 8, I consider the Tower of Babel story as the fundamental religious myth that simultaneously stands behind his critique of Rationalism and underlies his more positive conception of politics. First, however, I turn in the next chapter to his thought on aesthetics.

46. Maurice Cowling, *Religion and Public Doctrine in Modern England,* 268.

5

Oakeshott's Aesthetics

"A man's greatest works differ from his lesser works in degree and not in kind: they may be more perfect, but they express the same idea."[1] So Michael Oakeshott observed in a short essay written for his college magazine in 1921. There is ample evidence to support the view that this is an accurate description of Oakeshott's own works. For although he developed as a thinker—often revising, adapting, and refining his ideas—certain fundamental insights into the human condition remained consistent throughout his writings. One of the most important of these insights is grounded in a particular understanding of aesthetic experience, and it may be expressed as a belief that certain human activities—among them poetry, conversation, love, and friendship—have an intrinsic and indisputable value.[2] Their value does not stem from their utility; indeed, these activities are resolutely nonutilitarian. They are valuable because they may be engaged in as ends in themselves, and as such they express in the fullest sense what it is to be a human being. To experience something "aesthetically" is to put aside all thoughts of past and future, of productivity and consequences, and to focus instead on the experience entirely for its own sake. Insofar as conversation, love, and friendship may be approached in this manner they have much in common with pure aesthetic experience. These activities provide temporary liberation from the constant demands of the practical realm. One is thus invited to respond in terms not of "pleasure" but of delight.[3]

1. SJ, 62.
2. The terms *aesthetics, poetry,* and *art* will be used interchangeably throughout this chapter, since Oakeshott is quite clear that he means *poetry* to encompass all kinds of art: "[P]ainting, sculpting, acting, dancing, singing, literary and musical compositions are different kinds of poetic activity" ("The Voice of Poetry in the Conversation of Mankind," in *RP,* 509).
3. In this context *delight* is *not* the equivalent of *pleasure.* I am consciously echoing Oakeshott's use of this word in "The Voice of Poetry," where he designates "delight" and

This insight—that certain human activities have an intrinsic, "aesthetic" value—may not be immediately apparent to those who read only Oakeshott's more explicitly political work, though it lies beneath the surface of these essays too. It is most clearly expressed in a number of book reviews Oakeshott published as a young man in the 1920s and 1930s in such journals as the *Cambridge Review* and the *Journal of Theological Studies,* as well as in several essays that remained unpublished until 1993.[4] During these early decades Oakeshott was concerned with religion and poetry, and in these reviews he explored such questions as how to understand the Christian faith, the relationship between religion and morality, and the character of poetry as an expression of a kind of spiritual life. Because of their recent publication, the other essays have not yet received the full critical treatment they deserve, although an insightful article by Glenn Worthington has partially remedied this deficiency by considering the relationship between Oakeshott's aesthetics and his view of morality. Worthington ultimately finds that Oakeshott's view of poetry is equivocal and contradictory, but that in spite of some apparent deficiencies poetry "appreciates and expresses the qualities of the moral life . . . in their most comprehensive terms."[5]

The present chapter approaches these topics from a different perspective. Although I agree with Worthington that poetry indeed contributes to a richer understanding of the possibilities of moral life, I do not agree that Oakeshott's account of poetry (aesthetic experience) is equivocal and contradictory. There is, so I argue, a way of understanding Oakeshott's religious and aesthetic thought as a consistent development in a single direction. This development culminates in his 1959 essay "The Voice of Poetry in the Conversation of Mankind," in which poetry embodies an ideal unity of form and content. The second section of this chapter discusses the nature and purpose of "The Voice of Poetry." I consider whether it should be interpreted not so much as a comprehensive theory of aesthetics, but instead primarily as a description of a particular

---

"contemplation" as ways of responding to the poetic experience, whereas pleasure is part of the practical realm.

4. See *RPML.*

5. Glenn Worthington, "The Voice of Poetry in Oakeshott's Moral Philosophy," 286. Another student of Oakeshott's thought, Robert Grant, seems inclined to view Oakeshott's description of poetry in a less favorable light. Grant argues that Oakeshott's understanding of poetry is "ambiguous, paradoxical and plural" (*Oakeshott,* 109).

kind of human experience. In the third section I consider the question
of how poetry relates to moral conduct. Are the two kinds of experience
categorically distinct, as Oakeshott sometimes implies, or is there a certain kind of link between them? I make the case that there is such a link,
and I take up and expand this theme in Chapter 6. I conclude by suggesting that Oakeshott's insight into the satisfactoriness of certain kinds
of experiences—what may be termed a poetic, or aesthetic, insight—lies
behind his critique of Rationalism in his famous essays in *Rationalism in
Politics.* Moreover, this aesthetic insight forms the basis for his unique
view of what it means to be conservative.

Oakeshott's View of Aesthetic Experience: A Consistent Development

An important question to address at the outset is whether there is a consistent line of development in Oakeshott's thought about aesthetics.
Several previous commentators have answered "no" to this question. But
if Oakeshott's reflections on aesthetics are indeed variable and inconsis-
tent, this would seem to call into question the value of his thought on
the subject as a whole. In short, how could a view that is fundamentally
ill considered provide the basis for what I (and others) argue is one of
Oakeshott's fundamental insights into the human condition?[6]

On the other hand, W. H. Greenleaf's brief account of the matter implies a more consistent development in which Oakeshott's later designa-
tion of poetry as a unique kind of experience develops naturally out of
his earlier thought on modality.[7] It is not Greenleaf's purpose, however,
to make clear precisely how Oakeshott's thought develops in this regard.
Nor, indeed, were many of the crucial early essays available to Greenleaf
when he wrote his 1965 monograph. Thus it is the burden of the present

---

6. Wendell John Coats Jr. has addressed the importance of poetry in Oakeshott's
thought in the final chapter of *Oakeshott and His Contemporaries.* And in "The Voice of
Poetry in Oakeshott's Moral Philosophy," Worthington agrees that "poetic imagination
encompasses all aspects of Oakeshott's characterization of human conduct" (310).
Neither Coats nor Worthington, however, has attempted to explain the precise link between the two kinds of experience. Worthington admits that he does not claim to resolve
what he calls "the ambiguities, equivocations, and outright contradictions that litter
Oakeshott's references to the character of poetic experience" (310).

7. See Greenleaf, *Oakeshott's Philosophical Politics,* 30–35.

chapter to show that Oakeshott's thought on aesthetics indeed exhibits a steady and consistent progress and that this aesthetic insight is an important part of Oakeshott's political thought. The general development may be explained as follows.

In the writings of Oakeshott's early years, religion and poetry are bound up together as part of a cluster of similar experiences that share a "spiritual" element. Poetry and religion are described as experiences that transcend everyday concerns. They promise a unity of form and content, of what is done and how it is done, and a kind of satisfaction and fulfillment not available in ordinary experience. But although poetry and religion are similar, they are not identical, and Oakeshott was aware of their differences. The development of Oakeshott's thought on aesthetics may thus be described as a gradual sifting out of these differences, in which poetry (which includes all aesthetic experience) eventually takes on a radically nonpurposive, nonutilitarian character. Religion, on the other hand, remains part of "practice," addressing the human needs that arise in the course of moral life. In Oakeshott's mature thought, poetry and religion are no longer allied experiences. Poetry stands instead as an autonomous, explicitly nonpractical mode of activity offering a particular kind of satisfaction. This is the view set out in Oakeshott's "The Voice of Poetry in the Conversation of Mankind." For the sake of explaining this development clearly, it is helpful to think of Oakeshott's thought on these matters as comprising three distinct stages.[8] The first stage encompasses the years from the early 1920s through the 1933 publication of *Experience and Its Modes.* The second stage begins just after *Experience and Its Modes* and ends in 1958. And the third stage commences with the publication of "The Voice of Poetry in the Conversation of Mankind" in 1959, which marks the culmination of his thought on aesthetics.

In the first of these stages, Oakeshott classifies religion and poetry as part of a cluster of experiences that falls under the rubric of "spirit." He sets out this view most clearly in an early, undated paper.[9] We should keep in mind that this was (until 2004) an unpublished paper, perhaps even a student essay. The extensive bibliography appended at the end implies such a possibility. But although his argument in *Experience and Its Modes*

8. I agree with Worthington's classification. See "The Voice of Poetry in Oakeshott's Moral Philosophy," 300.
9. "An Essay on the Relations of Philosophy, Poetry and Reality," in *WIH,* 67–116.

repudiates much of this early view, this essay is important documentation of Oakeshott's early ideas on religion and aesthetics. Here he makes a stark distinction between two alternative ways of apprehending the world: intellect and intuition. Intellect (philosophy), he expounds, "enquires whether there be a rational whole, and if so, what is its nature. It seeks to formulate a 'theoria' of the whole universe, it is a systematic enquiry into the ultimate nature of Reality." Intellect is concerned with "analysis, classification and synthesis" and is wholly empirical. Oakeshott points out intellect's rather significant limitations in understanding the entirety of experience, and he concludes this section of the essay by highlighting philosophy's careful and restricted employment of language. "[T]he attitude of philosophy in the use of language cannot be too firmly insisted upon. Clearly, if it is to remain consistent with itself, philosophy cannot admit the validity of any use of words other than that which is designed to express a rational thought by means of the *meaning* of those words. Other uses of language may have their place, but they cannot express a rational idea and so far as philosophy is concerned they must always remain untruthful."[10] In other words, philosophical language must always aim at analysis and clarification. If it is to remain true to its character, it can never simply "delight" in poetic images.

But there is another way of apprehending the world, and this is the subject of the next section of Oakeshott's essay. It is what he calls intuition, or "poetry." The poet's knowledge is "of *being,* in distinction from the knowledge of knowing which belongs to the philosopher." The poet does not analyze or classify, but merely presents ideas that speak directly to the intuitive faculties of human beings. There are ideas of the spirit, Oakeshott explains, which "come to us in the way in which the emotion of pleasure comes, voices which are silent yet which speak, spiritual ideas which are not rational or cognizable by the mind." The poet seeks "to evoke within us a feeling of the reality of what is spiritual and of the poor shadowiness of even the greatest forms of expression. . . . the artist's life is a great conspiracy . . . for the establishment of the dominance of the spirit." For the poet, unlike for the philosopher, language has no intrinsic meaning. It has only the power to "evoke in others a feeling which the poet has already known. Often to [the poet] the sound of a word has as much value as its meaning, often a word will convey to

10. Ibid., 78, 80, 84.

the reader a sense which is beyond all sense that this same word would contain in conversation. The expressive content of language is increased a thousandfold, but if we were not all poets in some measure we should see in this only a hideous misuse of one of the finest of man's acquirements." Unlike philosophy, poetry cares nothing for analysis: "it desires only the soul, the thing itself, the truth behind the form. Its intuitive grasp can contain life itself, its fingers do not touch to kill but to feel the pulse of life beating at the center."[11]

Throughout this unusual essay Oakeshott describes these two ways of knowing (intellect/philosophy and intuition/poetry) as a "true economy" of human faculties.[12] He argues that neither intellect nor intuition can claim a superior position but that *both* have an important place in human experience. It is particularly striking that here Oakeshott describes poetry as a subset of religion:

> I have used, and shall continue to do so, the word poetry to represent all art. . . . But there is a yet wider term which seems to me to embrace the whole range of this side of man's activities. We may call it Mysticism or Religion. All art is mystical, all art is religious—in principle. The keenest appreciation of Beauty, the deepest understanding of the things of the spirit of which the artist always speaks, the most lively experience of the "realms of gold" cannot be stirred within a man except he be, in the profoundest sense, religious.

Religion is therefore the larger context in which poetry finds its place. But at other points in this essay Oakeshott characterizes poetry as by far the most spiritual of activities. One wonders if it might not have been more appropriate to place religion as a subset of the *poetic* experience. For poetry, Oakeshott observes, "does not propagate ideas but an immediate feeling and intuition of spirit."[13] Spiritual reality is constantly before the poet's eye, and he becomes a sort of creator and mediator. Indeed, Oakeshott goes so far as to describe the poet as the *point d'appui* between temporal and eternal, finite and infinite.

11. Ibid., 90, 86, 86, 95, 100.
12. Ibid., 68. Oakeshott's resemblance to Pascal here is striking. At the beginning of the *Pensées,* Pascal contrasts mathematics (intellect) with intuition, arguing that intuitive minds can judge "at a single glance," while mathematicians, like Oakeshott's philosophers, require systematic and reasoned proofs.
13. "An Essay on the Relations," in *WIH,* 87.

What is quite clear, however, is that Oakeshott is thinking of poetry religiously and religion poetically. "Religion is far more akin to Art than to pure morality with which it is so often confused," he argues. And yet even at this early stage Oakeshott is cognizant of the distinctions between these activities. Though they may be the same in *principle,* they are nonetheless different activities. "Where religion goes beyond Poetry, as such, is that it declares its oneness with a God, not merely with a spiritual world. Though in principle poetry and religion are identical, in result they may, and often do, differ."[14] Yet, in spite of their differences, poetry and religion are both subsets of the category "spirit."

The views expressed in this early essay in certain respects anticipate Oakeshott's mature view of poetry in "The Voice of Poetry in the Conversation of Mankind." They also provide support for the thesis that Oakeshott's thought on aesthetics developed in a single direction. Most notably, in the early essay Oakeshott emphasizes the "immediately present" nature of poetry: "there is no beginning and no end in [poetry's] quest," he observes; "a week's search will not bring it nearer than the work of an instant. Poetry knows reality all at once; process is foreign to its method." The conceptions of time and distance are foreign to poetry; and its "end is achieved so soon as the search is begun." Unlike other kinds of experience, which are concerned with past and future, poetry has the unique characteristic of being fully in and for itself. This is a striking anticipation of his later essay, in which Oakeshott describes the images in poetry as having "no antecedents or consequents; they are not recognized as causes or conditions or signs . . . or as . . . products or effects." Images in contemplation, he contends, are "merely present; they provoke neither speculation nor inquiry about the occasion or condition of their appearing but only delight in their having appeared."[15] Thus throughout Oakeshott's corpus poetry possesses a kind of timelessness.

There is another anticipation of Oakeshott's mature view of poetry in his first published essay. In "Shylock the Jew," written in 1921, Oakeshott praises Shakespeare's genius as a creator of fictional characters. These characters, he observes, are not merely "heroes and villains of the con-

---

14. Manuscript 1/1/33, "An Essay on the Relations of Philosophy, Poetry and Reality," 43n2, Oakeshott Collection, British Library of Political and Economic Science, London School of Economics and Political Science (this one sentence does not appear in the version of the essay published in *WIH*); "An Essay on the Relations," in *WIH,* 110n99.

15. "An Essay on the Relations," in *WIH,* 87, 100; "The Voice of Poetry," in *RP,* 510.

ventional type," but exist as fully formed persons who embody *both* good
and evil in varying degrees. Shakespeare's most outstanding characteristic, Oakeshott asserts, is his "human catholicity," which allows him to cast
aside preconceptions and to enter fully into the characters he creates.[16]
Oakeshott's short essay is an investigation of Shylock as a complex character in *The Merchant of Venice.*

In the context of Oakeshott's thought on poetry and aesthetics, the
most striking part of this particular essay is the distinction made in it between poetic appreciation and moral judgment. Oakeshott observes that
if, when considering Shylock, "we allow the natural, moral instincts of
justice to prevail, we necessarily obscure the real meaning of the character." And in order to engage in true poetic appreciation there must be a
"casting aside of all preconceptions which may colour our judgment, so
that we may, so far as is possible, be *at one* with him whom we wish to
know."[17] Here is the germ of a central idea expressed years later in "The
Voice of Poetry," namely, that moral considerations have no place in the
pure poetic experience. If one's aim is the most complete understanding
(what Oakeshott later calls contemplation) of a poetic image, then preoccupation with moral concerns must temporarily be put aside.[18] A fictional character must be "enjoyed," not judged. So far, then, these early
essays express two of the most central tenets of Oakeshott's mature view
of poetry: first, that poetry is a "fully present" experience, and second,
that moral considerations positively stand in the way of the full poetic
experience. In these respects, Oakeshott's view of poetry changes very
little over the course of his career, and the concepts present in his early
work need only be more explicitly set out in the later essay. However,
Oakeshott's early and late views of poetry are not simply equivalent, for
in the early essays poetry does not yet possess the kind of purity and independence that it does in his mature work. At this early stage, as I have

16. SJ, 63.
17. Ibid., 62, 63.
18. Worthington also observes this distinction, but argues that poetic appreciation and
moral judgment are only quantitatively (poetic appreciation tells *more* about a character
than moral judgment) not *qualitatively* distinct ("The Voice of Poetry in Oakeshott's
Moral Philosophy," 293). I agree; but I also argue that it would be impossible at this stage
for Oakeshott to have categorically separated the two, since he is not yet thinking of experience in the modal categories that he employs later. Thus I interpret this passage as an
important early intimation of his view, only later made fully explicit, that moral judgments are irrelevant to poetry.

mentioned, poetry and religion are still closely linked—different activities with a similar emphasis on spirit. At the very least, Oakeshott is satisfied at this stage that poetry and religion are similar enough to be grouped together as closely related experiences.

But by the mid-1920s Oakeshott's thought takes on a more Idealist cast. During these years he begins to distinguish poetry from religion, although the two experiences remain closely allied. In a 1927 essay entitled "Religion, Politics and the Moral Life," Oakeshott addresses the relationship between religion and morality. As I observed in Chapter 4, he follows F. H. Bradley almost to the letter, arguing that religion is "the completion of morality." And in his 1929 essay "Religion and the World," religion appears once again, defined as part of a "spiritual world" in which everything is valued as it is itself. The link between religion and aesthetics is made quite clear in this essay, where Oakeshott observes that living religiously is itself a kind of art. Moreover, as was the case with poetry, true religion is defined by its character as a wholly "present" activity. Life should not be oriented toward the future, but, if it is to be meaningful, must take place "here and now." Those who would be religious "must be courageous enough to achieve a life that is really contemporary."[19] It is *present* insight that constitutes religion, as it also does poetry. The commonalities between these two experiences are quite striking in Oakeshott's early essays.

However, Oakeshott's first definitive statement on the character of poetry and religion appears only in his 1933 *Experience and Its Modes,* which marks the culmination of what I have called the first stage of Oakeshott's thought on aesthetics. This work confirms the close alliance between poetry and religion, and both appear in it as part of the practical mode. And although Oakeshott later describes practice as a *bellum omnium contra omnes* in which individuals aim at satisfying an endless series of desires, in *Experience and Its Modes* he observes that practice is both more expansive as well as more inclusive. It is not a "mere miscellany of disconnected desires, random hopes and casual actions, nor is it confined to the attempt to satisfy vulgar ambitions." Practice can encompass "a life directed by an idea of the right and the good; it includes all that we mean by beauty." Therefore, the poet, the mystic, and the religious person must be called practical. This is, of course, a view that Oakeshott later

19. "Religion and the World," in *RPML,* 36.

revises, observing years later that "The Voice of Poetry" is meant as a "belated retraction of a foolish sentence in *Experience and Its Modes.*" This is the "foolish sentence": "The most thoroughly and positively practical life is that of the artist or the mystic."[20] But it is clear that in his early view religion and poetry are quite closely related and that they are both practical activities.

In what I designate as the second stage of Oakeshott's thought on aesthetics (roughly 1934–1958), there is evidence that Oakeshott's view on these matters begins to change. The first signal of this change is his 1939 essay "The Claims of Politics," where Oakeshott argues that political activity—that is, the activity of participating in campaigns, debates, protests, and so on—represents only one way of taking part in the life of a society. Moreover, such political activity is "a highly specialized and abstracted form of communal activity; it is conducted on the surface of the life of a society and except on rare occasions makes remarkably small impression below that surface." The more profound contributions to society are made not by politicians, but by those whose genius and interest lie in the fields of literature, art, and philosophy. This view appears to have been prompted, at least in part, by R. G. Collingwood's *The Principles of Art,* which Oakeshott reviewed. In the final pages of *The Principles of Art,* Collingwood asserts that art "is the community's medicine for the worst disease of mind, the corruption of consciousness." Oakeshott's subsequent observation that the "last corruption that can visit a society is a corruption of its consciousness" is a clear echo of Collingwood.[21] For the present discussion, there are several important points to emphasize about this essay.

First, "The Claims of Politics" signals the beginning of a move away from classifying poetry and religion as allied experiences. Religion is conspicuously absent in this essay, and those who "create and recreate" the values of society are now designated as the poet, the artist, and the philosopher. The philosopher, however, as we recall from *Experience and Its Modes,* is someone whose activity cannot ever be called practical. Philosophy, after all, is an attempt "to escape from the conduct of life" and to "throw off the responsibility of living."[22] Therefore, to associate

20. *EM,* 296; *RP,* xi; *EM,* 296.
21. "The Claims of Politics," in *RPML,* 93; R. G. Collingwood, *Principles of Art,* 336; "The Claims of Politics," in *RPML,* 95.
22. *EM,* 296–97.

the poet with the philosopher, as Oakeshott does here, would seem to signal that he has begun to question whether the poet ought to be classified unambiguously within practice. Indeed, he observes that the poet, artist, and philosopher must be *free* from the world in order to make their most profound contributions.

The ambiguity that commentators have noticed in this essay, however, concerns the question of what Oakeshott means by designating the poet or artist as someone who "creates and recreates" the values of a society. On the one hand, this might be read as a kind of encouragement for the poet, artist, and philosopher to make noble examples of themselves or to "inspire" other members of their society by their work. Such a reading would imply that the activities of the poet, artist, and philosopher are in some sense practical, in that they aim to make an impact on other members of their society—perhaps changing customs or reorienting ideals. But Oakeshott sees both the poet and the philosopher as engaged in another kind of activity that, if it is not altogether *removed* from practice, does not wholly take place there either. The task of artists, poets, and philosophers is to "remain true to their genius, which is to mitigate a little their society's ignorance of itself." Through their activity, society "becomes conscious and critical of itself, of its whole self," and not just of itself as a political entity.[23] Thus the activity of poets, artists, and philosophers takes place in a more profound sphere of consciousness. The poet, artist, and philosopher clearly have a connection to their society, but the precise nature of this connection is somewhat difficult to specify. On the one hand, they create and re-create the values of their society. But exactly *how* do they do this? It is certainly not through political activity, but instead by "remaining true to their genius" and being active in their particular spheres. "The Claims of Politics" marks the beginning of Oakeshott's move toward separating out the poet and artist as persons who, like the philosopher, are somehow different from ordinary folk. At the very least, he has begun to question the appropriateness of placing the poet and artist unambiguously within practice.

Oakeshott's 1948 "*Leviathan:* A Myth" is an appropriate companion piece to "The Claims of Politics." Oakeshott has already distinguished the poet, artist, and philosopher as persons whose work it is to mitigate the ignorance of their societies, and in "*Leviathan:* A Myth" he shows this

23. "The Claims of Politics," in *RPML,* 95.

kind of artist in action. Hobbes's *Leviathan,* he argues, "is a work of art in the proper sense," and Hobbes has given his reader a "gift of imagination" whose effect is "an expansion of our faculty of dreaming." When *Leviathan* is read as a myth, practical questions about the expediency or applicability of Hobbes's doctrines become inappropriate. For Hobbes's aim, so Oakeshott argues in this essay, is to convey the *mystery* of life, "not a pretended solution."[24] Whether or not one finds Oakeshott's unusual interpretation plausible, the essay conveys a sense of how Oakeshott is thinking of art: it is the perception of mystery and the expression of a common dream. But it is no longer allied with religion. Nor is its function to guide or protect society, but instead simply to make society aware of its own character. Oakeshott seems to be gradually singling out poetry as a unique type of experience—one whose function is only to enlighten, not to instruct. As such, it is becoming less and less practical.

In an undated essay from this period, "Work and Play," Oakeshott makes the distinction between poetry and other kinds of experience much more explicit. He divides human endeavors into two basic types: work is concerned with the satisfaction of wants, while play has no ulterior purpose and consists solely in enjoyment. Play, Oakeshott maintains, stands for an activity that "because it is not directed to the satisfaction of wants, entails an attitude to the world that is not concerned to use it, to get something out of it . . . and offers satisfactions that are not at the same time frustrations." It is not mere "fun" but should be understood as all leisure activities, including those that aim at understanding or illuminating the world (philosophy, science, and history). But it is poetry that is most securely insulated from the world of work. For poetry, in Oakeshott's view, is entirely an end in itself. Thus it may be distinguished not only from practice (work) but also from the explanatory (playful) modes of science, history, and philosophy. Poetry is now thoroughly distinct from religion—indeed from all other types of experience—and has taken on its own unique, nonpractical character. A footnote in Greenleaf's monograph marks the change in Oakeshott's view that has taken place over the decade of the 1950s. "In the first version of the essay on 'Rational Conduct,'" Greenleaf observes, "Oakeshott includes the 'artist'

24. "*Leviathan:* A Myth" should be distinguished from Oakeshott's more famous "Introduction to *Leviathan.*" Both pieces appear in *HCA.* "*Leviathan:* A Myth," 159, 160, 160, 162.

among a list of those (historian, scientist, politician or any one in the ordinary conduct of life) who are engaged in answering questions of a certain sort, i.e. dealing with argument, propositions, criteria of truth and
error, etc. When this passage was reprinted later [in 1962] . . . the 'artist'
was omitted from the list."[25]

All that remains is for the distinct nature of poetry to be set out, which
Oakeshott does in his 1959 essay "The Voice of Poetry in the Conversation of Mankind." This essay marks the beginning of the third stage of
Oakeshott's thought on aesthetics, but it should be clear by now that the
position he takes here is not unexpected or sudden. Indeed, although
Oakeshott describes his essay as a "belated retraction of a foolish sentence," it does not seem to be, as Grant has argued, a "volte-face."[26] It is,
as the present chapter has argued, the natural outcome of a progression
in Oakeshott's thought. Whereas poetry for the young Oakeshott was allied with religion in its expression of "spirit," poetry becomes, in his later
view, separate from religion. Indeed, in this essay poetry is separate from
all other activities and even constitutes a mode of its own. Far from
being ambiguous or paradoxical, poetry has acquired a kind of purity
that it did not have for Oakeshott in the 1920s and 1930s. No longer is
it merely a subset of the religious experience; it has gradually emerged as
an activity with a distinct modal identity. It is worth noting once again
that Oakeshott uses *poetry* as a technical term to encompass all kinds of
art: not only written verse, but all kinds of aesthetic activity. Moreover,
he understood the terms *poetry, contemplation,* and *delight* as synonyms.
Contemplation and delight are not the rewards that follow from enjoying poetry, but instead constitute the poetic experience itself. The activity of imagining poetically *is* contemplative activity.

When poetry takes written form, its essential characteristic is its non-
symbolic language. Whereas in practical life each word is valued for what
it symbolizes, in poetry words are valued in themselves for their delight-
ful sounds and images. But Oakeshott observes that it is extraordinarily
difficult to extricate oneself from the authority of "practical language"
because most of the time we are engaged in practical activity. And practical language is useful and effective precisely *because* of its symbolic nature; when we order food in a restaurant we are interested not in

25. WP, 32; Greenleaf, *Oakeshott's Philosophical Politics,* 33n3.
26. Grant, *Oakeshott,* 104.

exploring the subtleties of language but in getting something to eat. Practical, symbolic language is useful insofar as it points away from itself to something else that we desire to have or wish to avoid. But it is precisely this preoccupation with "usefulness" that must be overcome if poetry is to emerge. Against this view of language in the service of practical needs and wants, Oakeshott describes poetic language as something that is never a means to something else. The language of poetic imagining is valuable insofar as it "enlarges meaning" or "[sets] going a procession of reverberations." Or, as George Santayana has observed, "[I]t is when sound abandons the servile function of signification, and develops itself freely as music, that it becomes thoroughly vital and its own excuse for being."[27]

The heart of the poetic experience, in Oakeshott's view, is its character as something qualitatively different from everyday life. He understood the world of practical activity as good but limited, owing to the fact that in it humans can never find completion, permanence, or rest. Poetic experience, on the other hand, is an invitation to a type of activity in which there is a possibility of achieving these things, at least for a time. In contemplating and delighting, human beings do not aim at "getting" anything. They are concerned neither with questions of success and failure nor with saving or conserving resources. The experience, in short, is categorically different from almost everything else human beings do, and it is governed by altogether different considerations. Poetry, for Oakeshott, has thus taken over "whatever may be salvaged from the neo-Platonic ideal of contemplative participation in a divine order."[28] The following paragraphs consider what Oakeshott achieves in this essay and whether "The Voice of Poetry" succeeds as a theory of aesthetics.

Is "The Voice of Poetry" an Adequate Theory of Aesthetics?

Although "The Voice of Poetry in the Conversation of Mankind" is usually considered to express Oakeshott's mature theory of aesthetics, few commentators have recognized its importance to Oakeshott's thought as a whole. It is in this essay that Oakeshott once again sets out his modal

27. "The Voice of Poetry," in *RP,* 503; George Santayana, *Dominations and Powers,* 136.
28. Josiah Lee Auspitz, "Individuality, Civility and Theory: The Philosophical Imagination of Michael Oakeshott," 291.

theory, building on the groundwork he laid almost thirty years earlier in
Experience and Its Modes. The difference, of course, is that whereas in
Experience and Its Modes there were three modes (science, history, and
practice), now there are four: science, history, practice, and *poetry.* The
first several sections of the essay briefly restate the character of the three
familiar modes, and the balance of the essay examines the newcomer,
poetry.

Poetry is said to be a wholly self-sufficient activity. The poetic experience consists in "contemplating" or "delighting in" images for their own
sake. *Contemplation* and *delight* are synonymous in this essay, and such activity is thoroughly released from considerations of purpose or produc-
tiveness. Moral questions—should a fictional character act this way? ought
we to approve this poet's portrayal of a given situation?—are utterly inappropriate to poetry and indeed positively stand in the way of contemplating and delighting. After setting out his view of poetic experience,
Oakeshott then turns to the task of disabusing his reader of common
misconceptions about poetry. He emphasizes that the essence of poetry
does not consist in its representation of "truth" or in its attempt to express "emotion" or "beauty." The essence of poetry is its character as a
wholly self-sufficient experience in which images are delighted in *for
their own sake.* It is the ultimate example of "play."

And yet this essay is both odd and unsatisfying if it is understood simply as a theory of aesthetics. For although his is a provocative view,
Oakeshott does not adequately address many of the central questions of
aesthetics. And though readers of Oakeshott may not be surprised by
this—for Oakeshott often examines his subjects in original and unorthodox ways—it is worth considering whether it is indeed his *aim* to
set out a comprehensive theory of art. There is a clue to this puzzle in his
review of Collingwood's 1938 book *The Principles of Art.* Oakeshott observes that the book constitutes "the most profound and stimulating discussion I have ever read of the question, What is art? . . . [Collingwood's]
argument begins . . . with an attempt to distinguish Art from not Art, to
make certain that we know how to apply the word 'art' where it ought
to be applied and refuse where it ought to be refused." But there is no
consideration of this fundamental aesthetic question in "The Voice of
Poetry." Indeed, it seems that absolutely anything is fair game for poetic
contemplation. "[A]ny scene, shape, pattern, pose or movement in the
visible or audible world, any action, happening . . . habit or disposition

. . . thought or memory is a poetic image if the manner in which it is imagined is what I have called 'contemplating.'"[29] One wonders how Oakeshott could have recognized in Collingwood's work the importance of coming to a clear definition of art, and yet have failed to address this in his own consideration of the subject.

There is also no examination in "The Voice of Poetry" of the poet or artist's self-understanding. There is remarkably little discussion of the actual role of the poet and no discussion at all of the poet's place in society. Indeed, the actual person of the poet or artist is mentioned in only a handful of places throughout the essay, and Oakeshott observes (appropriately, I believe) that "neither the poet nor the critic of poetry will find very much to his purpose in what I have to say."[30] We have already observed that Oakeshott has failed to confront the fundamental definitional question of aesthetics—what is art?—and now he appears likewise to have omitted the question, who is the artist?

Perhaps most troubling of all to many readers is Oakeshott's categorical dismissal of all moral questions that may be put to art. He famously jettisons a host of inappropriate inquiries about such things as Hamlet's "normal bed-time" or the "true proportions" of Donatello's *David,* pointing out that these merely demonstrate a misunderstanding of the nature of art. But many would agree that there are more serious moral questions to be raised about poetry, modern equivalents of Plato's questions to the poets. Do not certain poetic images have the potential to harm the souls of those who view them? And what are we to make of the inescapable fact that certain artists clearly *intend* their creations to teach moral lessons? Indeed, many theorists positively insist on recognizing the moral content of art. "There is no such thing as art for art's sake, any more than science for science' sake," contends Tolstoy, "since every human function should be directed to increase morality and to suppress violence." And, from the Thomist perspective, one commentator observes that every "human activity, even art, is subject to the eternal law, and must be ultimately directed to God, else man plays false with his very nature."[31] Oakeshott is no doubt aware that serious questions exist

---

29. Oakeshott, "Collingwood's Philosophy of Art," 139–40; "The Voice of Poetry," in *RP,* 517.

30. "The Voice of Poetry," in *RP,* 495.

31. Leo Tolstoy, *What Is Art?* 287; Leonard Callahan, *A Theory of Esthetic according to the Principles of St. Thomas Aquinas,* 110.

about the moral status of art, and yet he has chosen not to address them. In the face of these considerations, then, "The Voice of Poetry" as a theory of aesthetics seems radically incomplete.

However, rather than conclude that Oakeshott has set forth an inadequate theory of aesthetics, we might consider an alternative hypothesis: that "The Voice of Poetry" is only *incidentally* a theory of aesthetics. I do not, of course, mean to imply that Oakeshott's essay does not concern itself with aesthetics (it certainly does), or that Oakeshott has nothing substantial to say about artistic experience. On the contrary: poetry and aesthetics were central concerns for Oakeshott and had been so since he was a young man. Nevertheless, there is a distinct sense in which it appears that Oakeshott's aim in "The Voice of Poetry" is not to give an empirical description of art or artist—nor even to give an empirical description of poetry as one finds it in the latest anthology—but instead to describe a particular kind of *experience* that he calls "contemplating" or "delighting." The essay's title, after all, does refer to the "voice" of poetry. Poetry here is a kind of conversation partner, someone who has something distinctive to say and who approaches human experience from a unique perspective. And the poetic disposition may even emerge in the absence of a work of art, properly speaking.

To approach the topic another way, we might ask ourselves what the question is to which Oakeshott's essay offers an answer. As R. G. Collingwood observes in his *Autobiography,* to discover an author's meaning "you must also know what the question was (a question in his own mind, and presumed by him to be in yours) to which the thing he has said or written was meant as an answer."[32] Until one has done this, one has not understood an author; and, of course, the most common mistake is for us to put our own questions to a text and then to complain that its author has failed to answer them. The question foremost in Oakeshott's mind must be something like, what kind of human experience might be said to be most satisfactory and least incomplete? His answer is poetry, and his essay is a defense of this answer. This is not primarily a theory of aesthetics; for poetry as it appears in this essay is not an artifact that may be empirically described. Instead it is a kind of human activity whose defining characteristics are self-sufficiency and insulation from the considerations of other kinds of experience. Since Oakeshott considers prac-

32. R. G. Collingwood, *An Autobiography,* 31.

tice to be by far the most dominant mode of experience, it is no wonder that he should spend most of his effort attempting to extricate poetry from practice's insistent moral questions.

To sum up my position thus far: "The Voice of Poetry" describes poetry or contemplation as a human *activity* that offers a kind of unity and completeness that can never be found unambiguously in other modes of experience. "At whatever point contemplation is broken off it is never incomplete," Oakeshott points out. Poetry is thus an "escape" from the considerations of these other modes.[33] The essay as a whole might be understood as a theory of art, but it is not *primarily* that. It represents what Oakeshott found to be a complete and rewarding kind of human experience—a kind of experience entirely removed from "the search for power after power" that constitutes the major part of practical life.

Evidence for the view that poetry is a type of self-sufficient activity comes from a neglected section of the essay in which Oakeshott describes the world as a place where "self and not-self divulge themselves to reflection." In this section, Oakeshott observes that the self is essentially activity. The not-self, as the other side of the equation, is "composed of images" that exist in partnership with the self. Now, it is possible to read this discussion of self and not-self as merely a prelude to the upcoming restatement of Oakeshott's modal theory. That is, whereas the young Oakeshott spoke of "ideas" and "coherent worlds of experience," this talk of "images" and "ways of imagining" might be understood as merely a restatement of his earlier thinking about modality. But it would seem to be more than this because of its function as an introduction to the essay. This discussion of self and not-self, and of the activity of imagining that takes place between the two, points the reader toward a particular way of interpreting the subsequent discussion of poetry. In no other mode is there such an intimate union of self and not-self, for while practice postulates a self and a world of "not-selves" to be made use of, in poetry self and not-self simply *exist* together in the activity designated "contemplating" or "delighting." The image that provokes contemplation is not to be "used," but apprehended. And in apprehending an image, a self takes no thought for what has come before or what will come after. The activity of contemplating is wholly self-sufficient, even if it is an intermittent experience. Listening to the voice of poetry

33. "The Voice of Poetry," in *RP,* 514, 535.

"is to enjoy, not a victory, but a momentary release, a brief enchant-ment."[34]

It is true that a relationship between self and not-self exists in all modes, but it reaches a particular state of completion in this activity Oakeshott calls contemplating and delighting. In poetry there is no "inquiry about the occasion or conditions of [images that appear]. . . . they have no antecedents or consequents." There is no premeditated end in poetry; at "whatever point contemplation is broken off it is never incomplete." The delight that comes with poetic experience "is not to be thought of as a reward which follows upon the activity. . . . 'delighting' is only another name for contemplating." Poetry may thus be understood to offer, as Wendell John Coats Jr. has put it, a unity in which "form and content . . . evolve simultaneously and are inseparable except in analysis." Practical life offers a distinct contrast to this kind of unity, for in practice, remarks Oakeshott, an image is always a "temporary resting-place in a necessarily endless process which is concluded only in death." In contemplation, on the other hand, images are "permanent and unique." Indeed, contempla-tion "does not use, or use-up or wear-out its images, or induce change in them: it rests in them, looking neither backwards nor forwards."[35] In the poetic experience, then, one achieves a sense of living wholly in the pres-ent. Considerations of practical life are thoroughly sublimated, and thus the moral questions of practice are simply irrelevant.

The Relation between Poetry and Morality

But if poetry is indeed self-sufficient and unique—in principle, incor-ruptible—why do we have the distinct sense that it also has something to do with morality?[36] Oakeshott repeatedly emphasizes that aesthetic ex-perience cannot be corrupted by the moral considerations that play such a large part in practice. Moral approval and disapproval "are alike inap-plicable to these images; [the 'conduct' of a fictional character] cannot be

---

34. Ibid., 495–97, 540.
35. Ibid., 510, 514; Coats, *Oakeshott and His Contemporaries,* 104; "The Voice of Poetry," in *RP,* 510.
36. I develop this argument at length in Chapter 6. *Morality* is meant here to convey the idea of human conduct in general—not to designate specific decisions in which "right and wrong" are necessarily at issue.

either 'right' or 'wrong' nor their dispositions 'good' or 'bad.'" And yet he simultaneously provides intimations (for example, when he describes human conduct as having a "poetic character") that *something* about the poetic experience relates to conduct. In a number of places Oakeshott observes that human activity has a "poetic character."[37] This apparent contradiction is the source of the confusion upon which several commentators have remarked.

I argued in the preceding section that Oakeshott saw poetry as a complete and satisfactory form of human experience, and as such it may serve as a kind of model for what all experience hints at but cannot achieve. Perfect completion is, by definition, impossible in other modes of experience—particularly so in practice, where "is" and "ought" can never be fully reconciled. In poetry, however, the desiring practical self is sublimated or temporarily lost, and what emerges is a self that engages images as fully present. In this engagement, desire and aversion, approval and disapproval are alike absent. As Oakeshott observes, images in contemplation are "merely present; they provoke neither speculation nor inquiry about the occasion or conditions of their appearing but only delight in their having appeared. They have no antecedents or consequents; they are not recognized as causes or conditions or signs of some other image to follow, or as the products or effects of one that went before. . . . they are neither 'useful' nor 'useless.'"[38] In short, images in poetic contemplation exist separately from all practical endeavors. And yet poetry appears to be related to conduct. How can this be? The relationship may be explained by using the Aristotelian language of essence and accident. Even though this language is not Oakeshott's, it captures his intention of identifying clearly the most crucial postulates of any activity. In the same way that morality sometimes has the "accidental" characteristic of seeming fully poetic, so poetry may at times appear fully practical (when its intention is to instruct, for instance). And yet we would not say that poetry's essence is to instruct any more than morality's essence is pure contemplative delight.

On the one hand, Oakeshott finds the essence of poetic experience to be its self-sufficiency, its character as a wholly satisfactory activity that

---

37. "The Voice of Poetry," in *RP,* 520, 479, 485.

38. An excellent discussion of the lack of unity in practice appears in Bernard Bosanquet's *What Religion Is,* chap. 1; "The Voice of Poetry," in *RP,* 509–10.

stands apart from all practical considerations. On the other hand, the essence of morality is to satisfy desires, as Oakeshott observes: "the aspect of practical imagining which calls first for our attention is its character as desire and aversion." It is true that the higher forms of morality may sometimes temporarily escape "desire satisfaction," as I discuss below in the examples of love and friendship. And morality takes place, of course, within the context of social interaction, where other people also wish to satisfy their desires (what Oakeshott refers to in *On Human Conduct* as a moral practice). It is also true that the desires of moral agents range widely, from base to exalted. But the essential principle of moral conduct would seem to be its aim of satisfying desires. Moral conduct is concerned with agents seeking to procure "imagined and wished-for satisfactions (which need not be self-gratifications) and each seeking them in responses of another or of others."[39]

And yet there are times when moral conduct takes on a high degree of self-sufficiency, as it does in love, friendship, and certain forms of self-enactment.[40] At these times it appears—like aesthetic experience—to be a complete and satisfactory activity. But this does not mean that morality actually becomes poetry, only that it is very much *like* poetry. Morality's relationship to poetry thus can only be accidental—that is to say, any moral action (though some lend themselves to this more than others) may be regarded from a poetic point of view, delighted in as an end in itself. But this would be accidental to its *essential* character as a moral act, an act whose primary characteristic is to satisfy a desire. Poetry thus offers an ideal unity that morality may sometimes approximate. When conduct exhibits, as it sometimes does, a true unity of manner and motive, it may be said to partake of a poetic character. Moral action, like poetry, becomes something to be valued in itself. So Oakeshott could celebrate a certain kind of activity that is "moral" and yet enacted in a virtuosic performance by someone who has *learned* how to act. It is moral and yet aesthetic—indeed, it is (almost) poetic. Nonetheless we should be clear: the two kinds of experience—poetry and conduct—remain theoretically and modally separate.

---

39. "The Voice of Poetry," in *RP,* 497; *OHC,* 70.

40. *Self-enactment* is a term that Oakeshott introduces in *On Human Conduct*. He speaks of it there as actions understood "in terms of the motives in which they are performed," not (as in self-disclosure) in terms of the looked-for responses from others. See *OHC,* 70.

Oakeshott illustrates this delicate relationship between art and conduct in his 1948 essay "The Tower of Babel." There is a "freedom and inventiveness" at the heart of every traditional morality, he observes, and this moral inventiveness "may be likened to the sort of innovation introduced into a plastic art by the fortuitous appearance in an individual of a specially high degree of manual skill, or to the sort of change a great stylist may make in a language."[41] Artistic creativity thus stands as the model for a certain kind of moral activity, and yet they are not the same activity. Oakeshott is nevertheless at pains to show that it would be better if moral activity *were* more often characterized as poetic. For the problem with commonplace morality—and particularly with Rationalist morality—is precisely that it denies the poetic character of human activity. I shall return to this point in Chapters 6 and 7.

This view of the relationship between poetry and morality—that moral conduct sometimes seems to approximate art—is confirmed by Oakeshott's discussion of self-enactment in *On Human Conduct*. There he describes moral conduct as "like an art in having to be learned . . . in allowing almost endless opportunity for individual style." Oakeshott goes far here toward a view that would link poetry and morality ever more closely, maintaining that in self-enactment "conduct is released from its character as a response to a contingent situation and is emancipated from liability to the frustration of adverse circumstances." Speaking the language of self-enactment is "to be as unconcerned as may be with the brittle pursuit and enjoyment of satisfactions and therefore as indifferent as may be to its frustration." And yet conduct can never be *fully* poetic because human beings must continuously seek "practical" satisfactions. Oakeshott clarifies this point a few pages later in a section concerning religious self-enactment, explaining that self-enactment "is itself an episodic and an inconclusive engagement, as *ondoyant* and as full of unresolved tensions as any other. It is never separable from the deadly engagement of agents disclosing themselves in responding to their contingent situations and achieving their passing satisfactions or suffering their transitory disappointments."[42] Thus even when morality is most "poetic" it is nevertheless distinct from the *pure* poetic experience.

There are certain activities in which the poetic character of human

41. "The Tower of Babel," in *RP*, 472.
42. *OHC,* 62, 73, 75, 84.

conduct is more likely to manifest itself. As Oakeshott concludes in the final pages of "The Voice of Poetry," foremost among these are the relationships between persons in love and in friendship. These relationships are "still unmistakably practical" and yet they contain "intimations of contemplative imagining" that may be pursued. A friend, asserts Oakeshott, "is somebody who engages the imagination, who excites contemplation." If friendship can never be true contemplation, it may yet be "ambiguously practical" and can therefore constitute "a connection between the voices of poetry and practice, a channel of common understanding."[43] In short, friendship is poised ambiguously between two modes. Viewed in one aspect, it is part of practice—an effort to address, through our relationship with others, our own desires, fears, anxieties, and so on. Viewed in another aspect, it is part of poetry—one of those rare opportunities to delight in something, another human being, in and for itself.

Thus poetry appears as the ideal of activity: an ideal in which form and content are unified in the activity of imagining poetically. It may inform morality as a model, but it should be clear that morality (as a less unified experience) can have nothing relevant to say to poetry—at least not to the experience of "contemplating" and "delighting" that Oakeshott has designated as poetry. In this view he echoes the writings of many authors he read extensively as a young man, authors such as George Santayana and Walter Pater. It is Pater who best expresses this view of poetry, and the following quotation illustrates the function of poetic experience in a way that Oakeshott would surely have approved. Here, in an essay on Wordsworth, Pater describes the office of the poet:

> Wordsworth, and other poets who have been like him . . . are the masters, the experts, in this art of impassioned contemplation. Their work is, not to teach lessons, or enforce rules, or even to stimulate us to noble ends; but to withdraw the thoughts for a little while from the mere machinery of life, to fix them, with appropriate emotions, on the spectacle of those great facts in man's existence which no machinery affects. . . . [T]he end of life is not action but contemplation—*being* as distinct from *doing*. . . . In poetry, in art, if you enter into their true spirit at all, you touch this principle, in a measure: these, by their very sterility, are a type of beholding for the mere joy of beholding.

43. "The Voice of Poetry," in *RP,* 538; "On Being Conservative," in *RP,* 417; "The Voice of Poetry," in *RP,* 538.

Pater likewise makes explicit the connection between the aesthetic experience and moral conduct when he argues that "to treat life in the spirit of art, is to make life a thing in which means and ends are identified: to encourage such treatment, the true moral significance of art and poetry."[44] To treat life "in the spirit of art" would seem to be a way of resolving what has often been seen as an ambiguous relationship between poetry and morality in Oakeshott's work. To put it as succinctly as possible: the unity found in artistic experience is untouched by the moral considerations of practical life. Yet moral conduct, when it is most fully satisfying, may sometimes take on the character of an artistic performance.

Poetry as an Alternative to Rationalism

This chapter has so far argued three points: first, that Oakeshott's thought on aesthetics develops in a single, consistent direction; second, that "The Voice of Poetry in the Conversation of Mankind" is not primarily a comprehensive theory of art, but rather a description of a particular kind of human experience; and third, that there is a definite relationship between poetic experience and morality, even though the two remain separate activities. The third of these arguments provides an important link to Oakeshott's moral and political theory. To treat life in the spirit of art and to pursue activities in which human conduct may best display its "poetic character" is to reject the Rationalistic conception of life that Oakeshott criticizes so incisively throughout his corpus. I discuss this in greater detail in Chapter 7, but it is worth suggesting its general contours here as well.

In *Rationalism in Politics* Oakeshott launches an argument against a certain cast of mind that appears both in individual conduct and in politics. At the heart of Rationalist morality is the idea that experience may be understood as a set of problems calling out for solution. For the Rationalist, the conduct of affairs is a matter of solving these problems by the application of "reason," unclouded by habit or tradition. He thinks, moreover, that such reason may be learned by anyone at will, through a handbook or a technical course of study. The mind of the Rationalist is a "finely-tempered, neutral instrument" and perfectionist in character. Such

---

44. Walter Pater, *Appreciations,* 62.

a person always aims at certainty and is impatient when the world does
not satisfy his compulsion for order. When he turns to politics he is like
an engineer. What the Rationalist cannot imagine is "politics which do
not consist in solving problems, or a political problem of which there is
no 'rational' solution at all." He displays an "irritable nervousness in the
face of everything topical and transitory" and tries to reduce the "tangle
and variety of experience" to a set of principles. What the Rationalist
specifically eschews is the idea of mystery—that there might be experiences not susceptible to formulation in clear, logical propositions. He has
no ear for poetry and is not intrigued by the ineffable elements of artistic creation. His "cast of mind is gnostic," and as such he would rather
formulate and categorize than contemplate and delight.[45]

When Rationalism infects morality, as it often does, it appears as a
propensity to formulate dogmatic moral rules. These rules are believed
to exist in advance of activity itself and must simply be applied as various
circumstances arise in an individual's life. Oakeshott observes that such
Rationalist morality consists primarily in "the self-conscious pursuit of
moral ideals." It is the "solution of a stream of problems, the mastery of a
succession of crises," "what other peoples have recognized as 'idolatry.' "
It calls those who practice it to orient themselves by a "vision of perfection."[46] But this view denies the fundamental characteristic of moral
activity, according to Oakeshott: its freedom and inventiveness. The constant pursuit of moral ideals positively stands in the way of recognizing
the poetic character of human activity. For, like the poet, who does not
first have an idea and seek to realize it in his composition, moral action—
when it is most coherent—simply and effortlessly unifies manner and
motive. This is not to say that moral action is thoughtless, for there may
have been a great deal of antecedent thought preceding any given action. But it is to say that at times authentic moral activity may approach
the unity of poetic experience. The Rationalist pursuit of moral ideals
explicitly denies this. It divides morality in half: one part conceiving and
accepting a set of moral rules, the other part observing them or "putting
them into practice." The Rationalist does not allow himself to act spon-

45. "Rationalism in Politics," in *RP,* 7, 9–10, 6.
46. Ibid., 40, 41; "The Voice of Poetry," in *RP,* 475. In *On Human Conduct* Oakeshott
describes in greater detail the character of moral rules. Rules, he observes, are abridgments that express "considerations of adverbial desirability." They are not commands that
must be obeyed, but "relatively precise considerations to be subscribed to" (66–68).

taneously, without clearly formulated reasons, and always seeks either a precept for action or a rule to prohibit it. Oakeshott does not necessarily mean to imply that this is how moral conduct *actually* takes place; indeed, it is almost a caricature of Rationalist morality. But if even the Rationalist cannot constantly hold to his ideals, this would seem to confirm that morality as it takes place in the world shares some element of creativity with poetry. Authentic moral conduct is thus neither problem-solving nor rule-following; it is "agents continuously and colloquially related to one another in the idiom of a familiar language of moral converse."[47] But while much has been made of the trenchant criticism of Rationalism displayed in the essays in *Rationalism in Politics,* it is important to consider what Oakeshott might have regarded as a positive *alternative.* We should be on guard against the view that Oakeshott somehow offers a "solution" to the "problem" of Rationalism, for already in using these terms we have entered into the Rationalist mind-set. But it is clear, if one considers the whole of Oakeshott's corpus, that there is such an alternative.

His alternative, as I have argued, is a life that takes aesthetic insight as its ideal or, at least, as a model that conduct may sometimes approximate. If Rationalism presupposes a lack of unity in experience, poetry offers an ideal unity of form and content. If the ends of the Rationalist are thrown ever forward into the future, poetry may be engaged in as a fully "present" experience. In such a life moral conduct is not subscription to standing rules, but is instead a kind of unity between knowing what to do and doing it. Like the poet, who simply "imagines poetically," a person acting in this manner "improvises" a response to a given situation. Just as a musician has a feel for his instrument and for his own capabilities, the language of moral intercourse "is an instrument which may be played upon with varying degrees of sensibility to its resources. There is room for the individual idiom, it affords opportunity to inventiveness. . . . it has rhythms which remain when the words are forgotten." And yet this poetic alternative cannot be constantly or dogmatically maintained, for there are many situations where it is proper to be concerned with utility. Nor would adopting a philosophy of "living poetically" be appropriate in moral life, for Oakeshott speaks in a number of places about the misunderstanding this entails. In *Experience and Its Modes,* for instance,

47. *OHC,* 64.

Oakeshott observes that a philosophy of life is a "meaningless contradiction," because philosophy is the engagement to be continually *en voyage.* A philosophy of life, on the other hand, seems to be—whether simple or more sophisticated—merely a set of precepts for action.[48]

And despite Worthington's claim that poetic imagination "encompasses all aspects of Oakeshott's characterization of human conduct," there would seem to be many situations in the moral life where more prosaic considerations take precedence. As Oakeshott famously observes, "[T]o go on changing one's butcher until one gets the meat one likes . . . is conduct not inappropriate to the relationship concerned." Moreover, it is easy to imagine situations in which the poetic ideal of unified experience might be impossible—as, for instance, when a person must fight the *desire* to act in a way that he *knows* to be wrong. Oakeshott's discussion of the concept of self-disclosure is instructive in this regard, for his description of this activity certainly points away from poetry. In self-disclosure, a person acts in ways that require responses from other agents, and this kind of activity occurs "in transactions with others and it is a hazardous adventure; it is immersed in contingency, it is interminable, and it is liable to frustration, disappointment, and defeat."[49] Such a description once again highlights the essence of morality: its concern with the satisfaction of desires. And although at its best moments conduct may exhibit a poetic character, it can never wholly shake off its practical character.

We may conclude, therefore, by observing that poetry and morality are linked. And yet this link is a delicate one, for it would be an overstatement to argue that all morality is by definition poetic. It is true that in his 1948 "Tower of Babel" Oakeshott attributes a poetic character to "all human moral activity." However, nowhere else in his corpus does Oakeshott make this claim, and in *On Human Conduct,* as I have argued above, there would seem to be a significant distinction between ordinary moral conduct and the rarer kind of conduct that may approach poetry. As Oakeshott observes in a number of places, morality's preoccupation with satisfying desires means it can never achieve the perfect self-sufficiency of poetry. Moral relationship exists "solely in respect of conditions to be subscribed to in seeking the satisfaction of any want."[50] It becomes po-

---

48. *OHC,* 65; *EM,* 354.
49. Worthington, "The Voice of Poetry in Oakeshott's Moral Philosophy," 310; "On Being Conservative," in *RP,* 416; *OHC,* 73.
50. "The Tower of Babel," in *RP,* 479; *OHC,* 62.

etic only at those times and in those activities in which the desiring self is temporarily sublimated. In such situations ordinary concerns recede and what emerges is a self disposed to contemplate, to delight, to live for the moment. This aesthetic insight—that there is a unity of experience sometimes available to human beings—is the fundamental counter position to Rationalism. As I have observed above, Oakeshott saw Rationalism as an intellectual pathology that works to constrict the range of experience, since Rationalists value only those things and activities that encourage modern man in his goals of maximizing utility. Oakeshott's work is a continual protest against the world's demand for productivity and progress.

There is one other respect in which this "aesthetic" ideal of conduct is an important part of Oakeshott's thought on morality and politics. This aesthetic unity of form and content provides the basis for his view of conservatism. Much has been written about Oakeshott's rather unorthodox view of conservatism, and many commentators have been inclined to distrust him since he grounds his conservatism neither in metaphysics nor by appeal to tradition. Instead, Oakeshott's conservatism, I would argue, is grounded in a particular kind of experience that in its ideal form may be seen as "aesthetic." I have observed throughout this chapter that aesthetic experience offers the ultimate unity of form and content. It consists in the propensity to "delight" and to "enjoy"—to put aside considerations of consequences and to live fully in the present. This is precisely what Oakeshott calls the conservative disposition, and it may appear both in morality and in politics.

In his 1956 essay "On Being Conservative," Oakeshott describes conservatism as the propensity to "use and to enjoy what is available rather than to wish for or to look for something else; to delight in what is present rather than what was or what may be." There is no "mere idolizing of what is past and gone. What is esteemed is the present." The conservative disposition, for Oakeshott, consists in *present enjoyment;* and in this it is at times far from many other prevalent conservative attitudes. Oakeshott avoids a reverential attitude toward "history" or "the past," and he has no hostility toward or fear of change. A major difference between Oakeshott and many other conservatives is his focus on the present, not the past; on enjoyment, not preservation per se. Friendship is the ultimate emblem of this kind of conservatism, consisting in the "ready acceptance of what is and the absence of any desire to change or to improve." The relationship of friend to friend is "dramatic, not utilitarian; the tie is one of familiarity, not usefulness; the disposition engaged is conservative, not 'progressive.' "[51]

As I noted in the introduction to this chapter, this view of Oakeshott may appear unusual to readers who are familiar only with his more explicitly political works. But as I have argued above, I believe this aesthetic insight lays the groundwork for his reflections on morality and politics. Indeed, we may observe in his mature political theory an emphasis on a kind of civil association that allows—perhaps requires—the kind of moral persons who know how to engage in the sorts of activities that make one most fully human. Poetry and other kinds of "play" express this highest part of human experience. In the early essay to which I have referred throughout this chapter, "An Essay on the Relations of Philosophy, Poetry and Reality," Oakeshott observes that "the key words to life are always small words, easily passed over in a hasty reading; and yet if we fail to recognize them the whole vast drama is well nigh meaningless. At the beginning of the play the key note is struck, and if we are not waiting with minds alert we shall miss this first intimation."[52] The key note for properly appreciating Oakeshott's work is, so I argue, to recognize that this insight—in essence, an aesthetic insight—lies at the very core of Oakeshott's thought on human conduct. I elaborate upon this point in the following chapter.

51. "On Being Conservative," in *RP,* 408, 417.
52. "An Essay on the Relations," in *WIH,* 96.

6

The Tower of Babel and the Moral Life

In Chapter 5, I made the argument that aesthetic experience stands as the fulfillment of all the "intimations" Oakeshott gives his readers about what is ultimately satisfactory in experience. If practical activity does not constitute the whole of life (and Oakeshott states clearly that it cannot), can there be any kind of experience that rejects the demands of practice and offers some greater satisfaction? The realm of aesthetics—where images are delighted in for their own sake, and all considerations of past and future are temporarily abrogated—fits this bill, even if it offers only a temporary escape from practical life. Aesthetic contemplation provides a full unity of form and content, and as such it seems to satisfy Oakeshott's desire to identify a kind of activity that is wholly self-sufficient. It is the kind of activity we might engage in if we were to renounce, for a time, the pursuit of practical satisfactions.

Aesthetic experience also stands as a model for a certain type of morality that rejects utility and is fundamentally creative. Oakeshott hints at this link between aesthetics and morality in at least three places: his 1948 "Tower of Babel," "The Voice of Poetry in the Conversation of Mankind," and *On Human Conduct*. I discuss these below. However, there is another sort of morality that does not approach any kind of aesthetic unity at all. Such is the morality of the Rationalist, the "anti-individual," and the ideologue, all targets of Oakeshott's incisive criticism.

The task of the current chapter is to set out the two kinds of moral character that appear time and again throughout Oakeshott's corpus. The first type is what I designate "servile morality." The primary characteristics of this morality are its markedly utilitarian character, its rejection of the task of self-understanding, its pursuit of perfection, and its propensity to favor a ready-made code of conduct. This is the morality of the Rationalist. Oakeshott elucidates this kind of morality in two distinct essays, both entitled "The Tower of Babel," written in 1948 and 1979, respectively. The first is a philosophical exposition of two kinds of morality, and the second is a modern retelling of the Tower of Babel story. Both, in markedly different ways, are emblematic of a certain conception of morality that Oakeshott finds unsatisfactory.

However, Oakeshott does more than find fault with what he considers to be common misunderstandings of the moral life. Lying behind his critique of servile morality is a positive alternative, a view of human conduct that he finds better suited to the constitution of human beings. This I designate "liberal morality." Briefly, liberal morality is not merely obeying rules. Nor is it loyal adherence to an ideology, or the postponement of all satisfactions to the future. It is morality that consists in the cultivation of a personal sensibility and that strives to live fully in the present. Such morality is learned through observation and action, not by internalizing a set of intellectual principles that are then "applied" to conduct. This kind of morality is natural, creative, and habitual. At its highest reaches, it may almost be called aesthetic.

These, then, are the two "ideal types" I consider in the paragraphs to follow: servile and liberal morality. I begin by examining closely Oakeshott's view of morality as filtered through the story of the Tower of Babel, which is, for Oakeshott, a profound myth that "the circumstances of human life constantly suggest."[1] This story discloses several of the central ideas that make up what I have called "servile" morality: the dangers inherent in the pursuit of perfection, the "illusion of affairs" as a substitute for self-understanding, the human inclination toward greed, and the tendency for people to be insecure about their relationship to God. I begin by giving an account of exactly how Oakeshott proceeds in each of these two works.

Next, I set out a view of what "liberal" morality looks like, and show how it is quite different from the morality I have thus far been examining. I make the case that this view of morality depends upon an idea of unified conduct that takes its bearings from Oakeshott's aesthetic theory. I focus on Oakeshott's discussion of morality in *On Human Conduct,* where moral activity is described in markedly artistic terms, as well as the 1948 "Tower of Babel" and "The Voice of Poetry in the Conversation of Mankind." Oakeshott makes a connection between aesthetics (poetry) and

1. "The Tower of Babel," in *RP,* 465.

morality in all three of these works. In setting out this particular "liberal" and "aesthetic" view, he presents the kind of moral character that can embrace the freedom of civil association under a rule of law.

"The Tower of Babel": 1979

I begin with an examination of the second of the two essays that bear the title "The Tower of Babel." Oakeshott observes in this essay that various versions of the Tower of Babel myth have existed among all peoples of the world, and that its most important aspect is its universal expression of an "unchanging human predicament."[2] He summarizes the classic version of the story as follows.

The theme of this myth is "a titanic assault upon heaven" (188) led by a proud but insecure leader named Nimrod, who fears God and is uncertain of his status in relation to God. Thus Nimrod determines to mount an attack upon heaven so that he can eliminate the cause of his anxiety and appropriate heaven's riches for himself. He does so by building a tower from which to engage in his campaign. When his people first hear of his idea they are apprehensive, but they soon come to agree that Nimrod has hatched a plan worth carrying out. Once the project begins, all their energies are directed to its successful completion, and they work with unprecedented determination and energy. With the project fully under way, the Babelians think only of the security that will surely follow from its accomplishment—the completion of the tower and subsequent conquest of heaven—and of the renown they will garner by being part of such an important and historical endeavor. The end of the story is, of course, well known. God frustrates Nimrod's endeavor by "confounding the tongues" (186) of those who work on the project so that they can accomplish nothing.

This, however, is only the prologue to Oakeshott's essay, the bulk of which is a specifically *contemporary* retelling of the myth. Oakeshott's story takes place in the modern-day city of Babel, whose inhabitants are fully engaged in the "getting and spending" (191) of practical life. The Babelians are remarkable for their fickleness and are "easily seduced by

---

2. "The Tower of Babel," in *OH,* 179 (hereafter page numbers from this essay will be cited parenthetically in the text).

novelty" (191). Like most busy people they rarely stop to reflect on the reasons for engaging in their activities; they know only that there are many things to be done and that they must accomplish them efficiently. And yet there is an undercurrent of dissatisfaction running beneath the surface of this society. The Babelians are constantly searching for more and better of whatever it is that they currently want. They feel strangely deprived and are prone to resent those who appear to have more than they. Babel is, in short, a *civitas cupiditatis.*

Nimrod, a young duke, is the ruler of Babel, and like his people he is engaged in the endeavor to satisfy his limitless wants. He feels a lack of goods even more keenly than his subjects, and he sees God as a miser purposefully withholding benefits from human beings. He thus addresses his people and makes the case that their frustrations are due to God's stinginess. "Are we not," asks Nimrod, "the victims of a cosmic conspiracy?" (194). He convinces them that they ought to oust God from his seat in heaven and appropriate the goods of heaven for themselves. And while the Babelians are not the sort of people who would normally be inclined to attempt such an undertaking, their greed and excitement get the better of them and they assent to the project of building a tower to heaven.

The work begins with great energy and enthusiasm. Tremendous resources are devoted to it, and little by little all the consolations and conveniences of civil society begin to decay. The local tobacco and sweet shop is torn down to provide a place for the tower. Private convenience, after all, "must yield to public good" (197), and such an important project will no doubt involve numerous personal sacrifices for the sake of the community. Oakeshott provides many amusing details about the sorts of things that take place during this transition from a civil society of free individuals to a mobilized, purposive community. New postage stamps are issued, featuring a tower motif. Bumper stickers conveying such messages as "Build for the People's Paradise" become commonplace on Babelian cars. The universities even begin to offer a degree in "Tower Studies."

And yet this amusement with the new project begins to give way as construction drags on, and the early enthusiasm becomes tired resignation. For where there is "only one subject of talk, imagination and language [become] impoverished" (199). As the years go by the social life of Babel degenerates further, since no one does anything other than work on the project or talk about the common purpose. There is no diversity, no art or literature, not even any popular entertainment—nothing but anxiety about the status of the project and impatience for its completion. Eventually, the physical resources of the area are exhausted and the builders must quarry the homes of the Babelians themselves. The inhabitants of Babel are reduced to living in tents and caves as they wait for the glorious day when they can finally storm heaven and seize its treasures.

At long last the project appears nearly finished. But there has been a troubling development in the meantime. Nimrod, now quite a bit older, has taken to mounting to the summit of the tower and staying there for hours on end. The townspeople begin to think that he is communicating directly with God, perhaps making some kind of deal that would leave the Babelians to fend for themselves. They begin to suspect that he no longer has their interests at heart, and these suspicions soon turn to explicit doubt. Finally, at the sound of an alarm all the townspeople rush to the tower, certain that the time has come for war with Nimrod. They want only, of course, to claim what should rightfully be theirs. All the inhabitants of Babel rush up the tower, and when it can no longer support their great weight, the tower tumbles to the ground, killing every last citizen.

Such is Oakeshott's retelling of the Tower of Babel story for the modern age. In a few short pages he has set out the central elements of his critique of a certain kind of morality—what I have called servile morality. In the following paragraphs I highlight the most important parts of this Babelian servile morality and attempt to begin sketching out what a more genuine, "liberal" morality might look like.

THE PURSUIT OF PERFECTION

At the heart of Babelian morality is the idea that the world is manifestly imperfect and that it calls out for some human remedy. Mistakes, sin, and inefficiency abound, and humans can never be completely secure in their happiness. The world encourages desires that are difficult to obtain, and even should these be obtained people will want more and better of everything. There is no stopping point for this progress of wants, nor can they be ignored. One is left with a sense of permanent dissatisfaction. The only solution to such manifest imperfection, some would say, is to better our condition once and for all. Such is the mindset of the Babelians as they embark upon building their tower. Yet this pursuit of perfection—of a condition that would permanently remedy the frustrations of living—is an impious activity. Engagement in such a pursuit assumes both limitless knowledge and ability on the part of human beings as well as a God who is either flawed, spiteful, or both.

Oakeshott nevertheless acknowledges that the pursuit of perfection is an unavoidable part of human life, an activity that suggests itself to every generation of human beings. Its danger, however, lies not so much in its implications for an individual (who may perhaps be successful in his pursuit) but in its implications for a society as a whole. The pursuit of perfection, whether economic, moral, or cultural, can never be a suitable endeavor for an entire society because this would involve it in undertakings such as building towers to heaven—purposeful, all-consuming projects that mobilize the entirety of a society's resources to realize an end that not all may agree is worth pursuing or even possible. In a massive mobilization of this kind, a society will necessarily sacrifice the variety that makes civil society something worth having. In the context of the Tower of Babel myth, if each person is a tower builder, then he cannot engage in meaningful conversation with his fellows. Such comrades would have nothing substantive to say to each other precisely because they lack any diversity of experience. Thus the Babelian pursuit of perfection—society conceived as an enterprise association—cuts off the sources of the richer "civil association" that Oakeshott prefers. In building the Tower of Babel the humbler enjoyments of the *vita temporalis* are permanently eschewed in favor of a grander—but always postponed—perfect and final satisfaction.

IDEALS, COMMUNITY, AND PURPOSE

But there are other problems that result from viewing the Tower of Babel as an appropriate model for moral life. In Oakeshott's version of this story, the tower also symbolizes the human desire to escape the difficult task of self-understanding by becoming part of a project that is thought to be great and noble. An individual's hopes for the future are thus tied to the success of a grand undertaking with which he has allied himself. And yet by allying himself in this way he has, in a sense, relinquished the difficult task of self-understanding: he is now the recipient of a ready-made purpose in life. In just this way the Babelians have become "priests of an ideal" (196). But it is no great leap to recall what

Oakeshott says about this kind of self-deception. Confidence "in the nobility of a long and difficult enterprise may go far to sustain its pursuit, and it may even make its collapse endurable. Indeed, an illusion of nobility may suffice. But those who invest all their energies and hopes in an undertaking even tinged with depravity are bound to its success and are apt to acquire an obscure self-contempt which qualifies their faith, first in their fellows, and then in themselves" (205). This is the familiar "illusion of affairs" to which Oakeshott returns many times as he considers the human condition. People are constantly inclined to ignore or avoid the episodic nature of human life, believing that the "greatness of an agent's devotion to his aims and . . . his singleness of purpose" suffice to cover up the emptiness of achievement without understanding. But investing all one's energies in the pursuit of any ideal is, according to Oakeshott, one of the most serious mistakes a human being can make. Human beings are not simply the sum of their achievements, and no amount of worldly accomplishment can make up for a lack of self-understanding. Anyone who misses this point misses the most fundamental part of being a human being and, as Augustine and Oakeshott both observe, "understands neither what he seeks nor what he is who seeks it."[3]

Of course, the emptiness that comes with this kind of endeavor is partially hidden by the rhetoric of those who participate in and direct the project. For there is a great sense of comradeship among those who are involved in building the tower. There is much talk of common purpose and of "community." Babel thus acquires a communal identity instead of the distinct individualities that its citizens had formerly possessed. It is quite clear that Oakeshott perceives the loss of individuality as a precipitous decline in the moral character of the Babelians. It is always a corrupting enterprise to force all citizens into a single overarching project, and the consequence of this enterprise is to kill the diversity from which civil conversation springs. The story is a fictional illustration of the emptiness of life oriented only toward achievement.

GREED

There is, however, another feature central to the Babelian moral character: greed. Dissatisfied with their lot, the citizens of Babel long for

---

3. *OHC,* 84.

more and better of what they already have. "Careless of its beauty, contemptuous of its gifts and persuaded of its hostility, they laid waste the world, seeking only to gratify their perverse and insatiable desires" (181). Even prior to the onset of the tower project the Babelians are greedy, and their lives revolve around satisfying their desires. Babel is "full of the bustle of getting and spending" and in it there is an "endless proliferation of wants and satisfactions" (191). The Babelians conceive of God as the stingy proprietor of a vast estate who, when he might give them their hearts' desires, instead chooses to withhold satisfactions.

The Babelians also possess a certain greed for results, and tend to disdain the process that yields those results. They prefer "to arrive rather than to travel, and they would naturally have wished others to undertake [the tower project] and that they would come in at the end to enjoy the fruits" (195). They are an impatient lot, much like spoiled children, who live for what they anticipate will be a "total satisfaction," a "final reward" (199). The Babelians are thus a dramatic illustration of the practical life taken to its furthest extreme. They are a people unable to find repose. They can never escape the practical life since they do not choose to ignore or put off the desires that constantly occur to them. Their hopes of getting and spending are distorted and magnified into the tower that will ultimately destroy them.

To sum up, there is a certain servile moral character expressed in Oakeshott's retelling of the Tower of Babel story, since the Babelians are clearly slaves to their desires. This character may be described as one that is impatient for perfection, one that is fundamentally dissatisfied with the human condition and aims to remedy it once and for all. It focuses on ideals and on overarching projects that eclipse an individual's need to cultivate his own self-understanding. It reassures the individual that he can find meaning by joining a larger, more "important" project. In it the difficult prospect of defining one's character may be avoided by becoming part of a purposive community. And finally, this moral character is defined by its greed: greed for satisfactions of all kinds, greed for results that may be obtained without too much pain or effort, and greed for the things that a miserly God withholds from deserving people. This kind of greed exemplifies the life of getting and spending, the "practical" life run rampant. The Babelians can never escape the tyranny of practice.

But Oakeshott is not merely critical in this essay. There are hints throughout of an alternative moral understanding that stands in stark contrast to the Babelian character. Oakeshott implicitly suggests, here and elsewhere, a different, "religious" or "aesthetic" view of the world that better accords with the human condition. Such a view entails taking the world as it is given and accepting it (and one's place in it) with a graceful humility, not with a constantly discontented sense that it could be better. This view calls us to enjoy the world "like poetic children," delighting in what is before us—not focusing always on perceived deficiencies. Constantly pursuing change and improvement will yield neither rest nor enjoyment.

But in Babel there is no possibility of suspending practical life. There is no enjoyment or delight, there are no provisional satisfactions, and everything is focused on the single goal of reaching heaven through human effort. The pursuit of perfection has overshadowed all those things that have the potential to provide human beings with more genuine happiness. A moral ideal has taken the place of what ought to be a more natural, habitual form of morality. I shall have more to say about this kind of morality below, but this requires, first, consideration of Oakeshott's other Tower of Babel essay.

"The Tower of Babel": 1948

In his 1948 version of "The Tower of Babel," Oakeshott proceeds in a manner quite different from that of the essay I have just examined. Unlike the later short story, this earlier essay is a straightforward philosophical examination of two ways of conceiving of moral life. Here Oakeshott sets out a dichotomy, contrasting morality as a "habit of affection and conduct" with morality as the "reflective application of a moral criterion."[4] This essay takes shape in classic Oakeshottian fashion, as two contrasting ideal types are set against each other and at least partially reconciled at the end of the essay. It is worth commenting that this standard procedure of Oakeshott's—that is, the setting out of ideal types—should not be taken to mean that he believed these types actually exist in pure form in the world. Oakeshott set them out rather as a way of illuminating the tendencies he saw in certain moral and political views, tendencies that

---

4. "The Tower of Babel," in *RP,* 467, 472 (hereafter page numbers from this essay will be cited parenthetically in the text).

may be mixed with other opposing tendencies, but that are strong enough to deserve careful examination on their own. In short, he used ideal types for the philosophical clarity they provide. We often see the inherent tendencies of moral and political types best when they are amplified for effect, and this is precisely what Oakeshott does in this essay.

The first view of morality that Oakeshott examines is one he describes as a "habit of affection and conduct" (467). In this kind of morality, actions are guided by a sensibility, by a way of acting that becomes second nature. Like a language, this kind of morality is learned by being observed and by being used. It may be used well or badly, elegantly or clumsily, and it allows opportunities for both brilliance and embarrassment. It does not require its practitioners to be particularly philosophical, nor that they justify their actions by appeal to principles. It asks only that they be somewhat sensitive to the innumerable contingencies of moral intercourse. It is a tradition, not an ideology—a habit born of use. In this form of moral conduct, actions do not spring from ideals that have been formulated in advance, nor are they thought of as solutions to problems that constantly arise. Action is far simpler than this, being only a way of responding to others that is acquired by observing one's elders. This kind of morality, however, is not (as some might suppose) static and unchanging. Nor is it uncreative. Indeed, as Oakeshott points out, it changes very much in the way a language does: subtly, and almost unnoticeably, but at a constant pace. And there is a "freedom and inventiveness" (472) at the heart of this morality that often goes unnoticed by those who advocate morality of a different sort.

The other kind of morality is what Oakeshott calls the "reflective application of a moral criterion" (472). In this form of the moral life, action springs from an appeal to ideals, to principles, and to rules. It is a form of the moral life "in which a special value is attributed to self-consciousness" (473). As opposed to habitual morality, which takes its bearings as it finds them, here and there, gleaned from numerous experiences, this reflective morality calls for significant intellectual gifts. Indeed, one must be something of a philosopher to engage in it at all. For the difficulties in this kind of morality exist on two levels: first, there is the problem of apprehending true and correct principles to begin with. One must arrive at these through reason, and be able to defend them by means of argument. But there is the additional problem of knowing how to apply these ideals to one's own actions: *how*, in a particular situation, ought we to act so that we carry out any particular ideal? This morality of ideals is a form of the moral life that calls for the person who practices it to know "at each moment exactly what he is doing and why" (475). It is oriented by a vision of perfection, by a conviction that any problems with human nature could be "solved" if only people were successful at putting their ideals into practice.

Both forms of morality—habitual and reflective—come about only through a process of learning, although the kinds of education they presuppose are quite different. In the habitual form of morality, learning how to act is something that begins during the earliest moments of consciousness. This learning is carried on ceaselessly. There is no special time set aside for it, nor does it ever end. It is unsought and unavoidable. The grounds for a reflective morality, on the other hand, must be intentionally pursued, and such morality depends on a philosophical education in ideals. It requires full understanding and assent as well as a corresponding ability to put these ideals into practice. Such education is consciously undertaken and aims at giving the agent an ability to defend himself by means of reasoned argument.

Perhaps the natural inclination is to think that the latter kind of morality (and its corresponding kind of education) is better, on balance. Is it not, after all, important to know and defend the principles that govern our actions? If we act merely out of habit, so this argument goes, are we not likely to be corrupted by others who either have different habits or come armed with persuasive arguments against our ways of living? Oakeshott would expect us to make such arguments, for he contends that this view favoring conscious, reflective morality constitutes the major part of our Western moral inheritance. Indeed, he observes, the remarkable thing about contemporary European morality "is not merely that its form is dominated by the self-conscious pursuit of ideals, but that this form is generally thought to be better and higher than any other" (486).

Oakeshott explains the genealogy of our modern view about the superiority of a morality of ideals by briefly recounting its origins in the Greco-Roman world and its development within the Christian tradition. The traditional Greco-Roman form of morality, he observes, had been primarily one of custom and habit. However, perhaps illustrating "the defect of a form of morality too securely insulated from the criticism of ideals" (483), this morality eventually began to lose its vitality.

Moral reformers such as Epictetus and Dio Chrysostom thus attempted to reform morality by teaching moral ideologies that could be applied to the situations of living. In a similar story, early Christian morality originally consisted in faith in a concrete person and hope in the world to come. It was, Oakeshott remarks, primarily a habitual morality that came about naturally in response to the events of Christ's life and death. But as the concrete experience of Christ receded further into the past, believers began more and more to depend on creeds and abstract propositions as expressions of their faith. Those who had not had the experience of Christ came to rely on a shorthand, on the "easily translatable prose of a moral ideal" (485), as a way of trying to recapture what was originally a lived experience. This accounts for the creation of a "Christian moral ideology," which has, in Oakeshott's view, eclipsed the "poetic character of human conduct" (485). In both cases—the Greco-Roman and the Christian—an original experience of a more natural form of morality hardened into an ideology and became the abstract pursuit of ideals. What remains in the present day of this tendency toward moral ideology is no longer explicitly Christian, but it *is* explicitly ideological. It is the inheritance of contemporary Western culture, and it accounts for our strong preference for a morality that is grounded in ideals. Such, at least, is Oakeshott's sketch of its development.

But this explanation, though helpful in understanding the modern drift toward ideals, is not provided as a justification for our current situation. For Oakeshott is quite critical of the type of morality that orients itself by ideals, looks constantly to the future, and is mediated through rules. He is inclined toward morality that is natural and habitual, not self-consciously reflective. Of course, Oakeshott does not dispute the fact that any existing morality will have elements of both habit and reflection—"[n]either, taken alone, recommends itself convincingly as a likely form of the moral life" (477). Nevertheless, on balance we ought to favor the naturalness, spontaneity, and "poetic character" of a habitual morality. A morality of ideals is unavoidably "prone to obsession and at war with itself" (486). Oakeshott develops this argument in several other works, as I discuss below.

Several conclusions may be drawn from the preceding consideration of the two Tower of Babel essays. It is clear that Oakeshott favors a particular conception of morality, one he sees as a reflection of the true springs of human conduct. This morality is one in which habit and affection take the lead and in which justification by principles is relegated to a distinctly secondary role. It is a kind of morality that Oakeshott calls "poetic," as opposed to "prosaic." It is not excessively intellectual; indeed, it does not depend on intellect at all in meeting most of the exigencies of life. It eschews grand projects in favor of cultivating personal self-understanding. And it is disposed toward present enjoyment rather than the constant quest to achieve. This is what I have called liberal, as opposed to servile, morality.

Yet in neither of these essays does Oakeshott provide much detail about precisely *why* he views the morality of habit and affection as better and more natural than the morality of ideals. While he does a masterful job in setting out the shortcomings of a morality of ideals, a reader cannot be blamed for asking what, exactly, he might offer as an alternative. To answer this question properly we must turn to another source that helps to explain Oakeshott's view of morality as a whole: *On Human Conduct*. In the paragraphs to follow I consider this work in concert with his Tower of Babel essays, as together providing a coherent view that stands opposite the morality of ideals. First, however, I consider the most common form of reflective morality, the form that Oakeshott most wished to dispute: morality as a subscription to rules.

Rule-Based Morality

The most widespread form of a morality of ideals consists in the use of rules as a purported guide to conduct. Rules act as the mediators of ideals, and a moral rule is "a cushion . . . between the behaviour it demands on each occasion and the complete moral response to the situation."[5] The ideal, of course, represents the complete moral response, but a rule makes it possible for an agent to approximate that ideal as much as possible. This idea that "morality consists in following the rules" is a view against which Oakeshott argued forcefully throughout his career.

The classic view goes as follows. There are, it is said, rules of conduct that, if followed, yield goodness. These rules are postulated in advance of conduct. Thus, before I act I should reflect on whether or not my action will stand as a satisfactory subscription to the rule that governs it. Only

5. "The Tower of Babel," in *RP*, 475.

then, having appropriately applied the rule, can I know that I am doing the right thing. Three distinct steps are required in this kind of morality: first, to construct and approve the rulebook; second, to be able to defend one's rules by reason; and third, to translate rules into behavior.[6] Oakeshott comments that in this kind of morality the situations of life appear as problems to be solved, and thus such conduct requires significant intellectual gifts as well as the patience (or stubbornness) to refer each action to its principle. It goes without saying that such an approach is both highly intellectual and lacking in spontaneity. For this is a view in which human life appears as an endless series of trials and crises. Life must be lived with guidebook in hand.

The desire for such rule-oriented morality springs from uneasiness about the contingency of things in the world and from uncertainty about the future. Rules, it is said, promise a certain kind of stability. They tell us that we may become good if we act as we are told. For, as Oakeshott observes, human beings "are apt to be disconcerted unless they feel themselves to be upheld by something more substantial than the emanations of their own contingent yearnings." And a morality that consists in following rules promises this more substantial security. But this is a gnostic view, for it is founded on a desire not to be reconciled to the human condition (which is by nature uncertain and contingent), but to overcome it. The basic desire here is to build on an unshakable rational foundation. A code of moral rules is a way of keeping uncertainty at bay, since the personal responsibility of deciding how to conduct oneself is subsumed under "subscription" to such rules. Oakeshott remarks on this tendency, observing that for people who are inclined this way mistake-proof certainty is only offered by "propositional knowledge," that is, rational rules postulated in advance—not by the kind of knowledge that arises from activity.[7]

Oakeshott refutes this view by pointing out its shortcomings, as I explain below. But he does more than merely illustrate that this view is incorrect, because (as I have hinted) he also wanted to show that there is a better, alternative way of understanding human conduct. To appreciate Oakeshott's alternative to the rule-bound morality that I have called "servile," we must consider his conception of "practices" (which are not the

6. Ibid., 473.
7. *OHC,* 80; "Rational Conduct," in *RP,* 113.

same as his earlier use of the word *practice* to designate a particular mode of experience). First, though, it is worthwhile to recount some of the criticisms he makes of morality conceived as a subscription to rules.

Most importantly, Oakeshott finds rule-based morality to be radically disjointed and overly intellectual, promoting reflection at the cost of spontaneous, natural activity. In such morality a "calculated observance of specified rules has taken the place of the singleness and spontaneity of morally educated conduct." For although propositional knowledge may yield certainty about how to *think* about moral ideals, it often results in a profound *un*certainty about how to act. And thus moral reflection may inhibit moral sensibility. It may even become "more important to have an intellectually defensible moral ideology than a ready habit of moral behaviour."[8]

But there is also, in rule-based morality, a false sense that rules exist wholly prior to activity, as if conduct (like a game of Monopoly) were an activity governed by a set of printed instructions. In fact, figuring out how to act comes about only through engaging in moral activity, by testing the waters and figuring out which actions are acceptable and which are not. Moral rules, such as they are, can arise only out of moral activity. Thus even if rules may be supposed to exist at present, they had at least to originate in *someone's* experience of moral conduct, so they cannot be said to be the absolutely rational, *a priori* foundations of activity.

There is also the obvious point—but one that bears mentioning—that "subscription to rules" is only the most exiguous description of moral activity. To say that someone has obeyed a rule tells us nothing about *why* he has obeyed that rule: Was it to avoid punishment? Did he want to impress someone else by acting as he did? Did he do it to obtain a reward from some third party? Only in the most superficial understanding of moral conduct can the bare subscription to rules be an adequate understanding of the moral life. The question of motives, of an agent's sentiment in performing an action, lies at the center of morality (rule-based or not), and it is only by taking account of motives that we can judge the essential goodness of an act.

The thorniest problem, however, that Oakeshott identifies in rule-based morality is the question of *how* exactly we might say that rules govern our actions. For moral rules are not like laws in the natural world,

8. *OHC,* 70; "The Tower of Babel," in *RP,* 478.

which exert irresistible force and compel obedience. In the moral realm we must first decide *which* rules we will subscribe to, and only then *how* we will make our subscription. For a rule specifies nothing in terms of the concrete action of a human being who acts in accordance with that rule. There is thus an unmistakable (and unavoidable) element of creativity inherent even in the activity of "subscribing to rules" that defies the Rationalist desire for certain knowledge of how to act.[9]

Oakeshott's argument on this question of "subscription" to rules is as follows. Rules are not the same as commands, which are addressed to designated persons and require specific action. A rule is more general than a command and is to be "used" in deliberation rather than blindly obeyed. Rules, according to Oakeshott, are adverbial considerations to be subscribed to in deciding how to act. In other words, they specify not *what* an agent should do, but the *manner in which* the agent should act— lawfully, politely, bravely, and so on. In truth, even such relatively undisputed rules such as "murder and arson are wrong" do not forbid all killing or all lighting of fires. Rather, they forbid killing that originates in hate or greed (for example) and starting fires with the intent to destroy.[10] An agent may choose to satisfy these adverbial conditions in multiple ways: he may avoid all killing in order to be certain that he has subscribed to the rule that proscribes murder. Alternatively, he may kill in a war or in self-defense, cases where it is clear that killing is (reluctantly) sanctioned. What nonetheless remains to him is the *choice* of what to do, and of how to satisfy the conditions that are enjoined in the moral rule to which he subscribes. Thus, as Oakeshott argues, the "appearance procedures and rules may have of excluding (forbidding), or more rarely of enjoining, substantive choices and actions is illusive." Rules, Oakeshott asserts, "cannot themselves designate choices."[11]

Thus the widespread view that moral conduct may be determined by a code of rules is, according to Oakeshott, a misunderstanding. As he observes in *Experience and Its Modes,* "so soon as moral action is reduced to mere reasoning, the calculation of chances, it has surrendered the very characteristic which most distinguishes it. Law is the enemy of the moral life." Moral rules may suggest courses of action, but a suggestion is not a

9. Terry Nardin, *The Philosophy of Michael Oakeshott,* 199–200.
10. See Oakeshott's footnote in *OHC,* 58.
11. *OHC,* 68.

command. Moral rules are to be taken account of in deliberation and subscribed to (or ignored) by people who have choices to make in conduct. Oakeshott remarks that such rules are "indeterminate, multiple, liable to conflict, and of unequal importance: none is categorical or is capable of 'specific performance.'" Moreover, the attempt to elicit actions from these conditional prescriptions is a "contorted endeavour."[12] Thus morality understood as "following the rules" can stand only as a grossly inadequate description of what actually goes on in conduct. This argument, however, should not be taken to imply that Oakeshott disregards rules altogether or that he thinks they have no part to play in morality. Quite the opposite is true. However, Oakeshott understands rules as considerations that inhere in what he calls "practices," and before proceeding further it will be worthwhile to consider exactly how he defines the concept of a practice.

Practices

As I have noted above, the word *practice* in *On Human Conduct* does not mean what it did in Oakeshott's early *Experience and Its Modes* or even in "The Voice of Poetry in the Conversation of Mankind." In these earlier works, practice is a distinguishable mode that presupposes a series of satisfactions to be pursued endlessly. It is the realm of work and wants, in which there is no escape from the deadliness of doing. But the idea of a practice as elaborated in *On Human Conduct* is quite a different concept, somewhat akin to the notion of a "tradition." Oakeshott describes it as a "relationship between agents articulated in terms of specific conditional prescriptions." Terry Nardin explains the concept of a practice somewhat less cryptically when he describes it as "a pattern of conduct emerging from the actions and responses of intelligent agents—doings condensed into ways of doing, into habit, custom, skill, prudence, and procedure."[13] Numerous examples of practices may be cited, from the less inclusive (the practice of acting politely) to the more inclusive (the practice of "morality" as a whole). One of Oakeshott's favorite examples is the practice of teaching and learning that takes place at a university. For the

12. *EM,* 301; *OHC,* 69, 64.
13. *OHC,* 56; Nardin, *Philosophy of Michael Oakeshott,* 76.

purposes of illustration, I shall consider the idea of "piano recitals" as a way of illustrating Oakeshott's idea of a practice.

In recitals as a practice, there is a set of relationships between the actors involved, such that each person has a name (performer, audience member, usher, etc.) and a generally understood role to play. The practice sets the boundaries of these relationships, and the relationships are defined "by the names of the *personae* concerned." For here persons are no longer mother, father, doctor, and electrician, but agents engaging in an activity that comes with "manners, uses, observances, customs, [and] standards" of its own. While they are at a recital, the actions of participants are governed (though not determined) by the general considerations that govern this practice: to clap when the performer appears on the stage, to remain quiet during the music, to refrain from clapping between movements, and so on. The practice provides a framework for "shared meanings" and is a system of durable relationships between agents.[14] However, it has arisen not out of someone's intentional desire to "create a practice," but rather from the natural and spontaneous purposive activities of human beings as they go about their daily activities. In this case, a practice has arisen as a result of the common desire to hear a musician's performance. In general, practices are the result of innumerable single actions taken by human beings, and they may be more or less complex.

I have chosen "piano recitals" as an example that is relatively bounded and has conventions that may be easily formulated. Now we must return to the question of "rules" and consider the place Oakeshott designates for rules within practices. We have already observed that Oakeshott distinguishes sharply between the ideas of rules and commands. Rules, once again, are general prescriptions that do not determine an agent's action although they aid in deliberation. Commands, on the other hand, are obligatory and require a specific performance on the part of the recipient. So far, however, we have not yet noted a key aspect of Oakeshott's discussion of rules—namely, that they arise only *within* practices. Rules of moral conduct, for instance, emerge among people who are accustomed to making moral decisions and taking moral action. The "rules" of piano recitals, likewise, came about when people began to play piano recitals. There was certainly no committee that—prior to the very first recital—decided that a performer must bow as he walks on and off the

14. *OHC*, 57, 55; Nardin, *Philosophy of Michael Oakeshott*, 76.

stage. Such conventions, or "rules," come about only in the lived experience of a given practice. They are "abridgments" that concentrate "into specific precepts considerations of adverbial desirability which lie dispersed in a moral language and thus transform invitations into prescriptions, allegiances to fellow practitioners into precise obligations."[15]

Rules do not provide a skeleton for a given practice, as the framing supports the structure of a house. On the contrary, they emerge as people "muddle through" and act in ways that come, only later, to be called practices. They are abstractions "which derive their authority from the practice itself as a spoken language in which they appear as passages of somewhat exaggerated emphasis." Rules are "passages of stringency" in a moral practice, but it is a perversion of a practice to reduce it merely to the "rules, the duties, or the 'ideals' it obtrudes." We may, for example, enumerate a list of rules for attending or performing in piano recitals, but this in no way captures anything approximating the total experience. This is the crux of Oakeshott's objection to a rule-based morality. It is a dramatic reduction of the tangle and variety of experience in favor of a (supposed) clear set of instructive principles. But rules do not "enjoin, prohibit, or warrant substantive actions or utterances; they cannot tell agents what to do or say," observes Oakeshott. Rather, they "prescribe norms of conduct; that is, abstract considerations proper to be subscribed to in choosing performances but which cannot themselves be either 'obeyed' or performed."[16]

Taking again our example of piano recitals as a practice, it should now be clearer how Oakeshott understood rules. There are, of course, general rules that should usually be observed during recitals, on the part of both the performer and the audience. One of these cardinal rules is that audience members should not clap between movements of a piece. Most of the time this rule ought to be followed, since applause between movements not only interrupts the continuity of a piece, but also shows a lack of knowledge of basic recital conventions and is simply contrary to an established and accepted tradition. Nevertheless, there may be times when it is appropriate. For example, if a performer plays particularly brilliantly, even an educated audience may be pardoned for bursting into spontaneous applause at the conclusion of a movement.

15. *OHC,* 66.
16. Ibid., 68, 126.

Similarly, another rule prescribes that a performer should acknowledge his audience by bowing as he enters and exits the stage. Yet there are conditions in which other forms of acknowledgment may suffice (a nod, a curtsy) or even no acknowledgment at all, as may be the case in some avant-garde performances. It seems, then, that even rules that are profitably observed most of the time may be disregarded under the proper circumstances. This does not mean that all rules should be thrown out, or that one ought to "reinvent" the rules or start anew. Nor does it mean that one ought not follow rules *most* of the time. Oakeshott himself, of course, came down strongly on the side of traditional modes of conduct. But it does illuminate the character of rules as Oakeshott understood them: they are adverbial considerations to be considered in conduct, but *not* binding commands or laws that tell us specifically what to do. It is "only in fantasy that a practice appears as a composition of rules claiming obedience which to learn is to acquire a familiarity with injunctive propositions and to understand is to know one's way about a rule-book." Rules are abridgments, Oakeshott repeatedly emphasizes, and as such they specify conclusions or considerations that govern a practice. They do not, however, absolve us from the task of choosing particular actions within that practice. They can neither "direct nor 'justify' the adventure of doing."[17]

Oakeshott was thus strongly opposed to the idea that complete morality consists in following rules. At the same time, however, he did not throw out rules altogether, since he believed that rules that arise within practices are a vital part of conduct, as I have just observed. Nevertheless, when the relationships of a moral practice come to be articulated in rules, "they lose some of their characteristic expansiveness," Oakeshott observes, and "the 'play' between agents is diminished." This use of the word *play* is important because it points to a realm of conduct in which Oakeshott had an abiding interest. The category of "play" encompasses all those things Oakeshott valued most highly: teaching and learning, poetry, love and friendship. This preference for the "playful," aesthetic, and creative may be identified as the distinguishing factor in Oakeshott's view of the moral life. Morality, in Oakeshott's view, is undeniably creative, and it concerns not only right and wrong, good and bad, but other considerations as well: beautiful and ugly, authentic and inauthentic, ex-

17. Ibid., 91.

pert and inexperienced, creative and plodding. Morality is not an endeavor in which agents grudgingly (or dutifully) obey hard and fast rules that have been set out for them. It is an activity in which agents decide which rules to accept and *how* (that is, adverbially) to accept or reject them. There is an indefinable element of artistry involved in moral conduct. Thus, what must be learned is not a rule of life, but rather how to navigate within the multitude of practices in which a human being necessarily finds himself. We learn not what to do or say, but the "arts of agency."[18]

Oakeshott's Alternative: A "Creative" Morality

As I have suggested in the paragraphs above, one of Oakeshott's objectives in *On Human Conduct* and the Tower of Babel essays is to argue against several related conceptions of morality that he finds deeply flawed. The most prominent of these are the morality of ideals that looks constantly forward to a state of future perfection, as well as a modification of this, namely, the idea that morality consists in following a set of rules. Oakeshott's task, however, is not wholly negative—that is, he is not *merely* concerned to tear down faulty understandings, though this is no small part of his aim. He also describes an alternative to these misunderstandings of morality, and he does so primarily by using two distinct but related metaphors to convey his meaning: language and artistic expression.

Throughout *On Human Conduct* Oakeshott returns to the idea of morality as a language. Moral conduct, he maintains, is like a language "in being an instrument of understanding and a medium of intercourse, in having a vocabulary and a syntax of its own, and in being spoken well or ill." To speak any language is to engage in a practice that must be learned, and the language of morality is no different. Moral conduct understood in this way consists in "agents continuously and colloquially related to one another in the idiom of a familiar language of moral converse."[19] Like anything that is learned, this "language" of moral converse may be learned well or badly, more or less proficiently. Within it there are places

---

18. Ibid., 67; see Nardin, *Philosophy of Michael Oakeshott,* 78, and Oakeshott, *OHC,* 59.
19. *OHC,* 62, 64.

for both the virtuoso and the boor, and there is room for the poetic utterances of a master stylist as well as the prosaic statements of ordinary
people.

What is common to all who speak this language, however, is the element of creativity inherent in speaking it at all. In any language what is
important is not merely a mastery of grammar, but having something to
say. To say something substantive requires moving past passive learning. It
requires striking out with the intent to satisfy a want or to express some
aspect of one's character. And there is an infinite number of ways to do
these things. Unlike the chess player, who is faced with a fixed number
of possible alternatives, the moral agent chooses from proposed actions
that are "his own inventions." And the number and variety of these proposed actions is limited "only by the virtuosity of his imagination."
Oakeshott observes that the "conduct of some is no better than an adventure in verbiage; clutching at imperfectly recollected and vaguely understood expressions, their conversation is thick with pretention and
littered with moral malapropisms." Others, he notices, seize the opportunities for fraud inherent in moral conduct, while still others speak the
language with care for "its intimations of balance, sobriety and exact-
ness."[20] Women and men, old and young speak this language differently.
Everyone, however, must learn to speak it with some degree of profi-
ciency. And all are, to varying degrees, creative.

Yet, like ordinary language, which may be used for multiple purposes—to write a poem or to write a legal contract—the language of
moral converse may be understood either poetically or prosaically. It is
prosaic when it is put into the service of satisfying desires and therefore
becomes the common currency of those who must cooperate with one
another in all the transactions of ordinary life. And it is not just ordinary
practical life that tends toward prose rather than poetry. Moral *ideals* are
also prosaic, in Oakeshott's view, because they require "translation" of an
abstract idea into a practical reality and deny the spontaneity and creativity that is natural to poetry. As the Tower of Babel story reminds us, a
morality of ideals always gropes to find its proper expression in conduct
and tends to become either paralyzed or overly intellectual. For Oakeshott, the act of translating an ideal into an action is the very opposite of
poetry, which is in essence naturally spontaneous and immersed in

20. Ibid., 43, 66.

"present-living." The radical defect of this prosaic morality of ideals is that it denies "the poetic character of all human activity" and instead turns to "the easily translatable prose of a moral ideal."[21]

But when the language of moral converse is understood as a kind of poetry, the possibilities for human conduct widen dramatically. Although many of us speak only prose, or brush up against the poetic only rarely, we sometimes manage to achieve perfection in conduct in the way a poet composes a poem. By perfection in conduct I do not mean to imply that anyone could achieve enduring perfection and act "perfectly" throughout a lifetime. Instead, I mean the fleeting perfection that is inherent in certain natural, appropriate, spontaneous actions. It implies "knowing what to do or say" in a situation. Like a poet who imagines poetically and thus creates a poem, an agent may "imagine morally" and thus act effortlessly and well in a given situation. As Oakeshott observes of the poet in his 1948 Tower of Babel essay, nothing exists "in advance of the poem itself, except perhaps the poetic passion. And what is true of poetry is true also, I think, of all human moral activity."[22] Thus poetry stands as a model of the possibilities inherent in the language of moral converse—possibilities that are always present but rarely realized.

Certain activities lend themselves to this kind of understanding more easily than others. As Oakeshott notes in "The Voice of Poetry in the Conversation of Mankind," love and friendship are moral relationships in which we strive to satisfy desires—both our own and those of others. And yet they can suggest the kind of contemplation that is inherent in poetry and "constitute a connection between the voices of poetry and practice."[23] Our moral language, when conceived poetically, offers opportunities for categorically different kinds of satisfactions than those promised by the narrowly bounded "practical" realm.

So far I have discussed Oakeshott's use of the metaphor of "language" as a way of describing what takes place in moral conduct, that is, of acting within practices. Yet even more striking than this is his discussion of morality as akin to artistic expression. Throughout *On Human Conduct* Oakeshott repeatedly likens moral conduct to various kinds of art. Here, indeed, is strong evidence for the thesis that Oakeshott's aesthetic

21. "The Tower of Babel," in *RP,* 479, 485.
22. Ibid., 479.
23. "The Voice of Poetry in the Conversation of Mankind," in *RP,* 538.

sensibility lies just behind his characterization of moral conduct—indeed, that poetry (encompassing far more than written verse) stands as a model for what moral conduct can sometimes approximate.

In various places Oakeshott remarks that practices are like "instruments" that may be played more or less skillfully. Within them there is endless opportunity for individual "style," and agents must learn not to demonstrate, but to "illustrate" their understandings of action in practices. An agent is a "dramatic identity" and as such he engages in a "continually extemporized dance" with other agents as they take part in a moral practice.[24] In sum, an agent is a "performer" who may execute his performances with greater or less skill, just as do artists, musicians, and poets. It is worth noting these passages as a way of showing the importance of the aesthetic element in Oakeshott's moral theorizing.

Morality, Oakeshott explains near the middle of his first essay in *On Human Conduct,* is "like an art in having to be learned, in being learned better by some than by others, in allowing almost endless opportunity for individual style, and in which virtuosity and mastery are distinguishable."[25] It is, of course, true that morality is *unlike* an art insofar as it is not elective. That is, while some of us may choose to study poetry or music, no one can avoid "studying" and engaging in morality. Nevertheless, like an art, moral conduct offers opportunities for brilliance as well as for dullness and mediocrity.

In similar passages Oakeshott observes that a moral language (a practice) is an "instrument which may be played upon with varying degrees of sensibility. . . . there is room for the individual idiom, it affords opportunity to inventiveness. . . . it has rhythms which remain when the words are forgotten." To "play" this instrument well, one must have "the understanding of a performer." One must view the adventures of human conduct as "illustrations" of practices, not as "examples" of unchanging, lawlike processes.[26]

Perhaps the most essential part of this view of morality on the model of aesthetic experience is Oakeshott's focus on the somewhat indefinable concept that he designates variously as "style," "judgment," "connoisseurship," and "sensibility." All these terms point to a kind of knowledge—

24. *OHC,* 84, 63.
25. Ibid., 62.
26. Ibid., 65, 91, 90, 92.

akin to Aristotle's idea of a *hexis*—that cannot be formulated but is essential to all virtuosity, whether it be in art, music, poetry, or moral conduct. Most importantly, all these terms point to the characteristic that Oakeshott finds most vividly illustrated in poetic experience, namely, creativity. Creativity is no less important in moral conduct than it is in artistic expression. But it is precisely what is forgotten when morality is conceived of either as "following the rules" or as the never-ending attempt to approximate ideals. Creativity, spontaneity, judgment, having a feel for something—all these things are ways of bridging the gap between a "rule" and a particular action, in those "wide open spaces . . . where no rule runs." It is worth quoting Oakeshott at length on this point.

> [I]n every "ability" there is an ingredient of knowledge which cannot be resolved into information, and in some skills this may be the greater part of the knowledge required for their practice. . . . And each individual example [of an activity] has what may be called a style or idiom of its own which cannot be specified in propositions. Not to detect a man's style is to have missed three-quarters of the meaning of his actions and utterances; and not to have acquired a style is to have shut oneself off from the ability to convey any but the crudest meanings. . . . [Rules] set limits—often telling us only what *not* to do if we wish to speak any of the languages of our civilization; but they provide no prescription for all that must go on in the interval between these limits.

It is in this interval between limits that a performer demonstrates his artistry and a moral actor shows his true character. Although the practice of piano recitals specifies certain guidelines as profitable to be observed, the essence of this activity lies in a performer's style—in his interpretive judgment, his ability to convey a certain reading of his music, and his relationship to the audience. Technique, of course, is a prerequisite, but it is less than half the whole. What is required for success as an artist or as a human being is the cultivation of a sensibility—of a sensitiveness to the innumerable contingencies of moral interaction and the corresponding development of judgment to deal with these contingencies. To acquire a mastery of any art, or indeed of moral conduct, is "to acquire an appropriate connoisseurship."[27]

27. "Learning and Teaching," in *VLL,* 54, 56; "Rationalism in Politics," in *RP,* 29.

Conclusion

To sum up, Oakeshott developed an understanding of moral activity that directly contradicts the views of morality he criticized in the two Tower of Babel essays. Unlike the views of morality that consist in "rule-following" or "the pursuit of ideals," Oakeshott's preferred moral understanding depends upon activity within established practices. The moral agent must learn these practices and come to understand that they are governed by rules that must be taken account of in conduct. Nevertheless, conduct is not *determined* by such rules. Instead, it contains an indefinable element of aesthetic creativity. As Robert Sokolowski describes this approach to morality, "[T]he core of the being of the moral act is not something that comes before or something that comes after, but the performance itself. The befores and the afters, the anticipations and the consequences, are derivative upon the activity itself."[28] Like a performer, an artist, and a poet, the moral agent must therefore develop a "sensibility" about how to act, and in this there is great freedom in deciding what to do. Oakeshott offers his readers an alternative to the morality of the Rationalist and the ideologue. It is what I have called "liberal" and "aesthetic."

To return to the story with which this chapter began, the myth of the Tower of Babel represents the very antithesis of this kind of "creative" morality. At the beginning of his 1979 essay, Oakeshott remarks that the project of finding a shortcut to heaven "is as old as the human race." And conduct that orients itself by ideology or rules is precisely an attempt at this kind of shortcut. It is a misunderstanding of the true origins of moral activity, but a misunderstanding that claims to be better and higher than its alternative. Like the project of building a tower to heaven, people mistakenly believe that they may avoid the difficulties of life by engaging in a project in which the ends have been determined for them, and in which they need not cultivate personal resources for responding to circumstances. A morality of ideals *is* a Tower of Babel. It explicitly pursues a future state of perfection, all the while neglecting the joys and sorrows of the *vita temporalis*. It ignores the present and strives for an imagined, ideal future. It substitutes the "illusion of affairs" for self-understanding. "There is, indeed, no ideal the pursuit of which will not

28. Robert Sokolowski, *Moral Action: A Phenomenological Study*, 59.

lead to disillusion," Oakeshott asserts. "*[C]hagrin* waits at the end for all who take this path."[29]

In my discussion of this alternative "liberal" or "aesthetic" morality, I have remained close to the primary texts in which Oakeshott discusses its character. Moreover, this particular argument I have made about the relationship between aesthetics and morality is largely my own, so I can place it into no preexisting literature on the subject.[30] Nevertheless, Oakeshott's views on this kind of moral conduct can still be placed into a certain "conversation," as Victor Kestenbaum has done in his recent book *The Grace and the Severity of the Ideal*. Kestenbaum observes that Oakeshott's theory of moral conduct is much like those put forth by Polanyi and Husserl, characterizing this tradition as one that holds that the "coherence of our conduct does not necessarily derive from an explicitly held rule, principle or idea." Such a view stands in sharp contrast to a view held by Wittgensteinians like Peter Winch, who believe that moral action *always* implies a criterion (a rule) even if that criterion is not consciously applied. In moral activity, Winch observes, a person always applies "a criterion in what he does even though he does not, and perhaps cannot, formulate that criterion."[31]

Some readers may object, with Winch, to Oakeshott's characterization of morality as fundamentally creative and aesthetically inspired.[32] After all, are there not situations in which we are brought up short by a rule that restrains us from performing a certain action? I think Oakeshott would surely recognize such situations, but he would most likely qualify the idea that "morality is rule-following" by reminding us that the rules

29. "The Tower of Babel," in *RP,* 465, 475.

30. Glenn Worthington notes the connection between aesthetics and morality in his recent article "The Voice of Poetry in Oakeshott's Moral Philosophy," but his solution to the problem of how aesthetics and morality may be connected is, in my view, insufficient. First, he says that poetic imagination "encompasses all aspects of Oakeshott's characterization of human conduct," which I think is an overstatement of the case. Human conduct is sometimes nonpoetic and utilitarian, and Oakeshott recognized this. Moreover, Worthington sees Oakeshott's writings on aesthetics as both "equivocal" and "contradictory," a view I disputed in Chapter 5.

31. Victor Kestenbaum, *The Grace and the Severity of the Ideal,* chap. 5, 105, 106; Peter Winch, "The Nature of Meaningful Behavior," 58.

32. Maurice Cowling objects on slightly different grounds, observing that "morality often is constricting and has frequently to be compulsory, just as law has to be. Morality is objective; it is naïve to expect it not to be, and idle to suppose that there can be a form of morality, or of law, from which compulsion and arbitrariness has been removed" (*Religion and Public Doctrine in Modern England,* 280).

we choose to follow arise out of the activity in which we are engaged. Again, his argument about "practices" is instructive here. For like the "rules" of piano recitals, which came about as recitals were performed, the "rules" of morality arise from engagement in moral conduct. They do not, in his view, exist *prior* to the activity itself and are not something to which we may refer as we would a guidebook. There is an undeniable element of intelligence and creativity *even* in deciding which rules we shall follow.

Oakeshott's primary aim in all the places he considers morality is to provide a corrective to a certain modern moral tendency that looks for "cribs" and "shortcuts" in all kinds of activity. In our impatience for results (political, religious, or otherwise) we tend, like the Babelians and the Rationalists, to look for ideals and ideologies that will provide us with ready-made structure and purpose. Oakeshott recalls us to the opposite view, to a view that holds that each of us—like the poet or artist—must make or find meaning in our own lives. This moral view finds its best illustration in his description of the "religious man" in the 1929 essay "Religion and the World." Such a person measures his life's worth by its "sensibility" and sees all things "in the light of his own mind," desiring to possess "nothing save by present insight."[33]

The conception of morality that promotes such a view of life is what I have called "liberal." Liberal morality rejects "worldliness" and the pursuit of perfection in favor of living fully in the present. It rejects the view that life is wholly practical, preferring (when possible) those things that may be engaged in "playfully" and as ends in themselves. In liberal or "aesthetic" morality what is aimed at is learning to speak the language of moral conduct fully—to engage in it without hesitation, requiring no feats of "translation," but to act spontaneously, immediately, naturally, and well. This is the moral persona that Oakeshott admired, and for whom his idea of "politics as civil association" was designed, as I discuss in the next two chapters.

---

33. "Religion and the World," in *RPML*, 38.

7

Rationalism and the Politics of Faith

The previous chapter argued that Oakeshott's aesthetic approach to morality stands starkly at odds with the kind of morality I have designated as "servile." Oakeshott calls it Rationalist, gnostic, and Pelagian, to name a few of his more notable characterizations. In the present chapter, I discuss these characterizations and argue that his thoughts on a certain kind of moral character—one that is informed by his considerations of religion and aesthetics—stand as a foundation for his view of politics. First, however, it is worthwhile to consider once again the origins of Oakeshott's thought on these matters. For he did not begin his career as a philosopher of politics, but was concerned with broader questions about religion, ethics, and the human condition in general.

Oakeshott was exceedingly straightforward in expressing the questions with which he began his philosophical quest: "I desired to know what I ought to think about our life as human beings in society." As a young man he observed that genuine political philosophy must originate "not with institutions but with men." Oakeshott thus began his career by exploring questions of what it means to be a human being and how we might find our greatest happiness in this world. He believed that it was "as gross a fallacy to suppose that the whole of man's life as a social being can be summed up in terms of government as to suppose that the source of a poet's inspiration may be found in his *Belesenheit*."[1] His aim in examining religion and poetry was to come to terms with what he saw as the most vital parts of human experience, and to discover at what points these activities could temporarily remove human beings from the more mundane experience of pursuing desire after desire—the much-discussed "practical" mode of experience.

---

1. "The Cambridge School of Political Science," in *WIH*, 47, 52, 53.

Oakeshott understood politics, therefore, as an activity that must not lead but follow. It is a simple, if obvious, point: he did not think he should turn to theorizing politics until he had thought long and hard about the character of human beings, the kinds of satisfactions available to them, and the things that make them most fully "human." For to begin from the other side, that is, to ask, what part should government play in human life? either presupposes a view of human beings or simply assumes that they might be molded into whatever form their government chooses for them. The latter view is one of the principal errors Oakeshott saw in collectivist and tyrannical governments. He attempted to propound a markedly different view in his essays on religion and aesthetics and also, I want to argue, in his political theorizing.

The substance of this view is that human beings possess a significant degree of freedom, which manifests itself in the choices each person makes. This freedom is not merely something that stands in the service of some greater good—economic prosperity or "progress"—but is something to be valued on its own terms. Freedom is a good because it fosters the development of human beings *qua* human beings. Oakeshott's "aesthetic" view of morality is the ultimate expression of this freedom, for here human beings are encouraged to be endlessly creative, to pursue things that are satisfying as ends in themselves, and to consider skeptically the world's demands for ceaseless productivity. The appropriate political arrangements, for Oakeshott, are accordingly those that appreciate and celebrate the value of this kind of life for human beings. This is what Oakeshott describes as the "politics of skepticism" and "civil association."

Unfortunately, examples of *inappropriate* political arrangements are far more common in the modern world. Oakeshott therefore spends much effort in setting out damning critiques of certain modern approaches to politics and tracing their development through the last five centuries of European history. The focus of these critiques is a moral vision at odds with Oakeshott's own. If his favored view of morality is aesthetic, then the morality of Rationalism, of collectivism, and of the "politics of faith" is emphatically *not* aesthetic. It is the morality of those who would build a Tower of Babel, who look for ready-made codes of conduct, and who resent what they see as the burdens of individuality. This morality is perfectionist in character—Pelagian, as Oakeshott repeatedly puts it—and gnostic. It expresses a fundamental dissatisfaction with the world and an inability to live in the present.

Oakeshott sides with Augustine in arguing against the moral perfectionism and utopian politics of modern-day Pelagians. Indeed, not un-like Augustine's, Oakeshott's view of what government can and should achieve is remarkably limited and even pessimistic, despite the fact that he is simultaneously optimistic about the vast possibilities open to indi-viduals. The most important achievements result from people's making choices for themselves, not from a government that imposes a dominant order on the society as a whole. The question, what should government do? can only be answered by posing the companion question, what are the characters of the subjects the government is supposed to govern? This second question is of immense importance for answering the first, and as I have argued throughout this book, its answer lies in Oakeshott's conception of morality, which is in turn informed by his ideas about re-ligion and aesthetic experience.

I am proposing, in short, that Oakeshott's reflections on politics are founded on aesthetic and religious concerns that were present through-out the entirety of his career. His expression of religion is not ortho-dox—indeed, we may question whether the mature Oakeshott was a Christian—but in many important ways his views echo Christian, and particularly Augustinian, ideas about the imperfectibility of man, about human limitations, and about the vanity and pride inherent in searching for mundane perfection. His views on aesthetics are similarly unortho-dox though not altogether original, since they appear to be part of a tra-dition that includes such thinkers as Walter Pater and Edward Bullough. Nevertheless, as I argued in the previous chapter, a conception of moral-ity informed by aesthetics—that is, by the ideal of experience that is fully present and enjoyed for its own sake—appears to be at the core of Oake-shott's thought about the human condition.

There is strong evidence for this argument about religion and aesthet-ics in what has become Oakeshott's most famous work, his collection of essays entitled *Rationalism in Politics*. Indeed, the essay for which the book is named is an illustration of a particular kind of "Rationalist" politics that exemplifies everything to which Oakeshott objects. This characteri-zation is well known, but its essentials bear repeating. In the paragraphs that follow, I first consider some criticisms that have been leveled against Oakeshott's conception of Rationalism and then consider Rationalism on its own terms. Next, I consider Rationalism and "the politics of faith" as together expressing a vision of morality and politics of which Oakeshott strongly disapproves. I conclude this chapter by looking at two sources in which Oakeshott turns partially away from pure political philosophy and toward what might be better designated as the history of political thought. In both *The Social and Political Doctrines of Contemporary Europe* and *Morality and Politics in Modern Europe,* Oakeshott gives examples of how the ideas he has been developing ("faith" and Rationalism) have appeared in history. I put off consideration of his alternative, "preferred" vision of politics—the politics of skepticism and civil association—until Chapter 8.

The Response to *Rationalism in Politics*

The essay "Rationalism in Politics," published with several other essays in a book with the same title, is probably Oakeshott's most widely read work. And although it is brilliantly written and provocative, it consists of a mere forty pages in which he levies a damning critique of a particular modern cast of mind. However, Oakeshott offers no explicit alternative in the essay to what he criticizes, and consequently the essay has seemed contentious and polemical to many readers. Reviewers have arrived at vastly different conclusions about Oakeshott, sometimes on the basis of this essay alone.

Early reviews of the collected essays in *Rationalism in Politics* varied widely in tone. Some readers were inclined to be sympathetic to Oakeshott, but many were either puzzled by him or openly hostile to what they perceived as his unfounded criticism of the ideas they held nearest and dearest. Thus one reviewer took offense at Oakeshott's biting remarks about the place of science and, in particular, the social sciences, arguing, "I fail myself to see how a man can happily develop a subject [political science] unless he loves it—and certainly he cannot if he regards it with impassioned hate." Others found fault with the abstraction of Oakeshott's writing, pointing out that he gives too few political examples of what he means—indeed, that he often seems to be less concerned with politics than he is with other human activities, like cooking and poetry. Still others entirely missed Oakeshott's point about the profound differences between philosophy and practice, arguing (naively) that Oakeshott's "doctrine" about Rationalism could not be of the slightest "use" to the political actors of the day.[2]

2. George E. Catlin, review of *Rationalism in Politics,* 259; see Harry Jaffa, review of *Rationalism in Politics;* George Lichtheim, "A Settled Habit of Behavior: A Review of *Rationalism in Politics,* by Michael Oakeshott," 171.

Many commentators berated Oakeshott for his old-fashioned approach to learning and politics: "his political theory is about contemporary with Noah, that great navigator in the vasty general." His vision was called "antique and irrelevant, ignoring the key questions we face and our efforts to deal with them." One critic accused Oakeshott of having failed to advance "significantly beyond" the largely useless categories worked out by his classical ancestors, Plato and Aristotle. This so-called antique approach to political science was supposed to have led to other problems for Oakeshott, foremost among them his lack of ability to face current crises. His was seen as a "fair weather view, inapplicable in times of rapid change or crisis," and he was perceived as casually ignoring the imminent threats to the civilized world—fiddling while Rome burned.[3]

Other readers objected to Oakeshott's Rationalist as a mere caricature that could not possibly exist in the world. "Oakeshott opposes his own understanding of politics to a simplistic rationalism which no one takes seriously. . . . [his] fight against 'rationalism' is largely a fight against straw men." But perhaps the most outrageous misunderstanding of Oakeshott's thought was that of the critic who wrote that "Oakeshott is an opponent of any attempt to gain theoretical clarity concerning the most important [thing]: how we conduct our lives."[4]

While I am not so much interested in refuting or qualifying these criticisms point by point, as a group they illustrate the complexity of Oakeshott's thought. It is quite remarkable that he could be so widely, and diversely, misunderstood. Many of these criticisms result from an abbreviated reading of Oakeshott's corpus, for his early *Experience and Its Modes* provides answers to many of the objections about the connections (or lack of connections) between philosophy and science. Moreover, the argument that the Rationalist is a "straw man" mistakes completely Oakeshott's analytical method, which is to draw out the most notable characteristics of a given phenomenon and then to construct an "ideal" type that serves to illuminate the less extreme tendencies we see around us in ordinary life. Surely the religious man in Oakeshott's early "Religion and the World," for instance, could not live *entirely* in the present. He

3. Catlin, review of *Rationalism in Politics*, 261; David Kettler, "The Cheerful Discourses of Michael Oakeshott," 489; Lichtheim, "Settled Habit of Behavior," 172. For an interesting comparison, see C. S. Lewis's essay on education during times of crisis, "Learning in War-Time," in *The Weight of Glory*.
4. Kettler, "Cheerful Discourses," 488; Walter Berns, review of *Rationalism in Politics*, 670.

must take some thought for the future, if only about what to eat for dinner and how to pay his bills. But Oakeshott's point, in this illustration as well as in many others, is that the moral and political tendencies that crop up in daily life require the kind of *philosophical* clarification that comes only with a certain amount of exaggeration. If Oakeshott's Rationalist is cartoonish, as some allege, it nevertheless reveals important information about the conduct of human affairs in the same way as "a caricature reveals the potentialities of a face."[5]

The major shortcoming of these critical assessments is that they fail to perceive the aesthetic and religious vision that serves as the foundation for the moral understanding behind Oakeshott's critique of Rationalism. To be fair, it would have been nearly impossible for any of these commentators to perceive this about Oakeshott at the time they wrote. For as I have pointed out, much of this vision is spelled out only in Oakeshott's early essays, which remained unpublished until the early 1990s.

Nevertheless, it now seems clear that Oakeshott's "Rationalism in Politics" cannot be properly understood unless it is paired with (at the very least) the 1948 Tower of Babel essay, which provides its most direct moral underpinnings. Since I have already considered this second essay in the previous chapter, I shall now note the places where his argument depends on the moral vision articulated in it. An even clearer understanding of Oakeshott's views on politics, however, requires both these essays to be read in concert with *The Politics of Faith and the Politics of Scepticism,* a recently published work from this same period of Oakeshott's career. But prior to bringing in these other sources, it is worth clarifying briefly the nature of Rationalism.

Rationalism

First and foremost, the Rationalist (with a capital *R*) stands for "independence of mind on all occasions." He is skeptical as well as optimistic, inclined to doubt the pronouncements of tradition and certain that he will do better than his predecessors. He is full of desires, is impatient for satisfaction, and wants to engage in activities without having to undergo a long and extensive training or initiation. His ambition is "not so much

---

5. "Political Education," in *RP,* 58.

to share the experience of the race as to be demonstrably a self-made man." Thus in politics he adopts an ideology as a guide to action and eschews the kind of knowledge that can only come from practice and experience. He understands life as a succession of crises, a series of problems to be solved. Solutions to these problems come as a result of applying "principles" that are supposed to exist independently of activity. The Rationalist disparages habit and custom, preferring new construction on an absolutely "rational" foundation to the uncertainty of fixing an old structure. "To patch up, to repair (that is, to do anything which requires a patient knowledge of the material), [the Rationalist] regards as a waste of time; and he always prefers the invention of a new device to making use of a current and well-tried expedient."[6]

Rationalism presupposes a particular view of human knowledge that Oakeshott separates into two distinct kinds: "technical" and "practical." Technical knowledge is the kind of information contained in a rule-book, the sort of prescriptions in "how-to" manuals for cooking or playing the piano. Although it is an abridgment, this kind of knowledge claims to convey the ability to engage in an activity, and thus it is precisely what the Rationalist seeks: "You too can have a Harvard graduate's vocabulary by merely listening to our tapes for an hour a day," promises one such guide. It is a shortcut, or, as Oakeshott says, a "crib." Rationalists seek the shortcuts to expertness promised by technical knowledge, just as the inhabitants of Babel desire a shortcut to heaven.

Moreover, in theory this kind of knowledge is available to everyone. No special talents are required to engage in politics if one can master an ideology. But just as in "The Tower of Babel" Oakeshott demonstrated the inadequacy of following moral "rules" as a method of acting morally, so technical knowledge of rules or principles is also inadequate as a way of directing political action or, indeed, any kind of action. How often has a salesman learned a pitch for selling his product, yet remained unable to answer the first unforeseen question about a detail of that product? This shortcoming highlights the essence of technical knowledge: it equips one for superficial engagement in an activity, but it cannot penetrate beneath the surface.

Opposed to this priority on "technique" there is an alternative that Oakeshott calls "practical" knowledge, which is a radically different

6. "Rationalism in Politics," in *RP*, 6, 7, 8.

approach to learning. Here is yet another distinct meaning of the word
practice: if technical knowledge is akin to the "reflective" morality that
Oakeshott describes in "The Tower of Babel," then practical knowledge
is akin to the morality that is a "habit of affection and conduct." Practical
knowledge is acquired in precisely the manner that one comes to possess
habitual morality: by experience, that is, by practicing the activity. If the
technical knowledge of piano playing may be abridged in a book, practical knowledge comes only in sitting next to the expert pianist. It consists
in watching and attempting to reproduce what one has observed—not
only with respect to the physical activity of playing the piano, but also in
the manners, feelings, and habits involved in being a musician more generally. Oakeshott observes that this is the case in military training as well.
The intelligent civilian in war, he notes, may have "little difficulty in ac-
quiring the technique of military leadership and command," but he always
remains at a disadvantage "beside the regular officer, the man educated in
the feelings and emotions as well as the practices of his profession."[7]
Such "practical" knowledge is required in any activity worth pursuing.
But it is precisely what the Rationalist omits when he attempts to use
technical knowledge as a shortcut.

What lies behind this desire for a kind of certain knowledge that is
supposedly universal and accessible to all? Oakeshott suggests that it is, in
a sense, a perversion of the religious impulse. Augustine, of course, explains this perversion as original sin—man's attempt to "ignore his
Creator and his Ruler and to set up himself, his own will, as the hub of
the universe. Refusing to acknowledge his lacks and limitations as a creature, he tries to upset the whole order of the universe by his perverse im-
itation of God." This desire to outsmart God stems from a prideful sense
of one's own self-sufficiency. In a similar line of reasoning Oakeshott
finds the origins of Rationalism in an age "over-impressed with its own
accomplishment and liable to . . . illusions of intellectual grandeur."[8]

Moreover, he labels the Rationalist's cast of mind "gnostic," and observes that Rationalism is closely allied "with a decline in the belief in
Providence." For the Rationalist, argues Oakeshott, a "beneficent and infallible technique . . . replaced a beneficent and infallible God; and

7. Ibid., 39, see footnote.
8. Herbert A. Deane, *The Political and Social Ideas of St. Augustine,* 17; "Rationalism in
Politics," in *RP,* 23.

where Providence was not available to correct the mistakes of men it was all the more necessary to prevent such mistakes." Since faith has receded, so this argument goes, human beings are necessarily thrown back on their own resources and must solve problems by themselves. From this predicament springs the desire for certainty and for fail-safe solutions that is characteristic of Rationalist and gnostic minds. Technical knowledge poses as an answer to this desire, promising to be something that "not only ends with certainty but begins with certainty and is certain throughout." Rationalism is thus an attempt to abate the mystery that is an inescapable part of life, but it does so at the price of misrepresenting the nature of human knowledge and activity. It is, in Oakeshott's words, "a misconception with regard to the nature of human knowledge, which amounts to a corruption of the mind."[9]

But Rationalism is not just a distortion of religion. It is also based on a fundamental misunderstanding of morality. Not coincidentally, this is precisely the same misunderstanding Oakeshott describes in his 1948 Tower of Babel essay. There, as we recall, he distinguishes between two types of morality: morality as a habit of affection and conduct versus a rigorously reflective morality that relies for its coherence on ideals and rules. In "Rationalism in Politics" Oakeshott makes an explicit link between Rationalism and the latter form of morality, observing that the Rationalist's morality is "the morality of the self-conscious pursuit of moral ideals, and the appropriate form of moral education is by precept, by the presentation and explanation of moral principles." The Rationalist rejects a natural, habitual moral education as an "inherited nescience" that must be eliminated and replaced by absolutely rational principles. The moral life of the Rationalist is a "stream of problems . . . a succession of crises" that may be solved by appeal to these principles.[10]

What matters to the Rationalist is that he has finally "separated the ore of the ideal from the dross of the habit of behavior." But for Oakeshott this is a fundamentally misguided way of understanding morality. No moral ideals can exist prior to or independently of a tradition of moral conduct; the "rules" of practices, such as they are, come about only as a result of living and acting within these practices. Thus any moral ideals that we may have are "a sediment . . . suspended in a religious or

9. "Rationalism in Politics," in *RP,* 6, 23, 16, 37.
10. Ibid., 40, 41.

social tradition." But Rationalism has for so long been engaged in "draw-ing off the liquid in which our moral ideals were suspended" that the modern world is left with only "the dry and gritty residue which chokes us as we try to take it down."[11]

The Politics of Faith and the Politics of Scepticism

However, as suggestive as are the hints about religion and morality in "Rationalism in Politics," it is only in *The Politics of Faith and the Politics of Scepticism* that we see the full extent of Oakeshott's transposed Augustinianism and his religious objections to the Pelagian character of modern politics. *The Politics of Faith and the Politics of Scepticism* implicitly recalls Oakeshott's 1929 essay "Religion and the World," in which he presents a choice between "worldly" and "religious" ways of living. In the book he presents a similar pairing: faith and skepticism. Here, how-ever, the two alternatives are not presented as styles of government that might be explicitly chosen by an individual or a society. Instead, Oake-shott calls them the "poles" of an activity (politics), an activity that may at times swing from one extreme to the other but generally ends up somewhere in between. Faith and skepticism are thus necessarily "ideal" types and alternative visions of what politics might look like. Neither of these is a *style* of politics, per se, but rather, in Oakeshott's words, they are "logical opposites."[12] In reality, politics partakes of each type, and neither can exist without the other. Faith and skepticism sprang up together over the past five hundred years as a result of specifically modern conditions that Oakeshott describes over the course of the work.

It is important to be quite clear at the outset about exactly what *faith* and *skepticism* mean to Oakeshott. For at first glance, faith might appear to point toward a less-worldly conception of politics, while skepticism, if taken to an extreme, could potentially undermine all existing political arrangements. But these are not the terms in which Oakeshott describes faith and skepticism. He is quite critical in his assessment of the politics of faith, which he perceives as the "politics of perfection." Faith, in this context, is thus "virtually the opposite of traditional religious faith." In

11. Ibid., 41.
12. *PFPS*, 30.

this style of government, man is thought to be capable of achieving utopia on earth. There are no inherent limitations to human progress, and political activity therefore directs the progress toward perfection. Government becomes huge as it strains to direct the activities of its citizens in politics and in all other spheres of life. It is the "chief inspirer and sole director" of the improvement that is supposed to lead to perfection.[13] *Faith* means, in short, faith in *human* capabilities.

The politics of skepticism, on the other hand, makes no such claims. It has much in common with Oakeshott's idea of civil association, in which government is an umpire, ensuring that minimal rules are obeyed and that the rule of law is not jeopardized. As its name suggests, skepticism is profoundly dubious about undertakings that pursue mundane perfection. Far from the activist government promoted by the politics of faith, in skeptical politics governing is primarily a judicial activity that leaves human beings free to pursue their own purposes.

It is well worth examining these two types in greater detail, because it is here that the religious underpinnings of Oakeshott's thought are most evident. As I have repeatedly emphasized, observing that Oakeshott's critique of modern politics is grounded in a religious view does not mean that Oakeshott himself may be counted among the orthodox religious. Nevertheless, his critiques of the politics of faith and of "Rationalism" are so firmly rooted in religious ideas that to overlook these is to miss a vital part of his thought. Oakeshott takes a notably Augustinian position toward what he sees as modern-day Pelagianism, which I consider below. Moreover, his view of politics more generally—both of what it can achieve and its rather significant limits—is also directly in line with Augustine's views.

Modern Pelagianism

Oakeshott explicitly states that a kind of "Pelagianism" lies behind all versions of the politics of faith. In using this term Oakeshott recalls the famous heretic Pelagius, with whom Augustine argued over the doctrines of free will and original sin in the years following 411. Pelagius believed that moral perfection was possible for man; indeed, it was obligatory.

13. Timothy Fuller, introduction to *RPML*, xi; *PFPS*, 25.

Against a fatalistic view of original sin, Pelagius spoke to those who wished to reform their lives and "make a change for the better." He believed that man "was responsible for his every action" and that every sin "could only be a deliberate act of contempt for God." He had little patience for the weakness and failings of human beings, which could be remedied, he thought, through a determined exercise of will. He disdained what he perceived as the moral weakness in Augustine's *Confessions,* which seemed to him "merely to popularize the tendency toward a languid piety."[14]

Perfectibility, according to Pelagius, was therefore not only possible for human beings, but its pursuit was a duty that "rested with man 'according to his merits.'" Moreover, Pelagius considered himself capable of offering individuals "absolute certainty through absolute obedience [to God]." This desire for certainty is the constant companion of the impulse to perfectionism. But for Oakeshott, like Augustine, both perfectionism and the compulsive desire for certainty are hostile to the doctrine of providence and to the idea that the universe is a perfect creation. If Pelagius and his followers "seemed determined . . . to reform the whole Christian church," Oakeshott's Rationalism, likewise, seems determined to reform modern politics in its own image.[15]

Augustine differed from Pelagius on virtually all his assumptions and, consequently, also on his conclusions. What seems to have galled him most about Pelagian doctrine was its insistence on moral perfectionism. The idea that human beings, by mere exercise of will, could become perfect even as God is perfect struck Augustine as manifestly false and prideful. Writing against the teachings of Pelagius, he emphasized the degree to which human virtue, such as it is, depends upon God:

> For we assert that the human will is so far assisted by divine aid in the accomplishment of justice that, over and above the fact that man is created with the power of voluntary self-determination, over and above the teaching from which he derives precepts as to how he ought to live, he also receives the Holy Spirit, whereby there is engendered (*fiat*) in his mind the love for and delight in that supreme and immutable good which is God, even now while he still walks by faith and not yet by sight; that,

14. *PFPS,* 80; Peter Brown, *Augustine of Hippo,* 343, 351, 343.
15. Charles Cochrane, *Christianity and Classical Culture,* 452; Brown, *Augustine of Hippo,* 347; *PFPS,* 23; Brown, *Augustine of Hippo,* 348.

this being given to him as a free offering (*munus gratuitum*), he may be in-
flamed with desire to approach to participation in that true light.

Oakeshott, of course, would not write in such explicitly religious terms
as these, but against modern-day Pelagians he makes a similar point.
Those who (wisely) doubt the desirability of the politics of faith do so
because they understand the limitations of their own abilities. This humility springs from recognizing that the world is given to mankind not
merely to be exploited, but to be "contemplated" and "enjoyed." What
distinguishes skepticism from faith is the skeptic's "sense of mortality, that
amicitia rerum mortalium, which detracts from the allure of the gilded future foreseen in the vision of faith."[16]
Like Augustine, Oakeshott found the modern impulse to perfectionism inherently objectionable. A strong warning against perfectionism is,
of course, also the moral of Oakeshott's retelling of the Tower of Babel
story. It might be said, then, that a religious idea lies at the heart of
Oakeshott's critique of a certain kind of politics. This idea is Pelagianism,
or, in modern terms, moral and political perfectionism. This is evident in
"Rationalism in Politics," where he describes the two general characteristics of Rationalism as the "politics of perfection" and the "politics of
uniformity" and contends that Rationalism is indeed the combination of
both: "the imposition of a uniform condition of perfection upon human
conduct."[17] But Oakeshott is even more explicit about the Pelagianism
of modern politics in *The Politics of Faith and the Politics of Scepticism.*

The Politics of Faith

In *The Politics of Faith and the Politics of Scepticism* Oakeshott observes that
the fundamental characteristic of the politics of faith is a conception of
government as being "in the service of the perfection of mankind." To
achieve human perfection one need not "depend upon the working of
divine providence for . . . salvation." On the contrary, it may be achieved
"by human effort, and confidence in the evanescence of imperfection
springs here from faith in human power and not from trust in divine

16. Cochrane, *Christianity and Classical Culture,* 453; Augustine, *De Spiritu et Littera,* v,
quoted in Cochrane; *PFPS,* 76.
17. "Rationalism in Politics," in *RP,* 9–10.

providence." The politics of faith is "the politics of immortality, building for eternity."[18] It is the attempt to remedy once and for all the unsatisfactory character of the world and the human condition. It is precisely what the Babelians attempt as they build their tower.

This view of perfection is partnered with three other principles, the first two of which are closely related. First, the perfection longed for may be achieved in this world: "man is redeemable in history." This doctrine does *not* hold that any perfection available to man will occur only through faith, in a world to come. Second, this perfection is mundane and understood "to be a condition of human circumstances." It depends, therefore, upon organizing political affairs so that they encourage human beings in their pursuit of perfection. The third principle follows, then: that government itself must be the chief agent of this improvement. It must organize the resources of mankind into a comprehensive plan prioritizing efficiency and singleness of purpose. Government does not merely assist in the project of moving toward perfection; it is the "chief inspirer and sole director of the pursuit."[19] Thus it takes upon itself the duty of directing action from a comprehensive perspective and becomes omnicompetent, radically limiting the spheres in which subjects may express themselves.

Such is the politics of faith. Human life is understood to be a condition in which people strive for a mundane perfection not merely individually, but as a society. In this striving they are oriented and organized by a government that steps in to enforce a plan. Dissent is discouraged, for who could doubt the goodness of transforming the human condition from one of manifest ills to one of perfection? The great virtue of this style of politics—and indeed, its great vice, from Oakeshott's perspective—is that it pursues perfection in one direction. It posits a "single road" and is "content with the certainty that perfection lies wherever it leads." The politics of faith presumes not only that "human power is sufficient . . . to procure salvation," but that perfection denotes a "single, comprehensive condition of human circumstances."[20] Clearly, this view is diametrically opposed to Oakeshott's view of politics, in which self-determined agents pursue a variety of chosen purposes within the framework of a settled rule of law. If the politics of faith is about the spir-

18. *PFPS,* 23, 114.
19. Ibid., 23, 24, 25.
20. Ibid., 26.

itual conquest of the world, the politics of skepticism studiously avoids such grandiose posturing.

Faith, Morality, and Politics in Modern Europe

Oakeshott does not, however, make his argument about the politics of faith solely in abstract, theoretical terms. As I have argued, his objections to certain political tendencies are grounded in his views about the character of human beings, views that are religious and aesthetic. Like all legitimate theories of politics or of human conduct, they have concrete manifestations in the world, and as valid theories they depend on a clear-sighted assessment of human beings. Oakeshott therefore brings his theory decisively to bear on the contemporary political arrangements of modern Europe. He analyzes modern forms of government in light of their approximation to the politics of faith, on the one hand, or to the politics of skepticism, on the other.

Oakeshott argues in the introduction to *The Social and Political Doctrines of Contemporary Europe* (1939) that the differences between various doctrines—Liberalism, Catholicism, Communism, Fascism, and National Socialism—are not so much between those that offer "spiritual" or "material" ideals, but between those "which hand over to the arbitrary will of a society's self-appointed leaders the planning of its entire life, and those which not only refuse to hand over the destiny of a society to any set of officials but also consider the whole notion of planning the destiny of a society to be both stupid and immoral." Oakeshott observes that on one side there are "the three modern authoritarian doctrines, Communism, Fascism and National Socialism; on the other Catholicism and Liberalism. To the Liberal and the Catholic mind alike the notion that men can authoritatively plan and impose a way of life upon a society appears to be a piece of pretentious ignorance; it can be entertained only by men who have no respect for human beings and are willing to make them the means to the realization of their own ambitions."[21] Once again, the fundamental difference is between those governments that have "faith" in their ability to direct the activities of human beings and those that are "skeptical" about this endeavor.

In a series of lectures Oakeshott gave at Harvard in 1958, now published

21. *SPDCE,* xxii.

as *Morality and Politics in Modern Europe,* he casts the faith/skepticism distinction in the terms of collectivism versus individuality, even going so far as to call these categories (as he does faith and skepticism) "the poles of the modern European political character." Collectivism postulates a common good that is chosen by government for the individuals who compose a society. This good is "preferred above all other possible conditions of human circumstance" and is believed "to be at least the emblem of a 'perfect' manner of human existence."[22] In other words, it is the politics of faith.

The politics of individuality, on the other hand, springs from an entirely different conception of the role of government. Indeed, it has no "vision of another, different and better, world," but takes its bearings from observation of "the self-government practiced . . . by men of passion in the conduct of their enterprises." It calls not for great concentrations of power, but for an authoritative "ritual" that can minimize the chances for great collisions between individuals. The government is thus merely "custodian" of this ritual, called "law." Government's functions, on this reading, are to minimize circumstances in which violent collisions of interest are likely to occur. It provides redress for those who have been wronged, maintains sufficient power to carry out its functions, and protects itself and its subjects from foreign threat.[23] But unlike collectivism, the government of individuality is not in the business of generating grand visions that would guide an entire people.

In *Morality and Politics in Modern Europe,* Oakeshott brings the somewhat abstract conceptions of collectivism and faith into sharper relief by giving examples from political history. He identifies three distinct versions of collectivism and describes the kinds of "perfection" they pursue: religious, productivist, and distributionist. The religious version, he believes, was exemplified in Calvin's Geneva, in which government's purpose was to channel every human activity into the pursuit of "righteousness." Calvin's design was to "impose upon the citizens of Geneva an exclusive and comprehensive pattern of activities from which no divergence was to be allowed." Moreover, government was oriented toward achievement of a substantive purpose: to guard the glory and honor of God and "to be the execution of God's will as displayed in the Scriptures."[24]

22. *MPME,* 110, 91.
23. *MPME,* 49, 50.
24. Ibid., 93.

Oakeshott's discussion of Calvinism as the quintessential example of the "politics of faith" is well worth reading in full. But the most striking part of the discussion in these pages is his analysis of Marxian politics as part of this same religious idiom. Oakeshott also locates Marx's politics in other versions of collectivism, but the essential features of Marxism seem to stem from a religious origin. It is worth quoting Oakeshott's analysis at length to see how a supposedly secular theory can be interpreted as fundamentally religious:

> Like the millenarian sectaries of the seventeenth century, the Marxist believes that a new age is emerging (a third epoch in world history) in which the dominion of "earthly" (that is, "capitalist") governments will be superseded by the rules of the Saints (the proletariat) over the Reprobate (the bourgeoisie), who have no rights save the rights to be ruled and who cannot be "saved" because they are not among the Elect. . . . [The Elect] must claim the right to propagate their beliefs ("the truth") without hindrance, and they will absolve themselves from all promises, contracts, engagements, treaties, oaths and debts. . . . [Soon] a "perfect" condition of human circumstance [will arise] about which little is known except that there will be no place in it for governing as a specific activity and that it cannot be established anywhere with certainty until it is established everywhere. In short, there is scarcely anything in the mythology and the anthropology of Marxism which does not have its counterpart in the writings of the seventeenth-century Puritan sectaries. The religious version of the politics of collectivism, the first version to appear in modern Europe, has survived almost unchanged . . . into our contemporary world in the political theory of Marxism.

It is worth noting that this analysis has much in common with Eric Voegelin's analysis of Marx's political theory, which I shall examine in Chapter 9. In *Science, Politics and Gnosticism,* Voegelin makes a similar case for Marx as a gnostic who wished to replace the true constitution of being with a "world-immanent order of being, the perfection of which lies in the realm of human action."[25] Indeed, Voegelin and Oakeshott agree that Marx's political theory, with its focus on the mundane search for perfection, is a distortion of religious impulses.

However, the "religious" version is only one type of collectivism. And the other two types Oakeshott identifies have assumed a dominant place

25. Ibid., 96–97; Eric Voegelin, *Science, Politics and Gnosticism,* 68.

in Western political thought over the past several centuries. The second kind of collectivism he considers is "productivist," which is a particular understanding of human purpose and association that emerged in the sixteenth century and finds its clearest expression in the writings of Francis Bacon. In brief, this is a view in which government directs its citizens not toward salvation (as in the religious version of collectivism), but toward economic prosperity. Work is the "preeminently proper oc-cupation of mankind," and all other activities should be subordinated to it. Government thus ought to aim at maximizing productivity: it ought "to promote research, to supervise industry and trade, to regulate prices and consumption, to distribute wealth where it might be most usefully employed," and so on.[26]

The third version of collectivism is "distributionist." Here the focus has shifted from economic prosperity to a vision of perfection that is dis-tinguished by its emphasis on the ideas of "security" and "welfare." Its desired state of perfection is one in which every person is fundamentally equal to everyone else, in which the immense quantity of goods and wealth that "productivism" yields are required to be divided up fairly among all people. The desired outcome is not merely legal equality, but a "real" equality, that is, equality of condition.[27] This version of collec-tivism emerged in the nineteenth century in those countries (such as France and England) that had the most wealth to distribute.

These three types of collectivism are illustrations of what Oakeshott meant when he described the politics of faith. As I have emphasized above, the politics of faith posits a uniform condition of mundane per-fection, as well as a government that leads the way to achieving it. In the religious version of collectivism the desired perfection is salvation that is to be worked out in the world. In the productivist version it is economic progress. And in the distributionist version it is equality of condition. In each of these a "single road" to perfection is chosen by government and imposed on a society. But each kind of perfection is a kind of idolatry, a Tower of Babel in which individual choice is stamped out in favor of what is supposed to be a greater good. As in the Tower of Babel story, dissent and disobedience are punished "not as troublesome conduct, but as 'error' and 'sin'. Lack of enthusiasm will be considered a crime, to be prevented by education and to be punished as treason."[28]

26. *MPME,* 103.
27. Ibid., 107, 108.
28. *PFPS,* 29.

But perhaps the greatest irony of all, given that these political systems aim at achieving human perfection, is that they produce not happiness, but a creeping dissatisfaction that cannot be remedied. For the promised perfection—religious, productivist, distributionist—lies always in the future and thus always out of reach. The politics of faith is preoccupied, indeed obsessed, with the future. The imbalance of contemporary politics, Oakeshott remarks, "springs from the preoccupation with the future which has been pressed upon it by the politics of faith." Just as Nimrod attempts to pacify his subjects in Babel, who are becoming impatient for their great reward, so governments of faith say to their subjects, "The pursuit of perfection is an arduous undertaking. You must not only expect to forego delights which those who will come after will enjoy, you must also expect to suffer the pains and deprivations inseparable from the enterprise." Present happiness is sacrificed to promises of *even greater* future happiness; but this, as Oakeshott makes clear throughout his work, is a fundamental misunderstanding of morality translated into a misunderstanding of politics. For Oakeshott believed that fulfillment in life comes only in living, so far as possible, in the present. If we postpone fulfillment to the future, when we expect finally to have accomplished our greatest works, most likely "death or disease will rob us of our harvest, and we shall have lived in vain."[29] The future, as Oakeshott is wont to remind us, is remarkably uncertain.

To sum up, Oakeshott's three related formulations of a particular kind of politics (Rationalism, "faith," and collectivism) all express a certain view of moral character and the kind of government appropriate to this moral character. The morality they presuppose is Oakeshott's least favored type, which I characterized in the previous chapter as "servile" rather than creative or "liberal." It is morality as the reflective application of ideals or rules. Just as servile morality imagines that it can achieve goodness by following rules, or "cribs," so the Rationalist in politics imagines that he can achieve political excellence by adhering to an ideology, and by sticking to principles. Servile morality is oriented toward ideals, and thus toward an ever-receding future; governments in the style of "faith" imagine that they can postulate a state of perfection for their societies, and this too is an endeavor that looks explicitly toward the future.

29. Ibid., 86 (see also his discussion on p. 96), 98; "Religion and the World," in *RPML*, 32.

To put it plainly, Rationalism, "faith," and collectivism spring from a faulty understanding of the character of human beings. These views of politics depend on the "servile" morality I have identified as dissatisfied, faithless, future-oriented, proud, and overconfident. It is the morality of the impatient and irritable, of those who are oriented solely toward accomplishment, and of those who do not value things as ends in themselves. The alternative vision, and indeed Oakeshott's favored vision, I shall discuss in the next chapter.

8

Skeptical Politics and Civil Association

As shown in the previous chapter, Oakeshott appears at his polemical best in "Rationalism in Politics," where he disparages a particular modern cast of mind. In *The Politics of Faith and the Politics of Scepticism,* on the other hand, he is more concerned with understanding the philosophical character of two dominant kinds of modern political arrangements. And in the lectures that make up *Morality and Politics in Modern Europe,* Oakeshott shows that these alternatives appear both in historical states (for instance, Calvin's Geneva) and in the writings of notable political thinkers (Marx). In all these works he emphasizes the shortcomings of understanding political activity as something imposed by overbearing governments on subjects who are thought to have neither the desire nor the will to choose for themselves. Such political arrangements, in his view, are perfectionist, Pelagian, Rationalist, and collectivist.

Oakeshott designates his alternative understanding of politics as skepticism, individualism, and, in his most mature thought, civil association. These are the poles that stand opposite the politics of faith, collectivism, and enterprise association, respectively. But, as Oakeshott repeatedly emphasizes, they are not simple alternatives that may be "chosen" or pursued while simultaneously rejecting their opposites. For while it is clear that he wanted to recover and to emphasize one of the members of each pair, Oakeshott did not think that any of these types could exist wholly on its own, nor that one is wholly desirable while the other ought to be completely avoided. Moreover, we should remember the gap between philosophy and practice that is a fundamental part of Oakeshott's thought: his aim was not to recommend *reform* in the direction of skepticism and civil association. He wanted rather to point out that these forms of government better reflect the true moral character of human beings. And the politics of skepticism and of civil association are, unfortunately, likely to be overlooked or ignored in a world that is more often concerned with achievement and enterprise than with the playful, contemplative aspects of human experience.

This chapter begins by examining the way in which Oakeshott sets out his interpretive categories and then moves to an explication of the politics of skepticism as an alternative to the "politics of faith." Next, I consider Oakeshott's definitive expression of skeptical politics, which he identifies in *On Human Conduct* as "civil association," and I conclude by linking this political view to the moral character of human beings he finds most satisfactory.

A Reflection on Method: Oakeshott and Ideal Characters

It is worthwhile to reflect on Oakeshott's method and to consider, for a moment, exactly why he worked with ideal types rather than giving a straightforward exposition of empirical political history. Oakeshott believed that only ideal types could escape the contingency that is part of every *actual* political association, and he was concerned more with a philosophical understanding of these types than with the particulars of any given regime. Ideal types emerge, of course, only as a result of an inductive process of observation and classification; and like Aristotle, Oakeshott moved from the particular to the general in a process of noetic investigation. But, again like Aristotle, Oakeshott recognized that the greatest clarity is gained when particulars crystallize into theories that may *themselves* reflect back on the concrete situation from which they emerged. Thus it is illuminating, when considering a political situation, to have these theoretical concepts (ideal types) as tools. Without them we notice only details: perhaps taxes are increasing and government seems ever more to appear in areas formerly left to individuals. With Oakeshott's concepts in mind we may classify such government action as more or less "Rationalist," or more or less "skeptical." In the absence of these kinds of interpretive categories, regimes would appear infinitely various and perplexing.

Oakeshott employed these ideal types, or "characters," from the beginning of his career, usually to identify certain polar opposites in moral or political conduct. This is precisely his approach in the early essay "Religion and the World," where he made clear that the religious life is

to be preferred to the worldly one and that each person must choose between two opposed orientations. But as Oakeshott's thought matured,
his writing on these ideal characters became more subtle, making the
question of how to understand them somewhat more difficult. Indeed, as
I have already remarked, Oakeshott did not believe that an individual or
society could choose either skepticism or faith. These characters are neither "options" nor concrete historical illustrations, though they may be
identified to greater or lesser degrees in actual historical states. They are,
rather, modes of association that stand as the poles of political activity.

Oakeshott's aim, then, in identifying ideal characters was to examine
them philosophically. He wished to use them "in *seeking to understand*
complex, ambiguous, historic human associations." The primary distinction here, one commentator observes, is akin to that between "a kind of
activity and an actual instance of that activity." Just as it is possible to distinguish baseball "as a game constituted by certain rules, from the play of
particular persons on a particular occasion, so we can distinguish law as a
practice from what is actually going on in this or that legal system."[1]
Oakeshott's method of setting out ideal political characters is thus a way
of gaining some degree of philosophical clarity about politics, an activity
that is often not at all philosophical.

It is also important to emphasize something that many of his critics
miss, namely, that Oakeshott himself never mistook ideal characters for
real persons or states. He was well aware—indeed, it is one of his primary
insights—that no ideal type exists unalloyed in the world.[2] In working
with these types, Oakeshott identified "an ideal character and a pro-
gramme of inquiry, not pointing to an assignable association and stipu-
lating this to be its character." Every existing state, he observed, is an
"ambiguous association," partaking to some degree of both civil and enterprise association. Likewise, faith and skepticism are two styles of governing "which are in abstract opposition to one another, but which
together compose our complex and ambivalent manner of governing."

---

1. *OHC,* 109 (emphasis added); Nardin, *Philosophy of Michael Oakeshott,* 196–97.
2. As Max Weber puts it, we can proceed only by examining ideal types as "constructed
concepts endowed with a degree of consistency seldom found in actual history."
Precisely because it is impossible to draw "sharp boundaries in historical reality, our only
hope of identifying the particular effects of [given ideas]," Weber observes, "must come
through an investigation of their *most consistent* [or 'ideal'] forms" (*The Protestant Ethic and
the Spirit of Capitalism,* 55).

But this mixture—or synthesis, to borrow a Hegelian term—is precisely why the method of constructing ideal types is necessary. As I have observed, Oakeshott saw "historical and practical life as pre-eminently contingent." Therefore, if philosophy does not achieve some distance from this contingency, "it will be led 'into all sorts of circumstantial considerations,' and its conclusions 'will be far from permanent.'"[3]

Yet although it is evident that Oakeshott preferred certain of these types to others, as he clearly preferred skepticism to faith, he was no unreserved partisan for an extreme form of skeptical politics. In the first place, as I have noted, Oakeshott did not recommend any sort of concrete program of reform that would move *toward* skepticism, since he doubted the ability of government to design and accomplish this kind of change. Secondly, Oakeshott recognized that one of the shortcomings of skepticism is that it is "preeminently suitable for a complex but relatively static condition of society."[4] That is, despite its general desirability, skeptical politics may be inappropriate for certain kinds of societies, either those that are just emerging or those that find themselves in times of war or crisis.

But most of all, Oakeshott warned against the wholehearted pursuit of either faith or skepticism, because they are extremes and because the pursuit of any extreme necessarily closes off other vital forms of experience. In the same way that Oakeshott warned against morality conceived as the pursuit of ideals (where, for example, the single-minded pursuit of "justice" may exclude mercy), so he condemned the pursuit of political ideals—whatever these may be—as equally misguided. The person who seeks perpetual summer, Oakeshott remarked, ceases to recognize anything other than his desired climate and its virtues. In his attempt to avoid the cold he misses not only the winter he hates, but also the more moderate seasons that intervene. For Oakeshott believed, in good Aristotelian fashion, that living at any extreme is an "insidious pursuit." Although one may "escape imprisonment in the particular extreme [he] has come to inhabit," one nevertheless becomes unable to recognize anything but an extreme "of some sort."[5]

---

3. *OHC,* 122, 128; *PFPS,* 31; Franco, *Political Philosophy of Michael Oakeshott,* 180. The quotes come from Oakeshott's review of *The State and the Citizen,* by J. D. Mabbott, 384–85.

4. *PFPS,* 107.

5. Ibid., 12.

The Politics of Skepticism

Even if extremes should be avoided, the politics of skepticism is, on balance, better than the politics of faith. Or, to put it in Oakeshott's terms, a mixture of the two in which skepticism is dominant is preferable to the alternatives. Thus skepticism deserves to be considered in its own right, just as I considered faith in the previous chapter. If the politics of faith is constituted by "the continuous reassertion of the unity of politics and religion," and may be described as "the politics of immortality, building for eternity," skeptical politics emphatically rejects the idea that government can assist in procuring an individual's salvation. In the politics of skepticism, governing is understood to be a specific and bounded activity. In particular "it is understood to be detached from the pursuit of human perfection." This is a skepticism rooted not in radical doubt, but in "prudent diffidence," a gentler form of skepticism, which hesitates to believe that government can be the savior of its people.[6]

This, indeed, is the primary difference between the politics of faith and of skepticism. For while faith believes perfection to be both possible and attainable *when its pursuit is directed by government,* skepticism, on the contrary, rejects this assumption. Skepticism either completely rejects the pursuit of mundane perfection or, if it recognizes it as appropriate at certain times, simultaneously acknowledges that government should play no part in its pursuit. This refusal to associate politics with perfection is a view Oakeshott derived directly from his reflections on Hobbes and (somewhat less directly) from Augustine. "For so far as political activity succeeds in modifying the reign of arbitrary violence in human affairs," Oakeshott observes, "there is clearly something to be said for it, and it may even be thought to be worth the cost." Consider, with this tradition in mind, Oakeshott's description of skeptical politics:

> The sceptic in politics observes that men live in proximity with one another and, pursuing various activities, are apt to come into conflict with each other. And this conflict, when it reaches certain dimensions, not only makes life barbaric and intolerable, but may even terminate it abruptly. In this understanding of politics, then, the activity of governing subsists not because it is good, but because it is necessary. Its chief office is to lessen the severity of human conflict by reducing the occasions of it. . . . This

6. Ibid., 81, 114, 31.

superficial order may seem insignificant [to some]. . . . But the sceptic understands order as a great and difficult achievement never beyond the reach of decay and dissolution.

This is a complex, subtle view of political activity. Unlike the politics of faith, which sees some form of perfection in its future, skeptical politics holds out no such hope. Indeed, mundane perfection guided by government is not something that the skeptic even desires. For he believes that certain activities are far more important than politics. As Oakeshott observes in a 1939 essay entitled "The Claims of Politics," although the achievements of politics are significant, they are by no means "the most valuable things in the communal life of a society." The "real" life of a society inheres in the activity of artists and poets and of all those who "create and recreate the values of their society."[7]

This insight—that political activity is important but by no means the *most* important human activity—is, in Oakeshott's view, fundamental to the work of all great political philosophers. The establishment of a stable political order, that is, "civil association," is necessarily something less than the "gift of salvation itself," which can never be provided by government. In the thinking of Plato and Aristotle, civil association is the necessary precondition for the "best life, which is a contemplative, intellectual life." In Augustine's view, civil association can bring peace, but never the highest good of a "perfectly ordered union of hearts in the enjoyment of God and one another in God." And in Spinoza's view, too, only "knowledge of the necessary workings of the universe" provides final fulfillment, though this cannot come about without the "second-best deliverance" of a mundane political order.[8] In short, for all these thinkers—as for Oakeshott and Hobbes—civil association is necessary but not sufficient for human fulfillment.

With this point in mind, one can begin to appreciate Oakeshott's reasons for turning from his early and, as I argue, abiding interests in religion and aesthetics toward politics. It is not, I believe, that these interests ever left him, but rather that he began to realize how crucial a proper understanding of politics was to achieving things of greater importance—the sorts of things pursued in religion, aesthetics, and scholarship

7. Ibid., 31, 19–20, 32, 93, 95.
8. *HCA,* 77.

for its own sake. Oakeshott's position, therefore, must be carefully stated. On the one hand, he observes the "unpleasing spectacle" of politics, which offends "most of our rational and all our artistic susceptibilities."[9] Political activity necessarily simplifies, trivializes, and may even deceive. It is emphatically not an activity in which to seek fulfillment. And yet we cannot do without it. Its goal—if formulated correctly and skeptically— is to establish the kind of stability necessary for human beings to achieve the things that *they* deem most important. A stable and free political order is, indeed, a great and difficult achievement.

But this understanding of politics, like any other, presupposes a particular kind of moral character in those who are to make up society. The vision implied by "skeptical" politics is clearly expressed in the work of such thinkers as Hobbes, Pascal, Montaigne, and other early modern philosophers, all of whom held certain distinct views about the possibilities and limitations of human beings. These thinkers, like Oakeshott himself, had a distinct sense of mortality that necessarily detracts "from the allure of the gilded future foreseen in the vision of faith." The future, since it is uncertain, is not where one ought to place one's hopes. Consequently, they were also dubious about the success of all human projects, "especially when they are largely designed," as well as about the wisdom of mankind's "committing itself to a single line of movement," as the politics of faith would recommend. But the most striking aspect of this skeptical moral vision is its idea that the earth is not merely a quarry to be mined, not a "world to be exploited," but, as Oakeshott contends, a "player's stage."[10] Human conduct, understood in this way, has a playful, aesthetic character that removes it from the "deadliness of doing" and from the interminable practical considerations of work.

Indeed, in *The Politics of Faith and the Politics of Scepticism* Oakeshott marks out a distinct place for "playfulness," not only where it might be expected—in teaching and learning, poetry, and certain human relationships—but in politics. He goes so far as to observe that play is the most complete "confession" or "revelation" of the character of skeptical politics. Whereas the politics of faith understands political activity as preeminently serious, as something that ought to be pursued to the exclusion of all other activities, skepticism sets aside special times and places for

9. *PFPS*, 19.
10. Ibid., 76.

engagement in politics. These times and places (for instance, parliaments and law courts) are deliberately separated from "ordinary life" and have special rituals and requirements for participation. According to this understanding, politics is an activity to be pursued not at all times but "on certain specified occasions." Its significance lies not in its result, but in the *manner* in which its participants engage in it.[11] This understanding does not trivialize political activity, for the outcome of this ritualized "play" certainly matters, but it does remove from it the tendency to consider itself more important than all other forms of human activity. It is worth noting, however, that this is an unusual characterization of politics, for Oakeshott. Nowhere else in his corpus does he equate politics with playfulness.

Just as for Oakeshott the "politics of faith" is reflected in the political theory of collectivism, for him the politics of skepticism is in certain kinds of political arrangements that he designates "individualist." As he makes clear in *Morality and Politics in Modern Europe,* skeptical politics depends upon the existence of a type of person who is a moral individualist, someone disposed "to make choices for [himself] to the maximum possible extent, choices concerning activities, occupations, beliefs" and so on. Moreover, the moral individualist finds this kind of conduct to be proper to human beings and seeks to bring about "the conditions in which it may be enjoyed most fully."[12] Oakeshott describes Locke, Smith, Burke, and Kant as theorists who, in different ways, helped to set out this connection between moral and political individuality.

Skepticism, Individualism, and Civil Association

However, if it was a reasonably straightforward task to elucidate Oakeshott's critique of "faith" and "collectivism" in the preceding chapter, it is not so simple to summarize his views about skepticism and individuality as well as the implications of these views for his political thought. It is difficult precisely because these are *the* fundamental ideas that underlie Oakeshott's conception of the character of modern morality and politics, and he expresses them in multiple ways. His particular moral vi-

11. Ibid., 91, 110, 111.
12. *MPME,* 20–21.

sion—a creative, aesthetic individualism—is the guiding principle in all his work on Hobbes, it illuminates most of the essays in *Rationalism in Politics,* and it is eloquently and comprehensively expressed in *On Human Conduct.* I cannot, therefore, exhaustively trace these ideas through the entirety of Oakeshott's corpus but will instead illustrate this "morality of individuality" by considering its connection to his most mature expression of politics as "civil association." Although Oakeshott uses the phrase *civil association* in his earlier work on Hobbes, it is only in *On Human Conduct* that it takes on the particular meaning that I explain below.

Civil association is Oakeshott's final formulation of the kind of politics he finds most adequate for human beings, but it is a difficult concept to grasp. Once again, it is an "ideal character," not a description of any existing political system. As a philosophical idea it "neither describes everything that goes on nor proposes slogans for actions: it elucidates organizing categories."[13] Civil association is an expressly *nonpurposive* association of human beings who are united in their agreement to observe certain rules of conduct as a system of law. It postulates no particular goods for the association as a whole, aside from the maintenance of the association itself. I discuss its characteristics in greater detail below, but it is helpful first to contrast it, as Oakeshott does, with its principal alternative, "enterprise association."

Throughout the second and third essays of *On Human Conduct* civil association appears as the antithesis of enterprise association, which is an association of human beings for a common, agreed-upon purpose. Enterprise association is by far the most familiar kind of human association, since it is the mode of association in which we most commonly engage. Enterprise associations have clear purposes, and these associations are not compulsory—that is, one can opt in or out. Oakeshott's favorite example of enterprise association is the "fire station," where there is no doubt about the group's purpose. But the term also describes associations of volunteers who engage in projects for community improvement, companies that produce products, missionary groups that aim at converting unbelievers, and even schools. In short, enterprise associations have goals.

Civil association, on the other hand, is peculiar in having no such

---

13. Josiah Lee Auspitz, "Individuality, Civility and Theory: The Philosophical Imagination of Michael Oakeshott," 283.

goals. Those who take part in this association, whom Oakeshott calls *cives,* may of course pursue their own individual ends and may even form enterprise associations amongst themselves in the pursuit of goals that certain members have intentionally chosen. But insofar as they are *cives* they are related only in terms of a moral practice, which postulates no substantive ends. Indeed, civil association rejects any understanding in which it is perceived to be "instrumental to the satisfaction of substantive wants." Most important to the relationship of *cives* is that they are self-determining individuals—"not neurophysiological organisms, genetic characters, psychological egos or components of a 'social process', but 'free' agents whose responses to one another's actions and utterances is one of understanding."[14] Thus there is ample room for *cives* to pursue a wide variety of self-chosen purposes: to become artists and poets, to live religious lives, or to pursue practical projects of all kinds. Conspicuously absent from this kind of association, however, is the directing hand of government. Civil association thus requires agents who are well prepared to face the "ordeal of consciousness," who embrace opportunities to make choices for themselves, and who are unafraid of the possibilities for failure that partner any potential success.

Oakeshott is explicit about the kind of moral character presupposed in civil association. He does not, of course, argue that it is a single, approved mode of behavior, but instead describes a disposition to recognize freedom as "the emblem of human dignity" and as something to be enjoyed rather than suffered as a burden. Freedom, in other words, not only is valuable as a means of achieving chosen ends but is *itself* a valuable end. Thus *cives* recognize that "imagining, deliberating, wanting, choosing, and acting" are not merely costs to be paid in seeking enjoyments but are "themselves enjoyments, the exercise of a gratifying self-determination or personal autonomy."[15] The very activity of coming to understand one's own abilities and limitations, choosing what to do and what not to do, and deciding upon the "manner" in which one will act *is* a kind of satisfaction. It is, as I have argued, Oakeshott's favored view of morality: at its best it is both creative and aesthetic—a continually extemporized dance, the world seen as a player's stage.

The characters who appear on this stage are, however, infinitely di-

---

14. *OHC,* 122, 112.
15. Ibid., 236.

verse. Though they share the disposition to enjoy freedom, they are not all masterful egoists in the image of Aristotle's magnanimous man or Nietzsche's *Übermensch*. Some, of course, may be of this type, "careless of the concerns of others" and disdaining "consequences or recognition" in their self-assured courses. But others embrace their freedom even as they display an "undismayed acknowledgement and admiration of the superiority of others" and a "humility devoid of humiliation." All these lovers of freedom, however, share the disposition to "prefer the road to the inn, ambulatory conversation to deliberation about means for achieving ends, the rules of the road to directions about how to reach a destination." And, as Oakeshott observes in a famous passage, the deity who corresponds to this view must be "an Augustinian god of majestic imagination, who, when he might have devised an untroublesome universe, had the nerve to create one composed of self-employed adventure[r]s of unpredictable fancy, to announce to them some rules of conduct, and thus to acquire convives capable of 'answering back' in civil tones with whom to pass eternity in conversation."[16] This, then, is the character of the *cives* who engage in civil association. They reject the constant pursuit of "goals" and "satisfactions" in favor of present enjoyment, preferring civil conversation to persuasion and argument. They have learned to enjoy the "purposelessness" that may be intentionally cultivated even in a world that prioritizes enterprise and achievement.

Many critics have commented on Oakeshott's unusual conception of the politics of civil association, which prioritizes "presentness" and goes so far as to celebrate the lack of a common purpose. Oakeshott did not view civil association as a means to social justice or to economic prosperity or, indeed, to any external end at all. It is, rather, an understanding of politics that grew out of his understanding of the moral character of human beings. Civil association—elsewhere designated the politics of skepticism and of individualism—fosters freedom and self-determination. Human beings are therefore not put into the service of achieving a particular political end; instead, *politics* serves the true needs of human beings. Indeed, as Paul Franco has noted, one of the major thrusts of *On Human Conduct* is to "purge liberalism of the materialism and economism with which it has been historically connected." And as Oakeshott himself observes, the most questionable element of current liberal

16. Ibid., 237, 238, 324.

democratic doctrine is its "moral ideal: 'the plausible ethics of productivity.'" In this Oakeshott may be distinguished from all those who see freedom as the best "means" to a variety of postulated ends. Civil association is never "instrumental to the achievement of any substantive purpose."[17] It is, rather, the view of politics that is best for those who understand themselves as engaged in adventures of self-determination.

Conclusion

In the nearly thirty years since Oakeshott wrote *On Human Conduct,* his conception of "civil association" has certainly found its defenders. Nevertheless, it is not an idea that all commentators have immediately rushed to embrace. In the eyes of many critics, civil association seems to discount all the substantive interests with which politics is usually associated: human wants and needs, economics, a notion of equality. As one commentator angrily puts it, "Oakeshott denies human need, economics, the body, and passion, in order to keep them out of morality and politics. . . . the result is to empty morality and politics of all value and meaning, all significant connection with our actual lives and the cares and commitments that really move us." It is all very noble, she continues, "but who wants it?"[18]

Another commentator takes the predictable route of bemoaning the lack of "practical" teachings in Oakeshott's political theory. "At a time [1976] when political discourse is heavily larded with the imagery of crisis and catastrophe and citizens are exhorted to sacrifice," this critic observes, "Oakeshott steadily, cheerfully, even maliciously, refuses to furnish solutions . . . [and] resolutely defends the cultivated life of private pleasures." His implication is that Oakeshott was unduly detached from the problems of his time and, moreover, that he blithely ignored these problems. This, such critics assert, is a symptom of his characteristically British intellectual and cultural elitism, and of his desire to cultivate the

---

17. Franco, *Political Philosophy of Michael Oakeshott,* 159; *SPDCE,* xx; Franco, *Political Philosophy of Michael Oakeshott,* 181. For an elaboration of the view that Oakeshott valued freedom for its own sake, see Jacob Segal, "Freedom and Normalization: Poststructuralism and the Liberalism of Michael Oakeshott."

18. Hannah F. Pitkin, "Inhuman Conduct and Unpolitical Theory: Michael Oakeshott's *On Human Conduct,*" 315–16.

effete life of a gentleman philosopher. It is, as a friendlier critic summarizes it, a view in which Oakeshott's thought is perceived as "too pure, formal, sterile, and negative to be morally satisfying or empirically workable."[19]

However, I believe that it is an overwhelming concern with "practical" considerations that gives rise to these and other criticisms of Oakeshott's work. Such concerns about usefulness and application highlight a widespread inability among many of Oakeshott's readers to extricate themselves from practice and to consider, with Oakeshott, what sorts of political arrangements best foster a particular moral understanding of human beings *qua* human beings. Oakeshott's concept of civil association is not concerned with human beings as "consumers" or "workers," but with what people do when they have the freedom to choose their activities. Moreover, Oakeshott's aim in *On Human Conduct* is not to recommend a particular political agenda, but to show that civil association (like the politics of skepticism) provides a framework in which individuals may best express their distinct individualities. Agents in civil association are joined not so that they may engage in a common enterprise, but rather so that they may exist "in that relation of somewhat 'watery' fidelity called civility . . . [that] does not define or even describe a common substantive purpose, interest, or 'good.'"[20]

I cannot end without at least mentioning the issue of "crisis," with which so many critics take issue in Oakeshott's work. They object to the fact that his theorizing provides no solution to the many problems that face society today. They are quite right. But he does not avoid this issue because he is irresponsible; that is, he is not simply the detached scholar and aesthete that certain commentators like to portray in their critiques. On the contrary: he had a particular view of human experience that I have been at pains to explain throughout this book, a vision that is grounded in religion and aesthetics. And he wished precisely to defend this vision against all those who can see nothing but the demands of practice and who foreshorten human character in order to address current, pressing problems. Oakeshott would answer that such problems will *always* be current and pressing, but abandoning our most essential and

---

19. Sheldon Wolin, "The Politics of Self-Disclosure," 323; Auspitz, "Individuality, Civility and Theory," 283.

20. *OHC,* 147. Oakeshott's use of the phrase *"watery" fidelity* to describe civil association comes from Aristotle's *Politics,* 1262b 16.

rewarding human pursuits is not the appropriate response. I quote at length C. S. Lewis, who discusses the importance of pursuing "useless things" during wartime, and with whom Oakeshott is in substantial agreement:

> The war creates no absolutely new situation; it simply aggravates the permanent human situation so that we can no longer ignore it. Human life has always been lived on the edge of a precipice. Human culture has always had to exist under the shadow of something infinitely more important than itself. If men had postponed the search for knowledge and beauty until they were secure, the search would never have begun. We are mistaken when we compare war with "normal life." Life has never been normal. Even those periods which we think most tranquil . . . turn out, on closer inspection, to be full of crises, alarms, difficulties, emergencies. Plausible reasons have never been lacking for putting off all merely cultural activities until some imminent danger has been averted or some crying injustice put right. But humanity long ago chose to neglect those plausible reasons. They wanted knowledge and beauty now, and would not wait for the suitable moment that never comes.

This, in sum, is Oakeshott's unspoken response to the sorts of criticisms I have quoted above. He is a defender of liberal education and philosophy, of love and friendship, of conversation and poetry. His political thought emerges as a response to the desire for a world in which these activities might be recognized and cultivated. Civil association is designed to foster a kind of moral character that is free to engage in self-determination within practices. And the relationship between agents who possess this character is one of intelligence, "enjoyed only in virtue of having been learned and understood or misunderstood."[21]

---

21. C. S. Lewis, "Learning in War-Time," 49–50; *OHC,* 112.

9

Rationalism and Gnosticism
Oakeshott and Voegelin

In the preceding chapters I have dwelt at length on Oakeshott's view of what it is to be a human being—specifically, what it means to exist with a sense of the impermanence of worldly goods and an accompanying desire to overcome this by achieving some sort of permanence or "presentness," as I called it in Chapter 3. In this attitude Oakeshott shares much with Augustine, especially regarding what might be called his "cheerful pessimism." This, I believe, is an attitude toward the world in which one maintains a clear-sighted recognition of human limitations but does not reject the goodness inherent in creation. It is an attitude in which one remains "otherworldly" in the world. To borrow a Voegelinian concept, it is to maintain the "balance of consciousness" in the face of circumstances that push inevitably toward imbalance.

I have also attempted to show that Oakeshott's most famous character—the Rationalist—is much more than a secular description of a certain kind of modern personality. Rationalism depends upon a view of morality that is both gnostic and perfectionist in character, a view that at once denies the uncertainty of existence and tries to arrange all of experience into logical, "rational" categories. It explicitly ignores the pervasiveness of the mystery in human life, arrogantly boasting that it can "fix" this mystery by constructing a system. To embrace Rationalism is to build a Tower of Babel. It is the attempt to avoid the anxiety that comes with living in the *metaxy*.

I use these Voegelinian terms quite intentionally, for I think there is a fruitful comparison to be made between Oakeshott and Voegelin regarding the nature of the human condition. Notwithstanding the obvious differences between the two thinkers, some of which I highlight at the conclusion of this chapter, the commonalities between "gnosticism" and "Rationalism" are remarkable and, to my knowledge, have gone largely unnoticed. Perhaps the reason for this lack of attention is that scholars have assumed that Oakeshott had no interest in religion, while Voegelin was *clearly* concerned with transcendence and the spiritual life.

Yet if we step past this facile separation between the two—which I hope my preceding chapters have begun to undermine—the similarities between Rationalism and gnosticism emerge strikingly. Perhaps the clearest way to introduce these is to quote at some length from one of Voegelin's most astute commentators, Glenn Hughes, who explains the situation to which both Oakeshott and Voegelin respond. Rationalism and gnosticism are their respective diagnoses of how human beings attempt to avoid the tension of existence, which may be described as follows:

> The mystery of reality is hard to bear. . . . We long for certainty: for absolute knowledge about what we are and where we came from, for assurance that our lives have some permanent meaning in the scheme of things, for immortality. The revelation of transcendence makes it certain merely that we *cannot* humanly know the ultimate truths about human origins and destiny; that our yearnings for truth, righteousness and goodness are uncertain of consummation; and that though we do participate as long as existence lasts in the permanence of transcendent meaning, we know nothing of our future or ultimate relation to imperishable being. . . . Nothing is more true of existence in the *metaxy* than that it has no resolution, no solution, in worldly time. All human accomplishment is an unfinished search within a horizon of divine mystery. This is a most disturbing fact to admit, one that understandably gives rise to anxiety. But to face this anxiety and respect the truth of the *metaxy* is precisely what is involved in maintaining the balance of consciousness.

When this balance is not maintained, various kinds of distortions occur. Some people choose to ignore the demands of this world, having come to recognize the importance of orienting themselves toward transcendence. "The conviction may then grow that only the transcendent source of the world is truly meaningful, and that the imperfect and perishing world does not deserve our deep concern." This attitude—and others related to it—leads to indifference toward many important problems. It also tends to reinforce a view of the world in which all immanence is seen as "evil."[1]

But it is the *other* form of imbalanced consciousness—that is, the de-

---

1. Glenn Hughes, "Balanced and Imbalanced Consciousness," 168–69, 171, 172.

sire to reject transcendence altogether—that appears in gnosticism and Rationalism. Gnostics and Rationalists tend to err on the side of immanence, praising the abilities of human beings to change and control their circumstances and largely discounting the mystery of existence. The gnostic tries to contract "divine order in reality to the sphere of personal existence" and desires "to bring the disorder of reality, as well as the salvation from it, into the form of a well-ordered, intelligible system." Oakeshott's Rationalist, likewise, has none of that "negative capability" that would allow him to accept "the mysteries and uncertainties of experience without any irritable search for order and distinctness." He has only "the capability of subjugating experience" and an "impatient hunger for eternity." His cast of mind is, indeed, "gnostic."[2]

In the paragraphs that follow I fill out these descriptions of gnosticism and Rationalism, noting the fundamental similarities between the two concepts. The second part of this chapter is a kind of "case study," examining the question of why, despite the similarity of their thinking on these concepts, Voegelin and Oakeshott approach Hobbes from such different vantage points, and suggesting a particular reading of Hobbes as a way of highlighting these differences. I conclude by observing several ways in which their differing views of Hobbes point to differences in their conceptions of philosophy—what exactly reason can accomplish, how reason ought to be oriented, and the limits of philosophical reflection.

Voegelin: Gnosticism

Voegelin describes gnosticism in two distinct ways: historically and psychologically. He sets out his conception of the historical emergence of gnosticism most explicitly in *The New Science of Politics,* where he locates its origin in the person of a twelfth-century monk, Joachim of Flora. It was Joachim who first conceptualized human history as a series of three successive stages, each superseding the one before it and culminating in a mystical and final "Third Realm." In his "trinitarian eschatology," contends Voegelin, "Joachim created the aggregate of symbols which govern the self-interpretation of modern political society to this day."[3]

Following closely upon this is the appearance of the "leader," who will

2. Eric Voegelin, *The Ecumenic Age,* 22; "Rationalism in Politics," in *RP,* 6–7.
3. Eric Voegelin, *The New Science of Politics,* 111.

emerge to guide all men toward the perfection of the final realm. Voegelin observes that the idea of this kind of dynamic leader began with the Franciscans, and he traces it through the Middle Ages, Renaissance, and Reformation to the "supermen" of Marx and Comte and the "paracletic leaders" of the present. Closely allied to this conception of a leader is the "prophet," whose task it is to make the inevitable course of history evident to all. Sometimes the leader and prophet blend together, though the prophet's main function is to convey to his society that the course of history is "an intelligible, meaningful whole."[4]

Voegelin identifies the final gnostic symbol as the "brotherhood of autonomous persons" that emerges to populate the final realm. No longer in need of grace, these autonomous agents will be able to perfect themselves and society through their own efforts. In Joachim's telling, the church will cease to exist because sacraments will no longer be necessary. It will be possible to achieve a perfect life without the cumbersome institutions that were formerly required, and people will live together as a "community of the spiritually perfect." It is precisely this idea that will later become the "dynamic core in the Marxian mysticism of the realm of freedom and the withering-away of the state."[5] These symbols—the Third Realm, the leader, the prophet, and the brotherhood of autonomous persons—compose the crucial parts of Voegelin's historical account of modern gnosticism as it has emerged since Joachim.

But this broad, historical description does not take account of the particular psychological characteristics of the gnostic personality, which are of the greatest importance for understanding the similarities between gnosticism and Rationalism. In *Science, Politics and Gnosticism* Voegelin addresses these psychological characteristics directly, listing them as follows. The first and most fundamental characteristic of the gnostic personality is a dissatisfaction with the world as it is and a desire to change it. Seeing the world as a "prison" from which he wishes to escape, the gnostic is fundamentally alienated from the world and desires to live in an alternative reality. "The imaginative game of liberation," explains Voegelin in *The Ecumenic Age*, "derives its momentum from an intensely experienced alienation and an equally intense revolt against it." Gnostic thinkers, he continues, "both ancient and modern, are the great psychol-

4. Ibid., 112.
5. Ibid., 113.

ogists of alienation, carriers of the Promethean revolt." Oakeshott's Rationalist, too, feels this profound sense of alienation. In his temperament one observes "a deep distrust of time" and "an irritable nervousness in the face of everything topical and transitory."[6]

Closely related to this dissatisfaction is the second characteristic Voegelin identifies, namely, the belief that the world is "intrinsically poorly organized." This assessment implicitly questions the goodness of God and His creation. For although it is quite possible that the order of being is good and it is humans who are deficient, Voegelin dryly observes that gnostics "are not inclined to discover that human beings in general and they themselves in particular are inadequate." Oakeshott's Rationalist, too, is not inclined toward self-examination but assumes that the *world* is faulty. Thus he brings the "social, political, legal and institutional inheritance of his society before the tribunal of his intellect" and attempts to reform and reorganize it.[7]

The next four characteristics Voegelin describes are closely related, all having to do with the idea of an inner-worldly salvation. The gnostic believes that "salvation from the evil of the world is possible." This is not the promised salvation that comes with faith, after death, but a transformation of the world through human action. For he thinks that a change in the order of being can take place in history. "From a wretched world," according to Voegelin, "a good one must evolve historically." Likewise, Oakeshott's Rationalist believes that final fulfillment may be achieved on earth, that through political activity a "uniform condition of perfection" may be imposed upon human conduct.[8]

The gnostic also believes, above all, that the salvation he seeks is possible through his own efforts. No longer need he depend upon a providential God; he sees the way to salvation on his own. By the same token, he no longer requires the Christian virtues of faith and hope. Moreover, he wishes to construct a "formula" for his own (and the world's) salvation. Seeing himself as a prophet, he will lead the way to the final realm of fulfillment. Once again, the Rationalist has similar tendencies. He is the consummate example of a "self-made man," someone who approves only changes that are "self-consciously induced" and

6. Eric Voegelin, *Science, Politics and Gnosticism,* 59–60; Voegelin, *Ecumenic Age,* 19; "Rationalism in Politics," in *RP,* 7.

7. Voegelin, *Science, Politics and Gnosticism,* 60; "Rationalism in Politics," in *RP,* 8.

8. Voegelin, *Science, Politics and Gnosticism,* 60; "Rationalism in Politics," in *RP,* 10.

for whom the "blank sheet of infinite possibility" lies waiting to be written upon.[9]

The crux of Voegelin's account of modern gnosticism is his contention that the gnostic has misapprehended the structure of reality and, furthermore, that this misapprehension is not naive, but deliberate. Because the gnostic lacks the strength to exist in the *metaxy* (which is the middle ground of human existence between the divine and material realms) and to endure the anxiety that comes with faith in a transcendent order, he denies transcendence altogether and attempts to save himself. But to do this, he must forget or ignore the fact that "the cosmos does not emerge from consciousness, but . . . man's consciousness emerges from the cosmos." The gnostic and the Rationalist both have inverted the proper order of things, vainly believing that they can change the order of being through their thought and action. The gnostic thus "displays his unawareness of destroying the mystery of reality by his speculative inversion" and engages in a venture that may be described as a "libidinous act of self-salvation."[10]

The attractiveness of this position derives from the sense of superiority it offers over a stubborn reality that refuses to conform. For gnosticism "surrounds the *libido dominandi* in man with a halo of spiritualism or idealism, and can always nourish its righteousness by pointing to the evil in the world." It is, at its core, a position that assumes a prideful reliance on one's own (limitless) potential, aiming at nothing less than the "transfiguration of man into superman." The gnostic believes that he has a "direct grasp of the ultimate human issues concerning human nature, human purpose, human meaning, and human destiny." With this knowledge he may attempt his escape "from the prison of the world."[11]

Oakeshott: Rationalism

The notion that life presents "a problem to be solved"—a predicament, as it were—has much in common with Oakeshott's conception of Ra-

---

9. "Rationalism in Politics," in *RP,* 8–9.

10. Voegelin, *Ecumenic Age,* 20; Ellis Sandoz, *The Voegelinian Revolution,* 241.

11. Sandoz, *The Voegelinian Revolution,* 28, 112; Stephen A. McKnight, "Voegelin's Challenge to Modernity's Claim to Be Scientific and Secular: The Ancient Theology and the Dream of Innerworldly Fulfillment," 186.

tionalism. The emphasis throughout Oakeshott's famous essay "Rationalism in Politics" is on the tendency of the Rationalist to conceive experience as a series of crises that call out for solution. Like the gnostic, the Rationalist sees experience as fundamentally flawed, and he attempts to change a world that appears unsatisfactory to him. I have already discussed Rationalism at some length in Chapter 7 and have alluded to its commonalities with gnosticism in the paragraphs above. Nevertheless, it is worthwhile briefly to summarize its essential features as a way of emphasizing its similarity to gnosticism.

Oakeshott locates the origins of Rationalism in the thought of Descartes and Bacon, the latter of whom he blames for developing a corrupting "technique" of inquiry. Bacon's technique requires that knowledge begin with a "purge of the mind" and end only with conclusions that can be demonstrably proven by means of "certain propositions." The talent or individuality of the inquirer is accordingly downplayed; the knowledge that Bacon values is to be attainable by all who seek it. Oakeshott sees this as the central epistemological assumption behind modern Rationalism: one can (and should) abandon habit, custom, and tradition as ways of knowing, since these are imprecise and uncertain. One should depend only on the sort of knowledge gained through a clearly formulated method of inquiry. But, Oakeshott argues, this is a misunderstanding of the sources of knowledge. There can be no "clean slate" in human experience, since we *always* depend on knowledge acquired in diverse ways. Moreover, the personality of the inquirer cannot help but influence the study of a given subject. According to Oakeshott, Bacon has thus misrepresented the character of intellectual inquiry.[12]

Unfortunately, this misrepresentation is widespread in the modern world. Oakeshott describes it clearly by making a distinction between what he terms "technical" and "practical" knowledge. Technical knowledge is the knowledge of the rulebook, the formulated procedure expressed in propositions and instructions for the novice (for example, "correspondence courses" and "do-it-yourself" manuals). No doubt such knowledge is valuable (a convenient way of learning to tile one's bathroom floor), but it is only one type of knowledge. A major problem with Rationalism is that it mistakes the part for the whole, by supposing that *everything* can be learned through technical instruction.

---

12. See "Rationalism in Politics," in *RP,* 18–22.

The more important (and more often ignored) type of knowledge is what Oakeshott calls "practical" knowledge. Practical knowledge is the knowledge of the apprentice, gained only by observation of a master or—in politics—of a tradition of conduct. Practical knowledge is not formulated in a rulebook, nor is it susceptible to propositions. Though it relies on technical knowledge (for example, one cannot learn how to play the piano *musically* without first being able to play scales) it adds something essential to this knowledge. What it adds is not more technical mastery, but rather "style," "prowess," or "expertness." Practical knowledge is thus "having a feel" for one's pursuit or being able to adapt on the spur of the moment to any new circumstance. It is, in Aristotelian terms, a *hexis* for any given activity. Rationalists tend to dislike this practical conception of knowledge and activity, because it is difficult to attain and there is no guarantee that one will be successful in its pursuit. It is somewhat mysterious, and does not conform to any sort of preconceived method. The Rationalist eschews this kind of knowledge, preferring the shortcut that is provided by the adoption of an ideology. "Better to appeal to certain principles," declares the Rationalist, "than to orient oneself by one's own experience." Arguing against this sort of thinking, Oakeshott suggests that true moral education comes only in the context of an "unselfconscious moral tradition."[13]

Oakeshott's Rationalist, therefore, may be described as follows: he favors the "clean slate" approach to knowledge, believes wholeheartedly in "technical" rather than "practical" knowledge, approaches experience as a series of problems to be solved, and relies on ideology as a shortcut to knowing how to conduct himself. The Rationalist, like the gnostic, grasps at certainty as a way of overcoming his anxiety about his place in the world. Although Oakeshott does not use the terms *immanent* and *transcendent* as ways of describing the poles of experience, it is clear that his Rationalist errs on the side of overconfidence in human ability. The idea that anything should remain inaccessible to the human mind—that some things are not susceptible to rational propositions—is an idea with which he has no patience.

In sum, both the gnostic and the Rationalist are driven by their desires to overcome the world and to make it conform to their own ideas of right order. They look toward "the eschatological Future in modernity,"

13. "Rationalism in Politics," in *RP,* 41.

where they expect to find perfection. In his review of Voegelin's *New Science of Politics*, Oakeshott describes gnosticism in a way that could apply equally well to Rationalism. The gnostic's aim, he explains, is to "secure the monopoly of existential representation which nevertheless is unavoidably destructive of that existential order." The "truth" of this order is "a dream that bears no relation to the *conditio humana* and in the end it can be maintained only by forcible suppression of whatever opposes it." Oakeshott saw Marx as the quintessential example of this kind of gnostic/Rationalist thinker. Marx believed in the emergence of a new age that would facilitate "a 'perfect' condition of human circumstance about which little is known except that there will be no place in it for governing as a specific activity." As is well known, Voegelin criticizes Marx along similar lines in *Science, Politics and Gnosticism*.[14]

It would seem likely, therefore, that, given their similar ideas about gnosticism and Rationalism, Oakeshott and Voegelin would also agree about the character of other thinkers. And yet their evaluations of Hobbes could not be more divergent. The question, therefore, with which the second part of this chapter will be concerned is this: Why should Oakeshott and Voegelin have reached such radically different understandings of Hobbes? In other words, why does Voegelin see Hobbes as the quintessential gnostic, while Oakeshott sees him as no Rationalist at all?

Voegelin on Hobbes

Voegelin's classification of Hobbes as a gnostic thinker intuitively seems correct. Hobbes, after all, is the creator of a "system" (that favorite pursuit of gnostics), and he goes so far as to suggest that this system can solve the problems of human nature.[15] With his typical rhetorical style and power, Voegelin thus makes a strong case for this reading of Hobbes, and I will recount here the major components of his argument. It centers around one major idea, namely, that Hobbes has collapsed the tension between immanent and transcendent being. He has, in other words, upset the "balance of consciousness." Voegelin analyzes this collapse on

---

14. Sandoz, *Voegelinian Revolution*, 242; Oakeshott, review of *The New Science of Politics*, in *WIH*, 232; *MPME*, 96; for Voegelin's criticism of Marx, see particularly *Science, Politics and Gnosticism*, 23–28.

15. *Science, Politics and Gnosticism*, 71.

two distinct levels: those of the individual and of society. Given the "anthropological principle" that the city is man writ large, the individual and society are of course inextricably linked. Yet it is worthwhile to clarify Voegelin's argument by considering each of these in turn.

The conception of a human being as composed of different types of being (ranging from apeirontic depth to the desire for godliness) is well known to all readers of Voegelin. It follows from this account of human nature that some parts of the psyche are oriented toward transcendence while others are oriented toward immanence. In a complete person all parts are constantly present and all are vital to the health of the psyche. If parts of the soul are ignored or denied, then the person suffers from various forms of deficiency and incompleteness. For man must participate in the *entirety* of experience, "noetically exploring the structure of reality as far as it is intelligible and spiritually coping with the insight into its movement from the divine Beginning to the divine Beyond of its structure."[16]

According to Voegelin, Hobbes has consciously and deliberately ignored the higher realms of spirit in man by describing the soul only in terms of its "passions." Passions require governance by reason, says Voegelin, and by constant recourse to transcendent reality. But Hobbes gives no such account of the soul. Hobbes moreover appears to Voegelin to have neglected the extent to which the passions are the source of corruption in man. Because Hobbes "did not . . . interpret passion as the source of corruption in the life of the spirit, . . . he could not interpret the nature of man from the vantage point of the maximum of differentiation through the experiences of transcendence." Furthermore, in focusing on passions Hobbes has chosen to ignore the objects of those passions and has thus placed himself in opposition to classic and Christian moral philosophy.[17] In other words, in Voegelin's view Hobbes misrepresented the nature of human beings in order to construct his gnostic vision.

It might have been possible for Hobbes to save himself in Voegelin's eyes had Hobbes argued that the passions were to be "rightly ordered," although this begs the question of how passions could order themselves without the aid of a governing faculty of reason. But Voegelin finds that Hobbes has made no attempt at orienting passions rightly; in fact, he has

16. Eric Voegelin, *Anamnesis,* 114; Voegelin, *Ecumenic Age,* 28.
17. Voegelin, *The New Science of Politics,* 180.

perverted the classic Augustinian distinction between *amor sui* and *amor dei*. Voegelin observes that Hobbes has completely removed the *amor dei* and "relied for his psychology on the *amor sui*, in his language the self-conceit or pride of the individual, alone."[18] Love of self—in the desire to avoid death, in the hope of preeminence, in the never-ceasing wish for more—is made the organizing principle of human personality. Hobbes has thus turned the natural order of things upside down.

The argument next moves to the level of "society," where Voegelin finds the same corruption that existed in Hobbes's account of the individual. A fully differentiated society, in Voegelin's account, is conscious of itself as existing in a tension between divine and human reality. Members of this society know—or ought to know—that they will not find their fulfillment solely in their existence as "citizens" but rather in another realm altogether. By its very nature Christianity is a truth of the soul that lies *beyond* immanent existence, and fulfillment comes not in this world but in another. But Hobbes's project of constructing a "civil theology" collapses the transcendent truth of divine reality into the immanent realm of political activity. He has attempted to eliminate the tension of life in this "in-between" state, but has succeeded only in eliminating the transcendent realm itself.

Specifically, Voegelin argues that Hobbes has eliminated the transcendent because Hobbes attempts to show that the immanent (civil law) can and should "contain" the transcendent (the law of nature). In other words, for Hobbes the law of nature derives its force over men *only secondarily* by being God-given law. Its primary force comes from the fact that it is promulgated by the sovereign. Voegelin summarizes Hobbes's argument as follows: "[The] law of nature, finally, is not a law actually governing human existence before the men, in whom it lives as a disposition toward peace, have followed its precept by combining in a civil society under a public representative, the sovereign." Thus divine law is made subject to a human ruler, all opportunity for public debate is eliminated, and the potentially positive tension caused by the conflict between divine and human law is removed. Hobbes has reverted back to the "compactness" of a society in which the distinction between immanent and transcendent is not recognized, denying the very existence "of a tension between the truth of the soul and the truth of society." As

18. Ibid., 184.

Voegelin reads Hobbes, "civil" theology now exhausts theology itself. This is the crucial element of Voegelin's interpretation of Hobbes as a gnostic. "With this idea . . . of abolishing the tensions of history by the spreading of a new truth, Hobbes reveals his own Gnostic intentions," explains Voegelin. "The attempt at freezing history into an everlasting constitution is an instance of the general class of Gnostic attempts at freezing history into an everlasting final realm on this earth."[19]

Oakeshott on Hobbes

It would appear that Oakeshott has set himself a difficult task in making the case that Hobbes is not a Rationalist. Oakeshott's case, however, is founded on a claim about the nature of knowledge. Oakeshott does not consider Hobbes a Rationalist because of Hobbes's deep skepticism and his belief in the limits of philosophy. For the Rationalist, we should recall, believes that reason is the answer to every problem and that the world can be explained and fixed by means of the reason that resides in the Rationalist himself. Nothing, of course, could be further from Hobbes's conception of reason. For while it is true that Hobbes uses reason to explain the causes of civil association and the necessary conditions for its survival, Hobbes's reason has little in common with that of Oakeshott's Rationalist. It will be instructive, therefore, to distinguish these two types of reason: Rationalist and Hobbesian.

As noted above, the Rationalist imbues reason with almost magical powers. It is available to all alike, requires little in the way of prior education, and is proposed as the solution to all problems. Rationalism in politics is the politics of ideology, of the rulebook, of the politically inexperienced. But "reason" for Hobbes is something quite different from this. Reason merely investigates causes and effects and does not concern itself with "final causes" because, asks Hobbes, how could one know these? Reason's aim, when turned to theorizing politics, is merely to provide the "minimum conditions" for the establishment and maintenance of civil association. In this endeavor, Oakeshott observes that Hobbes is in good company, for his aspiration is not unlike Augustine's. Civil association itself does not provide felicity or salvation; it is merely a "negative

19. Ibid., 154, 160, 161.

gift" that takes away some of the impediments that tend to inhibit an individual's search for fulfillment. In Oakeshott's view, Hobbes, like Augustine, aims merely at peace—not, like the Rationalist, at an immanent realm of perfection. Oakeshott maintains that Hobbes shows "no sign (indeed, quite the reverse) of understanding the activity of governing as an omnicompetent activity." Absent from Hobbes's thought is "any idea whatever of government as the agent of human improvement and perfection (the idea of human perfection is for him absurd), and there are present some very precise and far-reaching ideas about the limited, though very important, objects appropriate to the activity of governing."[20]

Given Hobbes's conception of reason as the investigation of cause and effect, it follows that things that do not lend themselves to this formulation are excluded from the realm of reason. And so, of course, theology is excluded. One cannot assert that God is "caused" nor say exactly what the "effects" of God's existence are, at least not in the normal language of cause and consequent. In speaking of God, one moves outside the realm of nature into the "supernatural" or "transcendent" or "divine." Whatever one chooses to call this realm, it is not part of philosophy as Hobbes approaches it. Yet this does not mean that Hobbes denies its *existence;* for as Oakeshott reminds us, Hobbes denies only its "rationality." We can have, Oakeshott quotes Hobbes, "no natural knowledge of man's estate after death." Philosophy, in Hobbes's view, "excludes the consideration of the universe as a whole, things infinite, things eternal, final causes and things known only by divine grace or revelation."[21] This means that "natural knowledge" of these things is limited, not that the things themselves do not exist or that we cannot apprehend them in other ways (meditation, prayer, intuition).

It does appear that meditation and prayer were not Hobbes's personal gifts or inclinations, though his ideas about civil association leave a significant realm of freedom for those who do wish to engage in such activities. But Hobbes clearly believed that transcendent reality stands at some remove from the practical political arrangements of a society. These must rest on some minimal and less-disputed foundation. The crux of Oakeshott's argument about Hobbes's skepticism is that he did not flatly *deny* the existence of God or transcendent reality, he merely questioned our

---

20. "Introduction to *Leviathan*," in *HCA,* 79; *PFPS,* 28.
21. "Introduction to *Leviathan*," in *HCA,* 25, 75, 18.

ability to know such things by means of philosophy. He was a skeptic, not a dogmatic atheist.[22] His idea of civil association does not deny the possibility of faith, but it does render it an individual matter.

Oakeshott seems to agree with this assessment of things in his own philosophical writings, since in general he focuses not on divine experience, but on human affairs and institutions. This focus, indeed, is what has caused casual readers of Oakeshott to conclude that he is not interested in religion. But I think the more accurate reading of Oakeshott is that he follows Augustine in observing the sharp differentiation between the "two cities." Politics, for Oakeshott, is the epitome of practical endeavor, something that must be addressed on its own terms. As he observes in *On Human Conduct,* "the theorist easily understands that nothing will come of questioning everything at the same time. . . . he has a heavenly home, but he is in no hurry to reach it. If he is concerned to theorize moral conduct or civil association he must forswear metaphysics." In other words, a theorist must forswear metaphysics until he turns his attention explicitly *to* metaphysics, as Oakeshott wished to do toward the end of his life.[23]

And yet even Oakeshott himself does not uphold this division absolutely. I have argued throughout this book that Oakeshott's understanding of the human condition derives from his reflections on religion and aesthetics, and that he praises a certain kind of moral personality that satisfies such reflection—someone who recognizes that the fundamental religious task is self-understanding, and that moral conduct results from that self-understanding. Oakeshott's political thought, then, revolves around a certain kind of human character: someone who has embraced individuality, who is unafraid to make choices, and who strives, so far as possible, to live fully in the present. Thus religion and politics are not *absolutely* divorced in his thought; they just lie at a far remove from each other.

The foregoing pages have suggested that the primary reasons that Oakeshott and Voegelin read Hobbes differently result from their quite different understandings of philosophy (reason) and transcendence. In

22. The question of Hobbes's position on religion is, of course, much debated. The dimensions of this debate are well summarized in Ronald Hepburn's essay "Hobbes on the Knowledge of God."

23. *OHC,* 25; see Patrick Riley, "In Appreciation: Michael Oakeshott, Philosopher of Individuality," 649.

Voegelin's view Hobbes ignored the fundamental structure of reality by collapsing immanent and transcendent and was therefore a gnostic, while Oakeshott sees Hobbes's reason as skeptical and his undertaking as limited, and so he was not a Rationalist. But such observations beg the questions of exactly *how* and *why* the two philosophers differ so dramatically, when their conceptions of gnosticism and Rationalism are so similar. What is it about transcendence that is essential for Voegelin's political theorizing but not for Oakeshott's? Why does Oakeshott contend that philosophy and practice are separate realms, while Voegelin argues that practice *must* be guided by a proper philosophical understanding? These are only some of the crucial questions that a comparison of Oakeshott and Voegelin brings to the fore. In the paragraphs that follow, I consider an alternative reading of Hobbes, a reading that is not exactly Oakeshott's own but that is suggested by his writings on Hobbes. I do this as a way of highlighting and suggesting some of the basic differences between Voegelin and Oakeshott, which I discuss in the conclusion of this chapter.

Hobbes, Religion, and the Rule of Law

There is little scholarly consensus on the question of Hobbes and his attitude toward religion.[24] Perhaps the most dominant view of Hobbes is that he wished to use religion for his own secular and political purposes. Both Voegelin and Leo Strauss set forth some version of this view. There are, however, legitimate reasons for thinking that Hobbes was out not to discredit religion absolutely, but rather to redefine it in such a way that it might become more compatible with individual reasoning.[25] There is, in addition, ample evidence in his writings that Hobbes's aim was not to found a "hedonist" political philosophy, but rather expressly to *prevent* hedonistic passions (which are always present in human beings) from

24. For summaries of this debate, see Keith Brown, *Hobbes Studies,* and Paul D. Cooke, *Hobbes and Christianity: Reassessing the Bible in* Leviathan. Several recent commentators make a strong case for taking Hobbes's religion seriously. Among them are Paul Dumochel, "The Political Problem of Religion: Hobbes's Reading of the Bible," and A. P. Martinich, *The Two Gods of* Leviathan. For the opposite view, see Charles D. Tarlton, "The Despotical Doctrine of Hobbes, Part I: The Liberalization of *Leviathan*."

25. For Strauss's view of Hobbes, see *The Political Philosophy of Hobbes: Its Basis and Genesis.*

dominating the better ones. I want to offer two points that might provide a foundation for a more positive reading of Hobbes.

The first point concerns the question of religion in Hobbes's *Leviathan*. While many readers agree with the dominant view of Hobbes's alleged impiety, others make the argument that in the *Leviathan* Hobbes is setting out a particular view of religion that, though not familiar or "orthodox," is nonetheless Christian. What does this sort of Christianity look like? First, it relies primarily on the natural reason of human beings and on their rational apprehension of God's word through natural laws and their reading of the Bible. It therefore places a great deal of responsibility on individuals to consider religious questions for themselves. Therefore, although obedience may yet be due to others, the "intellectual faculty" is not to be submitted to anyone else. It is true that Hobbes posits an all-powerful sovereign who is to legislate for the commonwealth, but at the beginning of the third part of the *Leviathan* ("Of a Christian Commonwealth") he reminds his readers that we should not "renounce our senses and experience, nor (that which is the undoubted word of God) our natural reason." These are the "talents which he hath put into our hands to negotiate till the coming again of our blessed Saviour; and therefore not to be folded up in the napkin of an implicit faith."[26] In other words, subjects owe their civil rulers obedience and respect, but these subjects retain the freedom to decide religious matters for themselves.

This understanding of Christianity depends, of course, upon Hobbes's idea that true Christian faith consists largely in "inward" persuasion, for Hobbes downplays the importance of external professions and actions and stresses the personal, interior character of belief.[27] If a ruler forbids faith in Christ, Hobbes asserts, "such forbidding is of no effect, because belief and unbelief never follow men's commands." Faith consists in each person's private belief, which neither a sovereign nor anyone else can

---

26. See Wendell John Coats Jr., *Oakeshott and His Contemporaries*, and Timothy Fuller, "The Idea of Christianity in Hobbes's *Leviathan*"; Hobbes, *Leviathan*, 246, 245.

27. A problem arises, of course, when one's inward religious beliefs conflict with what the sovereign commands. Hobbes addresses this problem in chapter 42 of *Leviathan* and gives an answer that is perhaps not satisfying to many readers: "This we may say: that whatsoever a subject . . . is compelled to [do] in obedience to his sovereign, and doth it not in order to his own mind, but in order to the laws of his country, that action is not his, but his sovereign's; nor is it he that in this case denieth Christ before men, but his governor, and the law of his country" (339).

perceive. "For internal faith is in its own nature invisible, and consequently exempted from all human jurisdiction," Hobbes continues, and the civil power has jurisdiction only over a person's *external* actions and words. "And of that which cannot be accused, there is no judge at all but God, that knoweth the heart." Thus the experience of transcendence is unique for each person, and as for "the inward *thought* and *belief* of men, which human governors can take no notice of . . . they are not voluntary, nor the effect of the laws, but of the unrevealed will, and of the power, of God, and consequently fall not under obligation." The sovereign may oblige me to be obedient to his laws but not "to think any otherwise than my reason persuades me."[28]

Moreover, in addition to his emphases on the individuality and inwardness of the religious experience, Hobbes seems to be attempting to define a sort of Christianity that does not look constantly to the future but rather insists on a type of immediacy in religious experience. This might be one way of accounting for Hobbes's rejection of the *summum bonum*. That is, he does so not because the idea of good is wholly unimportant, but because the orientation toward such a future good entails a lack of focus on *present* religious understanding. Such an idea is clearly echoed in Oakeshott's thinking. The future is a "fiction of the mind," Hobbes declares, and as Fuller has put it, what Hobbes actually requires is "an account of revelation that will show how to approach the future in a non-fictive way, or . . . to suspend people's preoccupation with the future in favor of the improvement of their spiritual strength."[29]

Religion, if it arises merely out of fear and anxiety about the future, is no better than superstition. For true religion, fear of the future must be downplayed as a motive force in favor of an individual's working out of his own religious understanding by reading the Bible and reflecting on what is found there. Rejecting the *summum bonum,* then, "is to begin to appreciate fully what the life of Christian faith really is," Fuller points out. "The transformative power of Christian faith is not seen by Hobbes to imply a radical transformation of the world as it now is, but rather to induce a radical transformation in our understanding of the significance, or insignificance, of the present world." Religion, if it is to have any effect on our lives, cannot be superstitious or based on fear of spirits, nor

28. Hobbes, *Leviathan,* 338, 354, 373, 318, 246.
29. Hobbes, *Leviathan,* 14; Fuller, "The Idea of Christianity," 142.

does it depend on some supposed state of future perfection. Hobbes down-plays the importance of tradition and church dogma in favor of a reformed version of Christianity that emphasizes personal, inward conviction. While Hobbes's understanding of Christianity does have the practical aim of reducing the conflict between people who claim to be divinely inspired, it does not thereby necessarily preclude the experience of transcendence altogether.[30]

There is another ground upon which Hobbes might be defended against his critics, and which may help to illuminate Oakeshott's debt to Hobbes. This concerns his notion of the rule of law. As I have already noted, Voegelin takes Hobbes to task for emphasizing man's passions at the expense of his reason. He implies that Hobbes *approves* a lack of governance for the passions. It is worth recalling what Voegelin says on this subject. In Hobbes's work, Voegelin observes, "the generic nature of man must be studied in terms of human passions; the objects of the passions are no legitimate object of inquiry. This is the fundamental counter position to classic and Christian moral philosophy. . . . Aristotelian ethics starts from the purposes of action and explores the order of human life in terms of the ordination of all actions toward a highest purpose, the *summum bonum*." When the *summum bonum* is taken away, however, the source of order disappears from human life, because for Voegelin social order depends on an Aristotelian and Christian *homonoia* ("community of spirit").[31] Rationality entails a sort of like-mindedness about the common good of a society. But although Voegelin is a forceful defender of the idea that a rationally ordered community must have a point of orientation—a common good for all—Oakeshott argues just as forcefully that there are alternative ways of conceiving rational political order.

How might this "nonteleological" conception of political order be described? Perhaps it would be best to return to Hobbes himself, since he so boldly rejects the classic tradition of philosophy.[32] First, although Hobbes forthrightly rejects the *summum bonum* early on in *Leviathan*, it does not necessarily follow that to do so is by definition to be "irrational." For while Voegelin argues for the *summum bonum* as necessary for rational ethics and politics, there remains the question of clarifying what

30. Fuller, "The Idea of Christianity," 172; Hobbes, *Leviathan,* chaps. 12 and 32.

31. Voegelin, *The New Science of Politics,* 180.

32. Note in particular his vitriolic criticisms of Aristotle and others in *Leviathan,* chap. 46.

we can say that it is. The idea of a *summum bonum* presupposes both that we could know what it is and that we could agree on it—premises that are questioned by Hobbes. As he famously observes, why has there been "such diversity of ways in running to the same mark, felicity, if it be not night amongst us, or at least a mist?"[33]

If there is a lack of public agreement about the *summum bonum,* as there certainly seems to have been in Hobbes's time, can there be an alternative solution that might yet provide the framework for a rationally ordered society? Hobbes answers that it is not necessary to agree on the "end" of a society. Instead, we ought merely to agree on the "formal" or "procedural" rules that govern that society so that individuals might be free to pursue their self-chosen purposes. This manifests itself in an accepted "rule of law" as an arrangement "that does not elevate, promote, or defend any particular conception of good. The variety of satisfactions human beings imagine to be desirable precludes the use of law to promote or discourage particular versions of fulfillment. Rather, law is an instrumentality indicating a virtue compatible with many different goods. Law maximizes the liberty of individuals to develop their lives as they see fit." In other words, resolving the question of the *summum bonum* is no longer necessary. What then *does* become necessary is the establishment of a legal framework that minimizes conflicts between individuals. Though this is not the traditional organization of society around a *summum bonum,* it is nevertheless a moral agreement in which the actors acknowledge that they will abide by the "rules of the game." Oakeshott makes this point in *On Human Conduct.* Civil association, he maintains, "is a moral condition; it is not concerned with the satisfaction of wants and with substantive outcomes but with the terms upon which the satisfaction of wants may be sought. And politics is concerned with determining the desirable norms of civil conduct and with the approval or disapproval of civil rules which, because they qualify the pursuit of purposes, cannot be inferred from the purposes pursued."[34] This is, indeed, a different way of thinking about politics, and it may be unsatisfactory to many. It does, however, provide a rational alternative to Voegelin's requirement that society be oriented toward a common good.

Furthermore, in the context of this "rule of law" society, the sovereign

---

33. Ibid., 412.
34. Fuller, "The Idea of Christianity," 113; *OHC,* 174.

is often understood by critics to be equivalent to a tyrant, but is instead merely the *emblem* of this rule of law and "not the trustee or director of a common substantive purpose." Hobbes maintains that it is in the sovereign's interest to follow the natural law as well as to make the laws. It is, of course, true that the sovereign's power is absolute, but this absolute power is not given so that the sovereign can abuse his subjects or take advantage of them. The interest of the sovereign and his people is one and the same, Hobbes says; and thus a prudent sovereign will act within strict limits.[35] William Connolly is especially clear on this point:

> What happens if the sovereign overreaches himself and tries to govern too many areas of life? First, Hobbes thinks that a sovereign power that over-reaches itself will fail eventually. Because the laws will become too many and too complicated, and many will be unenforceable. But second, the sovereign, though created by an earthly pact, is ultimately accountable to God. This is a central reason Hobbes prefers monarchy to either democ-racy or aristocratic rule. While the monarch does not sin against his sub-jects in acting capriciously or ruthlessly, he does sin against God in breaking a law of nature. This unity between the will of the sovereign and the will of the individual is not operative in other forms of rule; its pres-ence in this case makes it possible to hold the monarch responsible as an individual when sinning against God in his capacity as sovereign: But in a monarchy, if the monarch makes any decree against the laws of nature, he sins himself; because in him the civil will and the natural are all one.

The sovereign is compelled to protect the safety of his people "not by care applied to individuals, further than their protection from injuries when they shall complain, but by a general providence, contained in pub-lic instruction, both of doctrine and example, and in the making and ex-ecuting of good laws."[36] In short, there is to be no special treatment for certain people, just a general providence for all alike.

This, then, is the rule of law in Hobbes: a formal, procedural set of rules overseen by a sovereign who shares the interest of his people. The state thus no longer depends on a *summum bonum* and is understood in-stead as "the embodiment of rules of conduct for minimizing the colli-

---

35. *OHC,* 233; see *Leviathan:* "The riches, power, and honour of a monarch arise only from the riches, strength and reputation of his subjects. For no king can be rich, nor glor-ious, nor secure, whose subjects are either poor, or contemptible" (120).

36. William Connolly, *Political Theory and Modernity,* 36–37; Hobbes, *Leviathan,* 219.

sions and maximizing the forbearance among *individuals who cannot know one another's destinies.*" Virtue, here, is self-restraint. It is true, of course, that this is not an outwardly heroic virtue; but it does argue against the idea that Hobbes's emphasis on "passions" was meant to encourage the indiscriminate expression of those passions. As Peter Hayes observes, the "Hobbesian contract, the mutual renunciation of individual power to the sovereign, incorporates a renunciation of the right to seek unlimited power over others. The purpose of the state is not to encourage the oppression of the weak by the strong, but rather to give individuals the opportunity to use their peaceful, creative and non-adversarial powers to develop the benefits of civilization."[37] Hobbes thus set out the conditions for society organized around the "rule of law" in the absence of a *summum bonum*.

The purpose of this section has been to suggest two starting points for an alternative reading of Hobbes: that there is a conception of religion to be found in *Leviathan* and that Hobbes does not sanction all passions, but rather constructs a "rule of law" meant to rein in certain passions. Of course, this presentation begs two questions. First, does Hobbes's focus on the "inwardness" of religion neglect the outward religious actions that arise as a *result* of that inward belief? Can Christianity be understood as primarily an inward religion? And second, it may be good so far as it goes to discuss a rule of law in Hobbes, but what kind of safeguards does Hobbes provide against a sovereign who chooses to abuse his powers and to destroy that fragile rule of law? These are legitimate objections to the "alternative" reading I have set out above. Nevertheless, such a reading suggests that the persistent negative view of Hobbes is worth reconsidering. Hobbes's work seems to allow room for an interpretation that takes into account his discussion of religion in parts 3 and 4 of *Leviathan* as well as his significant emphasis on restraint and moderation within a rule of law. Oakeshott's largely sympathetic treatment of Hobbes encourages this view.[38]

I now return to the question of what we might conclude about

---

37. Coats, *Oakeshott and His Contemporaries,* 63; Peter Hayes, "Hobbes's Bourgeois Moderation," 74.

38. The best treatment of Oakeshott's views on Hobbes is Ian Tregenza's recent book *Michael Oakeshott on Hobbes.* Other good, article-length treatments are Bruce P. Frohnen, "Oakeshott's Hobbesian Myth: Pride, Character and the Limits of Reason," and Ted H. Miller, "Oakeshott's Hobbes and the Fear of Political Rationalism."

Oakeshott's and Voegelin's general approaches to philosophy on the basis of their conflicting analyses of Hobbes. For while their concepts of gnosticism and Rationalism are strikingly similar, other aspects of their philosophical outlooks differ significantly.

Teleology and the *Summum Bonum*

First, there is a general difference in "scope" between the two philosophers. Although Oakeshott discusses many types of experience—including poetry, religion, politics, history, and education—he tends to consider these topics in a rather circumscribed way, as is implied in his idea that there are "modes" of experience. His analyses focus on particular "levels of being" (to borrow a Voegelinian phrase), although Oakeshott does not distinguish levels in a vertical hierarchy. On the other hand, Voegelin tends to relate all phenomena to the "measuring stick" of the entire realm of experience, ranging from immanent to transcendent. Not to do so is, for Voegelin, a violation of the order of being that permeates all of existence. In simplest terms, Oakeshott focuses on particular problems—political activity, poetry, or education—without relating these to an overarching and governing purpose. Indeed, in his discussion of politics as "civil association," Oakeshott explicitly rejects the idea that there should be any common purpose for the members of a state. Voegelin, in contrast, suggests that a "community of spirit" (*homonoia*) is required for a society to be coherent.[39]

To put this point another way, the two philosophers differ over the question of teleology. Oakeshott has often been chided for following Hobbes in throwing out the *summum bonum,* for to do so is seen as rejecting the fundamental condition for rational political association. The *summum bonum,* according to Voegelin, is the essential condition of rationality itself. In his discussion of Hobbes, Voegelin makes this clear: "Now, Hobbes knows that human action can be considered rational only if it is oriented beyond all intermediate stages of ends and means to a last end, this same *summum bonum.* . . . if there is no *summum bonum,* however, there is no point of orientation that can endow human activity with rationality."[40] The question this raises, however, is twofold. First, *did* Hobbes

39. See *OHC,* 129; see Sandoz, *Voegelinian Revolution,* 20–21.
40. Voegelin, *Science, Politics and Gnosticism,* 70.

and Oakeshott "know" that human action is rational only if it is oriented to a last end? The possible answers are (a) that they did know this and purposely ignored it or (b) that they knew no such thing. If the latter is correct, we must consider a second question: if there are other ways of orienting one's action besides the *summum bonum,* what would these be? And what exactly was Hobbes's (and, for that matter, Oakeshott's) problem with the idea of a *telos*?

One possible answer immediately suggests itself. It relates, once again, to the thought of Hobbes, and particularly to his skepticism. The problem with teleology, for Hobbes and Oakeshott alike, lies in our ability to know what our *summum bonum* consists in. While there are any number of goods that one might aim at in a more intermediate fashion, postulating a final good for man lies beyond the scope of philosophy for both Hobbes and Oakeshott. Is our final good the life of pure contemplation? Or is it the life of the religious mystic? Or might it be a simple life lived in devotion to one's family? Selfless devotion to one's country? Any of these goods is admirable, but they are vastly different, and each requires distinct choices and sacrifices. Neither Oakeshott nor Hobbes could postulate one of these alternatives as the *summum bonum,* nor would either philosopher have found much use in talking abstractly about "the good" without specifying what it is for a concrete human being. Thus they conceived of rationality as something other than orienting oneself toward a far-off good. It is therefore possible for Hobbes *not* to have "known" that "action can be considered rational only if it is oriented . . . to a last end."[41] Voegelin certainly believed that action must be oriented this way, but it seems to remain a rather more open question than he allows. In simplest terms, the core question is as follows: how can we know our *summum bonum,* and if we know it, how exactly does it help us in choosing our actions?

Different Casts of Mind

But although contrasting approaches to the question of teleology are important in understanding Voegelin and Oakeshott's philosophical differences, there is another important contrast that has more to do with style than content. In his introduction to *Leviathan,* Oakeshott reminds his

41. Ibid.

readers that one would do well to consider the "temperament, cast of mind, and style of writing" of a philosopher as a means of better understanding him. And this holds true for readers of Oakeshott and Voegelin, too. It is a simple point: Voegelin saw philosophy as therapy for a disordered age, while Oakeshott saw it as a pursuit that offers us no *direct* guide to conduct. Voegelin observes that the gnostic impulse "may pervade a society with the weird, ghostly atmosphere of a lunatic asylum, as we experience it in our time in the Western crisis." The gnostic's attempt "at world destruction will not destroy the world, but will only increase the disorder in society."[42] Philosophy's task, therefore, is to combat this disorder. Voegelin's work is a forceful and direct response to the atrocities of the twentieth century, and he locates the roots of these atrocities in long-established intellectual currents.

Oakeshott, on the other hand, rarely speaks of crisis. His style is detached, urbane, skeptical—and, some would say, ultimately unsatisfying, since he offers us no solution to the "problem" of modernity.[43] But then again Oakeshott did not necessarily see modernity as a problem, and this distinguishes him from Voegelin and others of his generation. Oakeshott was not, however, uncritical, nor did he accept without question the values of modern society; but Oakeshott understood himself as a philosopher, and he understood philosophy itself to stand apart from politics, even as it considers politics a subject worthy of examination. Ultimately, the political philosopher, in Oakeshott's view, can do little to affect the politics of his own time. This is, admittedly, a very unusual view, and it has appeared to many critics as if it unduly discounts the position of the philosopher. But here it is possible to see clearly why he and Voegelin are at odds: Voegelin argues throughout his corpus that a proper understanding of philosophy is essential for understanding politics, and that without the right philosophical grounding society is in grave danger. Oakeshott, on the other hand, categorically separates philosophy and politics; and one should remember that Oakeshott offers us no "solution" to Rationalism, for to do so would be to concede the battle. Indeed, the problem/solution construct is largely absent in Oakeshott's thought, whereas it is central to Voegelin's.

42. "Introduction to *Leviathan,*" in *HCA,* 9; Voegelin, *The New Science of Politics,* 170; Voegelin, *Science, Politics and Gnosticism,* 9.
43. As one recent commentator has argued, he is, unlike Voegelin and Strauss, a *defender* of modernity. See Efraim Podoksik's *In Defence of Modernity.*

Transcendence

The question of transcendent experience in politics is, of course, an ex-traordinarily complex one; and it is also closely tied to the question of teleology, since on many accounts man's *telos* is his reconciliation with God. Voegelin's conception of transcendence is that it somehow permeates all of political activity, as explained in his famous "principle of complete-ness." Indeed, transcendence lies at the heart of all human experience, according to Voegelin: "Man experiences himself as tending beyond his human imperfection toward the perfection of the divine ground. . . . any construction of man as a world-immanent entity will destroy the meaning of existence, because it deprives man of his specific human-ity."[44] Now, it is hard to argue with this formulation; for certainly most human beings perceive that they are not complete in themselves, and that there exist realms of being of which they are only dimly aware. What is less clear is exactly *how* this transcendence ought to structure political existence in the world. It would seem to be possible to see tran-scendence as an essential part of human life, as I have argued Oakeshott does, without making it a part of all political theorizing. It is important to recall that for Hobbes and Oakeshott, political activity is one of the *least* transcendent of human undertakings; it provides the minimum con-ditions for peace so that people may be free to seek transcendence where they may find it. How ought one to reconcile the directly conflicting views of Voegelin, on the one hand, and Oakeshott, on the other?

Perhaps a starting point for thinking about this problem is to observe that Oakeshott and Voegelin come to political philosophy with quite dif-ferent assumptions. Voegelin's conception of politics might be called "broad" and Oakeshott's "narrow," in that when Voegelin speaks of polit-ical activity he seems to mean far more than attending to the institutional arrangements of a society. Political life for Voegelin seems to consist not only in politics as it is usually understood but also in moral and religious activity of all sorts. Indeed, as Voegelin puts it in his introduction to *The New Science of Politics,* his analysis of politics is an "exploration of the symbols by which political societies interpret themselves as representa-tives of a transcendent truth." Oakeshott, on the other hand, sees no such function for politics. The civil condition, in his view, is something that

44. Voegelin, *Anamnesis,* 114, 103–4.

exists for human beings in their particularly human situation; the philosopher's task is to discern "the mode of intelligent relationship it postulates."[45] In designating a limited scope for politics Oakeshott's thought appears particularly "modern," especially in contrast to Voegelin's expansive, "classical" conception. But the crucial questions regarding Oakeshott and Hobbes in this respect would have to be, first, *why* they limit politics in the way they do, and second, whether or not this limitation eliminates transcendence altogether from human life or, instead, somehow recasts it.

This chapter began by describing a similarity between Voegelin and Oakeshott (their constructs of gnosticism and Rationalism), but it has ended by observing that the two philosophers differ in significant ways. And yet it is worth pointing out their similarities on a number of issues: they object to the excesses of the modern scientific method in politics and find positivism a deeply flawed approach to inquiry; they are both fundamentally conservative; and they are both devoted to the life of philosophy. Moreover, they both clearly apprehend man's place in a "tension of existence," although their formulations of and responses to this tension are different. In other words, the two thinkers emerge from a common tradition and they speak directly to many of the same existential problems. There is, of course, much more to be said on these topics, and the present inquiry is merely a beginning. It has, however, presented a few of the substantive philosophical issues that distinguish these two philosophers as well as the fundamental ways in which they may be seen as fellow travelers.

---

45. Voegelin, *The New Science of Politics,* 1; *OHC,* 114.

10
Conclusion

To live in the moment would indeed be brutish and dangerous if
we narrowed to a moment the time embraced in our field of view,
since with the wider scope of thought come serenity and domin-
ion; but to live in the moment is the only possible life if we consider the spiritual activity itself. The most protracted life, in the
actual living, can be nothing but a chain of moments, each the seat
of its irrecoverable vision, each a dramatic perspective of the world,
seen in the light of a particular passion at a particular juncture. But
at each moment the wholeness of mind is spiritual and aesthetic,
the wholeness of a meaning or a picture, and no knife can divide it.

GEORGE SANTAYANA, "CLOUD CASTLES," *SOLILOQUIES IN*
ENGLAND

Oakeshott observes of both contemplation and conversation that "at
whatever point [they are] broken off" they are never incomplete.[1] There
is a sense in which I have conceived this book as a rather long "conversation," mostly with Oakeshott, but also with those writers who influenced him and with those, like Voegelin, who were his contemporaries.
And yet a book is not exactly a conversation, at least not in Oakeshott's
sense. For Oakeshott understood conversation as something that expressly lacks a governing purpose, unlike a book, and it is also a corruption of conversation to equate it with argument. Conversation does not,
properly speaking, conclude.

A book, however, *must* conclude. And it must show, in summing up its
argument, that it has contributed something both coherent and new to a
particular literature. Therefore, in the pages that follow I briefly recapitulate what I have done in the work as a whole. I then answer the question of what parts may be seen as substantially new—that is, in what

---

1. "The Voice of Poetry," in *RP,* 514.

respects my argument is original. And finally I draw out some of the major implications for Oakeshott's political theory and then for his philosophy as a whole.

In the final section of this chapter, however, I turn once again to my central idea about Oakeshott, that is, to his conception of human character as informed by both religion and aesthetics. I briefly examine this character in light of a very recently published essay entitled "The Voice of Conversation in the Education of Mankind" (2004). Here Oakeshott sets out an image of the most satisfactory life as a "conversation" and of the "conversationist" (Oakeshott's word) as a particular type of person suited for this kind of life. Conversation, observes Oakeshott, is "not only a manner of talk; it is also a manner of thinking, a disposition of the human soul, a reading of human life."[2] This "manner" or "disposition" toward life is precisely the one I have attempted to describe throughout this book, and Oakeshott's short essay beautifully encapsulates its primary features.

A Brief Recapitulation

I began by observing that Oakeshott is often misunderstood—or, perhaps, only *partially* understood. Readers who see him as merely a polemicist or right-wing apologist have missed something essential in his work. They have missed, on the one hand, his profound concern not with "opining," but with understanding; for however much Oakeshott is distinctively modern, he also stands in the tradition of classic philosophy. In an observation that might as accurately describe himself, Oakeshott observes that Plato "lived his philosophy." When Plato spoke, "his words were but the overflowing of his inner life. It was not so much a power of memory which kept all things connected but the fact that they formed a single whole in his life—a whole which he was ever rehearsing with himself."[3] Oakeshott's work, too, forms a whole of this kind, which, though it has many diverse expressions, conveys what is essentially a single (though rich) insight about the human condition.

2. "The Voice of Conversation in the Education of Mankind," in *WIH*, 197. This essay was probably written in about 1948. It is not to be confused with "The Voice of Poetry in the Conversation of Mankind."
3. Notebook 2/2 on Plato's *Republic*, 36.

But readers have also missed the profoundly "religious" character of Oakeshott's thought. They may be more easily forgiven for this omission precisely because Oakeshott's religious sensibility lies beneath the surface of his work and is far from obvious to the casual reader. Nevertheless, we must remedy this omission if we are to understand the essential character of his thought as a whole. William James observed that the most crucial task in coming to understand any writer consists in grasping the central vision around which his ideas revolve: "Place yourself at the center of a man's philosophic vision and you [will] understand at once all the different things it makes him write or say. But keep outside, use your post-mortem method, try to build the philosophy up out of the single phrases, taking first one and then another and seeking to make them fit, and of course you fail. You crawl over the thing like a myopic ant over a building, tumbling into every microscopic crack or fissure, finding nothing but inconsistencies, and never suspecting that a center exists."[4] The center of Oakeshott's thought might be characterized as an essentially religious insight about the limitations of human life—limitations exemplified in the story of the Tower of Babel—as well as its possibilities, which may be most fully explored on the model of aesthetic experience.

I am aware that it is important to clarify what I mean in using the word *religious* to characterize Oakeshott's thought. For as I have emphasized, Oakeshott was not religious in a conventional manner. Indeed, much of what I have shown about his immersion in the English Modernist movement during the 1920s points to a strikingly unorthodox approach. In his rejection of authority, dogma, and creeds, Oakeshott is at variance with traditional Christian beliefs, and his early equation of religion with "living in the present" seems to have little in common with the forward-looking nature of much religious observance. But one can make the case, I believe, that like Voegelin's and Santayana's—both of whom had a rather unconventional approach to what we might call the "spiritual life"—Oakeshott's outlook on the human condition is deeply informed by religious considerations.

Perhaps the best way to clarify what religion means for Oakeshott is by observing what are essentially two different aspects of his view. On the one hand, he is quite clear about the distinct limitations of human experience and human knowledge. Following in Augustine's footsteps,

4. William James, quoted in Ellis Sandoz, *The Voegelinian Revolution,* 217.

Oakeshott is attentive to all the things that constrain human action. Foremost among these are the frustrations of practical life and the unavoidable conditions of human mortality and imperfection. Like the inhabitants of Babel, people may attempt to ignore these limits, but they can never successfully overcome them, for death is the central fact of life.

And yet human beings often try to escape their limitations. Sometimes, as in the story of the Tower of Babel, they mistake greed and pride for virtues and attempt to overthrow a God who does not attend to their every wish. Sometimes they simply believe that the pursuit of perfection is a laudable goal, and that they may be pardoned for whatever inconveniences their single-minded pursuit imposes upon others. But in every case what is at issue is a fundamental misunderstanding of human character. This is precisely what Oakeshott argues so strongly against in his critique of Rationalism, and it is what he finds objectionable in the politics of "faith" and collectivism. Oakeshott is Augustine come again to argue against the neo-Pelagians, against all those who vainly place their hopes for salvation in immanent progress and projects.

But there is another aspect of Oakeshott's view that balances his strong sense of human limits. It is the recognition that *within* these limits there exists a distinct realm of human freedom. When human beings come to understand that they exist within bounds, and when they reject the mundane pursuit of perfection, they are suddenly free to explore the intimations that arise in their own experience. If they are fortunate enough to realize the vanity of living solely for the future, they will learn to value those pursuits that can be approached as ends in themselves. Not coincidentally, Oakeshott found these kinds of pursuits to be the most important human activities. It is the familiar list once again: love, friendship, contemplation, conversation, liberal learning, and philosophy. But this activity within limits is also a kind of self-enactment, a process of coming to know oneself and one's abilities; of facing one's personal limitations and strengths squarely and without illusion. It is the creation of a "personal sensibility" through engaging in the kind of "aesthetic" morality I discussed in Chapter 6.

To illustrate the two sides of his view by way of an analogy, it is much like assigning a specific essay topic to a group of students. Rather than demanding that these students write an essay on Plato's *Republic* as a whole, for example, we ask them instead to consider just a few lines, examining and clarifying the lines' meaning, and giving a thoughtful interpretation of what they have learned from the exercise. In short, we limit them.

Their responses are, of course, predictable. Many will ignore the assignment, preferring to bypass the set limits and endeavor to make a pronouncement on the *Republic* as a whole and on Plato's significance in the history of Western thought. Aiming at a grand and ambitious perfection, they miss the point entirely. They are the Rationalists of the classroom, those not content with the bounds that have been set for them but looking for quick success on a grand scale. Others—these are analogous to Oakeshott's "anti-individualists"—will wish the assignment had never been given, and that the teacher would simply *tell* them the correct answer. Thinking for oneself is so difficult, they complain, and they would be far more comfortable with a ready-made interpretation that they could simply memorize and use.

But there is a third group, which consists of those who face the assignment squarely. This group recognizes precisely the limits of the assignment and finds within those limits the freedom to explore with great depth the lines in question, creatively interpreting them in myriad ways. This group realizes that the limits offer a welcome constraint as well as the possibility for significant action. Their freedom lies not outside the limits, but within them. Now, in terms of Oakeshott's philosophy, the assignment is, of course, the human condition, and those who evade it are various kinds of Rationalists and collectivists, to use Oakeshott's terms. But the person who explores the assignment, understanding both the limits and the possibilities of the human condition, is the one who grasps Oakeshott's fundamental religious insight and can live according to it.

New Insights

Much of what I have argued in this book is substantially new. Although a handful of Oakeshott scholars have recognized the importance of his reflections on religion and aesthetics, the majority of commentators have noticed these only to pass them by on the way to examining some political or philosophical question. The reasons for this are not far to seek. First, Oakeshott made his name first as an Idealist philosopher and then as a philosopher of politics, and there is enough material in his major published works alone to keep scholars busy for years. But second, as I have noted elsewhere, much of what Oakeshott wrote about religion has only recently become available. And although there are numerous hints about the importance of religion in his two Tower of Babel essays,

Experience and Its Modes, and *On Human Conduct,* a full examination of his religious views requires consideration of the previously unpublished early essays. These are the practical considerations that help to explain why Oakeshott's views on religion and aesthetics are only now beginning to attract the attention they deserve.[5]

My book takes these early works quite seriously as evidence for the direction of Oakeshott's initial intellectual development. I recognize, of course, that some of these are clearly juvenilia, which Oakeshott never meant to publish. As such, these essays must be treated with caution, to be compared with Oakeshott's mature published work and recognized for what they are: often ambitious, idealistic, and less tempered than what we have come to expect from the mature Oakeshott. And yet these works provide vital clues about his early years. We know now that Oakeshott came under the influence of the neo-Platonists and Christian mystics, that he read Santayana and Pater as well as innumerable poets, and that he possessed a strong streak of Romanticism. In short, we now have a more complete view of Oakeshott's outlook on life, which should help to counter the view that Oakeshott was solely interested in politics. He was, as I have observed, primarily interested in politics as a means of facilitating pursuits that he considered more important than political activity.

The thesis that Oakeshott's favored view of morality is "aesthetic" is also my own.[6] For while Oakeshott suggests that there is something "poetic" about human conduct, he does not make this connection explicit. Moreover, in other places he appears to flatly contradict the idea that conduct can be poetic; for poetry and practice, he asserts, are modally distinct from one another. And yet there are too many connections between Oakeshott's description of moral activity and poetry for the question to be ignored. Why would Oakeshott use the vocabulary of aesthetics to describe moral conduct, if there was not *something* artistic about the moral agent who enacts himself like a virtuoso, knowing immediately both *what* to do and *how* to do it?

I have recently discovered a source that may help to make this idea of "aesthetic morality" much clearer. It is a book entitled *Aesthetics,* by Ed-

---

5. The following relevant essays came out just as this book was going to press: Martyn P. Thompson, "Intimations of Poetry in Practical Life"; Robert Grant, "Oakeshott on the Nature and Place of Aesthetic Experience: A Critique"; Wendell John Coats Jr., "Michael Oakeshott and the Poetic Character of Human Activity"; and Glenn Worthington, "Poetic Experience and the Good Life in the Writings of Michael Oakeshott."

6. I am aware of Glenn Worthington's similar view of Oakeshott's morality. But as I argued in Chapter 5, our interpretations are at odds in some significant ways.

ward Bullough, lecturer at Cambridge University from 1902 until his
death in 1934. His tenure includes the years in which Oakeshott was at
Cambridge, and in fact Bullough was elected Fellow of Oakeshott's own
Gonville and Caius College in 1912. Although his official position was
in Modern Languages, he had an abiding interest in aesthetics, which he
modestly spoke of as his "intellectual hobby." After Bullough died in
1934 Oakeshott published a lengthy obituary in his college paper, where
he mentions that Bullough had presented a series of lectures on aesthetics annually from 1907 until just before he died. Oakeshott certainly
would have attended these lectures, which were published as the book
Aesthetics in 1957.[7]

I mention Bullough here because it is highly likely that Oakeshott's
thought on aesthetics was at least partially formed by Bullough's lectures,
and Bullough presents explicitly what I have argued is *implicit* in Oakeshott's work. Consider one of Bullough's comments on the relationship
between aesthetics and moral action:

> [O]nly to the aesthetic consciousness is revealed what the act meant to
> the doer, the overflowing fullness of living energy and the clenched re-
> solve of its performance. Not so much to live happily rather than miser-
> ably, or to lead a godly rather than a wicked life, but to *live*, to force life of
> the highest quality in its deepest and intensest form into the span of a
> human existence, is an ideal purely aesthetic. Aesthetic consciousness dis-
> covers that innumerable acts are daily done, not for the sake of practical
> utility nor in conscious observance of ethical postulates, but because the
> doing of them was accompanied by that peculiar sense of enjoyment in
> doing them well, with all the strength, perfection and grace that could be
> imparted to them.[8]

Something very much like this view is exactly what I have identified in
Oakeshott's reflections on moral conduct, and it helps to explain why
Oakeshott is so vehemently opposed to morality understood as merely
following a set of rules.

Finally, this work, broadly conceived, is an attempt, in the spirit of the
William James passage I quoted above, to find the center of Oakeshott's
thought. And while I have not presented Oakeshott's work in its entirety—I have made only limited mention, for instance, of his views on

7. Efraim Podoksik, *In Defence of Modernity: Vision and Philosophy in Michael Oakeshott*, v.
8. Bullough, *Aesthetics*, 75.

Hobbes and of his extensive work on history—there is a sense in which Oakeshott's thought may be better understood by observing its religious and aesthetic character, as I have argued above. His corpus may, in a sense, be divided into the two categories I have proposed. On the one hand, in many of the essays in *Rationalism in Politics* and in *The Politics of Faith and the Politics of Scepticism* he is concerned with setting out the limits of the human condition. In these works he attempts to show the ways in which modernity has gone wrong, and how a fundamental misunderstanding of human limits leads inevitably to frustration and unhappiness.

In other works, however, such as *On Human Conduct* and *Religion, Politics and the Moral Life,* he is concerned with the other side of this religious view. In these works he sets out the expansive possibilities that are available to human beings, if they understand themselves rightly. It is in these works that he sets out his favored views of morality and of contemplation, and indeed of all those things that can go on in the realm of freedom he has defined for man.

Political and Philosophical Implications

There are a number of conclusions that may be drawn from this study of Oakeshott, and several of them are specifically political in nature. First, I have repeatedly emphasized that Oakeshott defends human freedom broadly understood, as well as a political freedom in which subjects are only minimally constrained by government. This freedom, however, is not to be understood as a kind of radical liberation from tradition, just as the freedom to cultivate self-understanding does not suggest that "man creates himself, with all of the schemes of unlimited possibilities that such visions usually imply."[9] The freedom Oakeshott applauds is something that must be learned and enjoyed within inherited traditions. It is therefore a freedom at once expansive and limited. This is important to note, because many people find Oakeshott's non-rule-based morality almost frighteningly liberating. If there are no hard and fast rules, they argue, what is to prevent people from acting immorally and badly? Oakeshott's answer would surely be that no rules *could* prevent this, and it is a misunderstanding of morality to imagine that any such ironclad rules exist. Nevertheless, he would also point out the constraining features of prac-

9. David Walsh, *The Growth of the Liberal Soul,* 60.

tices and traditions, which habituate people toward acting in morally acceptable ways.

The other point worth making about Oakeshott's idea of freedom is that for him freedom is something that is worthwhile entirely for its own sake. Human freedom can *never* be put in the service of any other goal—prosperity, equality, or progress, for example—no matter how noble that goal may appear. Oakeshott can thus be distinguished from those with whom he otherwise has much in common, like Friedrich Hayek and others who see freedom as the best means to economic prosperity.[10] For Oakeshott frankly repudiates any version of freedom that requires "the achievement of a premeditated utopia . . . an abstract ideal (such as happiness or prosperity), or as a preordained and inevitable end."[11]

This study has also yielded the conclusion that Oakeshott's conception of Rationalism is grounded in a fundamentally religious insight. Oakeshott himself recognizes that the Rationalist is gnostic, and that his search for demonstrable certainties is a sign of a disordered soul, of someone who cannot accept the tension of existence for what it is. Moreover, the Rationalistic search for perfection is a symptom of what Oakeshott describes as a new manifestation of the old Pelagian heresy. This is perhaps even more virulent in our modern world than it was in Augustine's, simply because the pursuit of perfection is now hardly ever recognized for its inherent cupidity and hubris. Instead, the impulse to pursue perfection is recognized as praiseworthy, and anyone who cautions against it is seen as a defeatist. The virtue of Oakeshott's philosophy—which translates into his political philosophy—is that his strong warnings against such pursuits go hand in hand with an expansive view of what individual moral agents may yet accomplish in their own lives.

But the religious basis of Oakeshott's thought is manifest in more than merely his reflections on Rationalism. I have discussed the phenomenon that Timothy Fuller has called Oakeshott's "transposed Augustinianism," observing that the conception of a fundamental choice to be made in conduct and politics runs throughout Oakeshott's theorizing. And while this choice is set out most starkly in "Religion and the World," similar alternative pairings appear throughout his corpus: faith and skepticism, civil and enterprise association, individualism and collectivism. And while Oakeshott surely does not argue that any of these choices can be

10. I do not doubt that Hayek also saw freedom as valuable in itself. But Oakeshott resolutely refused to link freedom with *any* substantive end.
11. "The Political Economy of Freedom," in *RP,* 396.

made unambiguously—indeed, this is the point of observing that these alternatives are "ideal types" designed to provide philosophical clarity—he is clearly inclined toward those choices that lead away from "worldliness."

Oakeshott's conception of worldliness appears most clearly in his meditations on the Tower of Babel story, a tale in his version of which he outlines the origins of our modern (and not so modern) pathologies. This story, for him, illustrates the danger of living at extremes, of pursuing immanent perfection, of orienting our lives toward ideals, and of attempting to permanently overcome all the dissatisfaction inherent in the practical life. The story is the apotheosis of pride and greed, all in the name of some greater good. It is, Oakeshott maintains, a view of life that has a permanent allure for human beings, but it is always dangerous. For it necessarily either truncates or eliminates the realm of freedom that Oakeshott contends is *truly* man's inheritance. In the process of building this tower, all the diversity of civil association and the humble satisfactions of the *vita temporalis* must be relinquished.

In light of these religious considerations, we can conclude that Oakeshott is part of a tradition that includes explicitly Christian religious thinkers like Josef Pieper and C. S. Lewis, despite the fact that Oakeshott is in no way a Christian apologist. Like these thinkers, Oakeshott constantly opposes the world's call for utility and progress. He celebrates the amateur, the poet, the philosopher, and the idea of liberal learning for its own sake. In another sense, Oakeshott also has much in common with philosophers like Voegelin and Santayana, and indeed with all those who are aware of the limits of living a "worldly" life. For while some may object to Oakeshott's lack of orthodoxy, to deny that his work emerges from a fundamentally religious view of the world is, I believe, simply mistaken. The challenge, of course, when reading Oakeshott, as with any original thinker, is to get him right—that is, to understand exactly what it is he means to convey even when this departs from our own cherished, familiar categories of experience.

Criticisms and Qualifications

In an essay entitled "Philosophy as a Branch of Literature," R. G. Collingwood observes that a good reader must approach a philosophical author "as if he were a poet, in the sense that he must seek in his work the expression of an individual experience, something which the writer has actually lived through, and something which the reader must live through in his turn by entering into the writer's mind with his own." The task of criticizing the author's doctrine, "or determining how far it is true and how far false," is altogether secondary to this primary task of understanding. "A good reader, like a good listener, must be quiet in order to be attentive; able to refrain from obtruding his own thoughts."[12] Such has been my aim in this book. And yet it is appropriate in concluding a work such as this to register—in a cautious and friendly manner—some questions and concerns about the author we have been studying. The following reflections stand, then, as the beginnings of a critique of Oakeshott's thought regarding religion and aesthetics.

It will be obvious to anyone who has read the entirety of this book that Oakeshott's religious views are unique and difficult to classify. If my reader had expected to discover an Oakeshott who considers theological questions and addresses the idea of transcendent experience directly, he will have realized by now that no such Oakeshott exists.[13] For the thesis that Oakeshott's thought is grounded in religious insights does not necessarily imply that Oakeshott was a *theologian*. We should recall that Oakeshott makes a clear distinction between religion and theology. Religion consists in the lived, practical experiences of consolation for sorrow, forgiveness of sins, and reconciliation to mortality. As such, it is within the realm of human conduct and intensely interesting to Oakeshott. Also, as I have pointed out, the religious ideas embodied in the myth of the Tower of Babel structure much of Oakeshott's political theorizing. But theology, on the other hand, is philosophy turned to theorizing the religious experience, and would seem to require consideration of metaphysical questions—the existence and nature of God being foremost among these. And Oakeshott was reticent about venturing into theological controversies—at least, he did not do so after 1930—preferring instead to consider those things that he believed he could grasp more directly and concretely, such as moral activity and politics.

But Oakeshott's move away from explicit consideration of such questions also means that his account of the human condition is perhaps less

12. R. G. Collingwood, "Philosophy as a Branch of Literature," in *An Essay on Philosophical Method,* 207–8.
13. According to Timothy Fuller, Oakeshott's reflections on theological works were remarkable for their insight. Unfortunately, he did not write them down.

full than accounts given by others who share his view. I have argued that he shares with Voegelin and Augustine a view of the human condition that recognizes both limits and possibilities, and in which man is poised between a variety of polar opposites: religion and worldliness, individualism and anti-individualism, and so on. But this perspective must be teased out of Oakeshott's work, and while I believe it is vital to understanding his thought as a whole, it is no wonder that people have tended to miss it. A thinker such as Eric Voegelin, by contrast, gives his readers a much richer account of man's experience in the *metaxy*, and a fuller account of the fundamental tension of existence in which human beings find themselves.

Secondly, Oakeshott's ideal of living so far as possible in the present will certainly have struck some readers as unattainable, and perhaps even undesirable. For this ideal is not one that is easy or perhaps even *possible* for most of us, since it requires the most thorough coming to terms with oneself, accepting one's imperfections, and it is a view that does not encourage faith in anything to come. It emphasizes one kind of human experience at the expense of others, such as planning for the future. No one could live wholly in the present, and to some it will seem merely a youthful, romantic ideal.

Notwithstanding these legitimate criticisms of the idea of "presentness," I think Oakeshott realized that we are in *no danger* of forgetting to plan for the future. What we *are* in danger of is forgetting to live right now. And there is indeed an element of faith in actually *living* the life we have been given. Humans are so apt to become caught up in the anxieties of worldly life that we cannot stop to enjoy the beauty of the created world around us, to explore the possibilities within the limits of our freedom. So I think the answer to this particular criticism is not that Oakeshott failed to understand the forward-looking nature of the human condition, but that he wanted to recall us to something we are very much in danger of forgetting, namely, that we should live a full and rich life even in the midst of present contingencies.

And yet there is a more serious charge that can be leveled against Oakeshott, which has to do with what it is that makes his outlook coherent. I observed in Chapter 2 that Oakeshott's reformulation of the "two cities" seems to lack the kind of external ordering principle that makes Augustine's view intelligible. In short, Oakeshott's religious man does not appear to need God. But can the choice between the two cities be maintained in the absence of God? What is to prevent the "religious" man, in Oakeshott's terms, from falling into despair when he discovers he cannot achieve a meaningful life by recourse to his own powers? Augustine's God offers hope to those who are discouraged and yet believe, but there seems to be nothing to bolster Oakeshott's religious man beyond his own hard-won self-understanding.

We might speculate that aesthetic experience steps in to offer a certain kind of transcendence for Oakeshott, that poetry is a self-forgetting, and that contemplation provides the possibility of apprehending a higher realm of spirit. Perhaps we need not postulate a transcendent realm, for as Santayana observes, "To double the world would unspiritualize the spiritual sphere; to double the truth would make both truths halting and false. There is only one world, the natural world, and only one truth about it; but this world has a spiritual life possible in it, which looks not to another world but to the beauty and perfection that this world suggests, approaches, and misses."[14] Some such view would seem to be very much in line with Oakeshott's view—that we can apprehend limitations but also a certain beauty and perfection only through our attentiveness to things in *this* world.

However, calling poetry transcendent does raise certain issues, and it is worth noting one of the most important of these. In short, the question is whether poetry and more "traditional" notions of transcendence *are,* in fact, equivalent experiences. Oakeshott's use of almost mystical language in describing poetry places it in line with some more orthodox descriptions of transcendence; but what it does not (and cannot) specify is an "object" for contemplation and delight. In traditional Christian formulations, God is what is ultimately contemplated; and even though one can never completely grasp God as a reality, there is the notion that one knows what one is looking for. But Oakeshott never names such an object as the goal of contemplation, for to do so would be to assume a *telos* for the activity of contemplation, which would be unacceptable to him. Moreover, it would corrupt the experience of contemplation by orienting it "religiously" and thus would place it in the practical realm.

Nevertheless, the question remains, and Josef Pieper has put it this way: "Can a Christian accept a thesis that puts poesy on the same level as revelation and inspiration?"[15] For while a Christian might be able to accept Oakeshott's characterization of poetry as a certain kind of transcendence

14. Quoted in Russell Kirk, *The Conservative Mind,* 444.
15. Josef Pieper, *"Divine Madness": Plato's Case against Secular Humanism,* 30–31.

so far as it goes, it would nonetheless seem a far cry from a fully Christian understanding of transcendence, which includes faith, revelation, and belief in a God with particular characteristics. In other words, Oakeshott's "poetry as contemplation" may arise from the same perception of the limitedness of the world, but it cannot serve as an adequate substitute for a fully developed Christian faith.

To sum up, I have observed three potential criticisms that may be leveled against Oakeshott: first, that his consideration of religion is not as full as it might have been, and that while a religious view lies at the core of his thought, readers must piece this view together, for he is not explicit about it. Second, his focus on the idea of "presentness" as a kind of religious and poetic way of conducting oneself will no doubt seem untenable for many readers. And finally, Oakeshott's idea of the two cities seems to lack the ordering principle that makes Augustine's thought intelligible.

Nevertheless, even with these criticisms in mind there is something to be said *in favor* of Oakeshott's approach to these topics, for in this approach he is much like the poet or artist himself who suggests but does not declare. If his discussions of poetry and religion are unsatisfying and vague to some readers, perhaps it is because Oakeshott is trying to describe an experience that is ultimately impossible to capture in ordinary philosophical language. Pieper has expressed the experience particularly well. "The philosophical act, the religious act, the aesthetic act, and, of course, the effect of love and death, or some other way in which man's relation to the world is convulsed and shaken—all these fundamental ways of acting belong naturally together, by reason of the power which they have in common of enabling a man to break through and transcend the workaday world. . . . the philosopher . . . is related to the poet in that both are concerned with *mirandum,* with wonder, with marveling and with that which makes us marvel."[16] And one thing we can be certain of is that Oakeshott was a philosopher through and through, someone concerned with wondering, marveling, and delighting in the world around him.

A Final Note: The Voice of Conversation

It is worth taking one final look at the kind of life Oakeshott recommends as most fully human, namely, a life that offers a certain happiness

16. Josef Pieper, *Leisure the Basis of Culture,* 68–69.

and fulfillment within the unavoidable limits of our mortal nature. Oakeshott was aware that he was going against the grain in recommending a way of life that at times explicitly repudiates purpose and achievement in favor of "play" and "purposelessness." Conversation, in his argument, provides a particularly good example of this kind of play, an activity in which there is no end besides present enjoyment. He distinguishes conversation from argument and inquiry, from demonstrating a point or giving a lecture, and observes that the value of conversation never lies in its having achieved a result or conclusion. "The sweetness of conversation," he maintains, "is not the aroma that rises from some long matured wine when at last, and with ceremony, the cork is drawn; it is the aroma of the wine-vat, the sweetness that belongs to the extemporary and the unrehearsed."[17] His short essay "The Voice of Conversation in the Education of Mankind" is an extended metaphor for his view of life as conversation. He knew well that this is an understanding that cannot constantly be pursued; but it offers the supreme image of civilized, human association for those who are willing to engage in it.

His metaphor of conversation, moreover, encapsulates all the characteristics I have described as religious and aesthetic: a focus on living in the present, a rejection of purpose and achievement in favor of enjoyment, a reading of the human condition that is both limited and expansive, and a description of the particular kind of human character best suited to live in this kind of world. Conversation, Oakeshott observes, "springs from the movement of present minds disposed to intellectual adventure," and since its achievements are transitory, "its pleasure is absolute in each moment" (190). It is a temporary abandonment of practice in favor of an activity that looks neither to the future nor the past.

Because of its focus on present enjoyment, conversation rejects all demands that it achieve something substantive. It is instead a kind of performance, like the activity of juggling that Oakeshott uses to illuminate its character: "Up go the balls, the plates, the hats, the whole miscellany of the juggler's box; up and over, in and out, spinning and leaping. Nobody asks where they have come from, or on what authority they have appeared" (187). The object of conversation is thus merely to keep going, and to speak "in such a manner that what is said leads on to something else" (190). In this "partnership in intellectual pleasure" (188) the

17. "The Voice of Conversation," in *WIH*, 188 (hereafter page numbers from this essay will be cited parenthetically in the text).

participants are neither adversaries nor lovers. For both argument and passion are modes of relationship that lack the necessary detachment required for conversation. What is required for this activity is a kind of "watery" fidelity to one's fellows.

This world of conversation is very much like our wider world. For, as I have observed, Oakeshott uses conversation as a metaphor for life, and thus it is not only "a manner of talk but a manner of thinking, a disposition of the human soul" (197). The world of conversation is "both in its greatness and in its littleness, fit for mortals" (191), one in which the "fixed shapes which practical men have imposed" (192) may be temporarily dissolved.

There is, moreover, a certain character required to engage in conversation, Oakeshott believed, a character that is at once virtuosic and amateur. We are no doubt unaccustomed to thinking of these two characteristics together, for *virtuoso* tends to imply "professional," and *amateur* often connotes a certain lack of seriousness with respect to a given activity. But Oakeshott wants to encourage the *spirit* of the amateur—that is, a spirit that loves its activity—combined with the *excellence* of the virtuoso. Such a person, in conversation, does not talk to win or to dominate. He is neither lazy and unresponsive, on the one hand, nor aggressive and overbearing, on the other. He has an "amused tolerance of himself" (193) and never takes himself too seriously. He is skeptical about all opinions, even his own, and is willing to examine himself candidly. Above all, such a person accepts "his own want of greater perfection" and forgives himself "for being what he [finds] himself to be" (193). It will be no surprise to readers of Oakeshott that he found the archetypal example of such a person in Michel de Montaigne, whose style of candid self-examination Oakeshott appreciated.

Finally, the true "conversationist" will lack both hubris and singleness of purpose, traits that encourage the development of an explicitly non-conversational character. He will have no illusions about perfection, since he will recognize that imperfection is a condition of human life. Indeed, "poise in imperfection is the only perfection" (198). And most of all, he will recognize himself as neither beast nor god, but as a mortal man "in a world of mortal men" (196).

Such is the human character that Oakeshott praised. For he recognized that to be solely a creature of wants in the prison of practice "is itself a curse, a condemnation to a life in which every achievement is also a frustration." In setting out this alternative Oakeshott revealed a bit of his own poetic nature, one that seemed to long for some kind of permanence even as he recognized that mortal things are bound up with change. His alternative is both religious and aesthetic, a way of living in which enjoyment is not to be sought in the end "but only in each flying moment."[18] It offers no "solution" to the problems of human life, but it is, we might suppose, a way of being otherworldly in the world and of finding such fulfillment as is available to human beings at present.

18. WP, 31; "The Voice of Conversation," in *WIH,* 198.

Works Cited

Works by Oakeshott

I. BOOKS AND ARTICLES

Experience and Its Modes. Cambridge: Cambridge University Press, 1933.

With G. T. Griffith. *A Guide to the Classics, or, How to Pick the Derby Winner.* London: Faber and Faber, 1936.

Hobbes on Civil Association. Oxford: Basil Blackwell, 1975.

Morality and Politics in Modern Europe. Ed. S. R. Letwin. New Haven: Yale University Press, 1993.

On History and Other Essays. Oxford: Basil Blackwell, 1983.

On Human Conduct. Oxford: Oxford University Press, 1975.

The Politics of Faith and the Politics of Scepticism. Ed. Timothy Fuller. New Haven: Yale University Press, 1996.

Rationalism in Politics and Other Essays. Ed. Timothy Fuller. Indianapolis: Liberty Press, 1991.

Religion, Politics and the Moral Life. Ed. Timothy Fuller. New Haven: Yale University Press, 1993.

"Shylock the Jew." *Caian* 30 (1921): 61–67.

The Social and Political Doctrines of Contemporary Europe. New York: Cambridge University Press, 1953.

The Voice of Liberal Learning. Ed. Timothy Fuller. New Haven: Yale University Press, 1989.

What Is History? and Other Essays. Ed. Luke O'Sullivan. Exeter: Imprint Academic, 2004.

"Work and Play." *First Things* 54 (1995): 29–33.

II. REVIEWS AND MISCELLANEOUS

"Collingwood's Philosophy of Art." Review of *The Principles of Art,* by

R. G. Collingwood. In *The Cambridge Mind,* ed. Eric Homberger, 139–41. Boston: Little, Brown, 1970.

Review of *Adventures of Ideas,* by A. N. Whitehead. *Journal of Theological Studies* 35 (1934): 73–75.

Review of *Can We Then Believe?* by Charles Gore; *Essays Catholic and Critical,* by E. G. Selwyn; and *The Inescapable Christ,* by W. R. Bowie. *Journal of Theological Studies* 28 (1926–27): 314–16.

Review of *The Christian Religion and Its Competitors To-day,* by A. C. Bouquet. *Journal of Theological Studies* 27 (1926): 440.

Review of *The Historical Element in Religion,* by Clement C. J. Webb. *Journal of Theological Studies* 37 (1936): 96–98.

Review of *The Making of the Christian Mind,* by G. G. Atkins. *Journal of Theological Studies* 31 (1930): 203–8.

Review of *Science, Religion, and Reality,* by J. Needham. *Journal of Theological Studies* 27 (1926): 317–19.

Review of *The State and the Citizen,* by J. D. Mabbott. *Mind* 58 (1949): 378–89.

Notebook 2/2, Detailed Commentary on Plato's *Republic.* Oakeshott Collection. British Library of Political and Economic Science, London School of Economics and Political Science.

Works by Other Authors

Aristotle. *Nicomachean Ethics.* Trans. Martin Ostwald. Upper Saddle River, NJ: Prentice Hall, 1999.

Augustine. *City of God.* Trans. Henry Bettenson. New York: Penguin, 1972.

———. *Confessions.* Trans. Maria Boulding. Hyde Park: New City Press, 1997.

———. *The Harmony of the Evangelists.* Trans. S. D. F. Salmond. Edinburgh: T and T Clark, 1873.

———. *On Free Choice of the Will.* Trans. Thomas Williams. Indianapolis: Hackett, 1993.

———. *The Political Writings of St. Augustine.* Ed. Dino Bigongiari. Washington, DC: Gateway, 1985.

Auspitz, Josiah Lee. "Individuality, Civility and Theory: The Philosophical Imagination of Michael Oakeshott." *Political Theory* 4 (1976): 261–94.

Berns, Walter. Review of *Rationalism in Politics,* by Michael Oakeshott. *American Political Science Review* 57 (1963): 670–71.

Bosanquet, Bernard. *What Religion Is.* London: Macmillan, 1920.

Boucher, David. "The Creation of the Past: British Idealism and Michael Oakeshott's Philosophy of History." *History and Theory* 23 (1984): 193–214.

———. "Human Conduct, History and Social Science in the Works of R. G. Collingwood and Michael Oakeshott." *New Literary History* 24 (1993): 697–717.

———. "The Idealism of Michael Oakeshott." *Collingwood and British Idealism Studies* 8 (2001): 73–98.

———. *Texts in Context: Revisionist Methods for Studying the History of Ideas.* Dordrecht, Netherlands: Marinus Nijhoff Publishers, 1985.

Boucher, David, and Andrew Vincent. *British Idealism and Political Theory.* Edinburgh: Edinburgh University Press, 2000.

Bradley, F. H. *Appearance and Reality.* Oxford: Clarendon Press, 1930.

———. *Ethical Studies.* Oxford: Oxford University Press, 1988.

Brown, Keith. *Hobbes Studies.* Cambridge: Harvard University Press, 1965.

Brown, Peter. *Augustine of Hippo.* London: Faber and Faber, 1967.

Bullough, Edward. *Aesthetics.* Stanford: Stanford University Press, 1957.

Callahan, Leonard. *A Theory of Esthetic according to the Principles of St. Thomas Aquinas.* Washington, DC: Catholic University, 1947.

Catlin, George E. Review of *Rationalism in Politics and Other Essays,* by Michael Oakeshott. *Western Political Quarterly* 16 (1963): 259–61.

Coats, Wendell John, Jr. "Michael Oakeshott and the Poetic Character of Human Activity." In *The Intellectual Legacy of Michael Oakeshott,* ed. Corey Abel and Timothy Fuller. Exeter: Imprint Academic, 2005.

———. *Oakeshott and His Contemporaries.* Selinsgrove, PA: Susquehanna University Press, 2000.

Cochrane, Charles. *Christianity and Classical Culture.* Oxford: Oxford University Press, 1940.

Collingwood, R. G. *An Autobiography.* Oxford: Oxford University Press, 1939.

———. *An Essay on Philosophical Method.* Bristol: Thoemmes Press, 1995.

———. *The Principles of Art.* Oxford: Clarendon Press, 1938.

———. *Speculum Mentis.* Oxford: Clarendon Press, 1924.

Connolly, William. *Political Theory and Modernity.* Oxford: Blackwell, 1988.

Cooke, Paul D. *Hobbes and Christianity: Reassessing the Bible in* Leviathan. Lanham, MD: Rowman and Littlefield, 1996.

Cowling, Maurice. *Religion and Public Doctrine in Modern England.* Cambridge: Cambridge University Press, 1980.

Davis, Howard. "Poetry and the Voice of Michael Oakeshott." *British Journal of Aesthetics* 15 (1975): 59–68.

Deane, Herbert A. *The Political and Social Ideas of St. Augustine.* New York: Columbia University Press, 1963.

Devigne, Robert. *Recasting Conservatism: Oakeshott, Strauss and the Response to Postmodernism.* New Haven: Yale University Press, 1994.

Dumochel, Paul. "The Political Problem of Religion: Hobbes's Reading of the Bible." In *English Philosophy in the Age of Locke,* ed. M. A. Stewart, 1–27. Oxford: Clarendon Press, 2000.

Franco, Paul. *Michael Oakeshott: An Introduction.* New Haven: Yale University Press, 2004.

———. *The Political Philosophy of Michael Oakeshott.* New Haven: Yale University Press, 1990.

Frohnen, Bruce P. "Oakeshott's Hobbesian Myth: Pride, Character and the Limits of Reason." *The Western Political Quarterly* 43 (1990): 789–809.

Fuller, Timothy. "The Idea of Christianity in Hobbes's *Leviathan.*" *Jewish Political Studies Review* 4 (1992): 139–178.

———. "The Work of Michael Oakeshott." *Political Theory* 19 (1991): 326–33.

Gardner, Percy. *Modernism in the English Church.* London: Methuen, 1926.

Gerencser, Stephen. *The Skeptic's Oakeshott.* New York: St. Martin's Press, 2000.

Grant, Robert. *Oakeshott.* London: Claridge Press, 1990.

———. "Oakeshott on the Nature and Place of Aesthetic Experience: A Critique." In *The Intellectual Legacy of Michael Oakeshott,* ed. Corey Abel and Timothy Fuller. Exeter: Imprint Academic, 2005.

Greenleaf, W. H. *Oakeshott's Philosophical Politics.* New York: Barnes and Noble, 1966.

Hayes, Peter. "Hobbes's Bourgeois Moderation." *Polity* 31 (1998): 53–74.

Hepburn, Ronald. "Hobbes on the Knowledge of God." In *Hobbes and*

Rousseau: A Collection of Critical Essays, ed. Maurice Cranston and Richard S. Peters, 85–108. New York: Doubleday, 1972.

Hobbes, Thomas. *Leviathan.* Ed. Edwin Curley. Indianapolis: Hackett, 1994.

Hughes, Glenn. "Balanced and Imbalanced Consciousness." In *The Politics of the Soul: Eric Voegelin on Religious Experience,* ed. Glenn Hughes, 163–84. Lanham, MD: Rowman and Littlefield, 1999.

Inge, W. R. *The Platonic Tradition in English Religious Thought.* London: Longmans, 1926.

Jaffa, Harry. Review of *Rationalism in Politics and Other Essays,* by Michael Oakeshott. *National Review* (October 22, 1963): 360–62.

Kestenbaum, Victor. *The Grace and the Severity of the Ideal.* Chicago: University of Chicago Press, 2002.

Kettler, David. "The Cheerful Discourses of Michael Oakeshott." *World Politics* 16 (1964): 483–89.

Kirk, Russell. *The Conservative Mind.* Washington, DC: Regnery, 1986.

Lewis, C. S. "Learning in War-Time." In *The Weight of Glory.* San Francisco: HarperCollins, 2001.

Lichtheim, George. "A Settled Habit of Behavior: A Review of *Rationalism in Politics,* by Michael Oakeshott." *Commentary* 35 (1963): 168–72.

Martinich, A. P. *The Two Gods of* Leviathan. Cambridge: Cambridge University Press, 1992.

McKnight, Stephen A. "Voegelin's Challenge to Modernity's Claim to Be Scientific and Secular: The Ancient Theology and the Dream of Innerworldly Fulfillment." In *The Politics of the Soul: Eric Voegelin on Religious Experience,* ed. Glenn Hughes, 185–206. Lanham, MD: Rowman and Littlefield, 1999.

Merton, Thomas. *The Way of Chuang Tzu.* Boston, MA: Shambhala, 2004.

Miller, Ted H. "Oakeshott's Hobbes and the Fear of Political Rationalism." *Political Theory* 29 (2000): 806–32.

Milne, A. J. M. *The Social Philosophy of British Idealism.* London: Allen and Unwin, 1962.

Montaigne, Michel de. *Essays.* Trans. Charles Cotton. New York: Doubleday, 1947.

Nardin, Terry. *The Philosophy of Michael Oakeshott.* University Park: Pennsylvania State University Press, 2001.

Oman, John. *Grace and Personality.* New York: Macmillan, 1925.

O'Sullivan, Luke. *Oakeshott on History.* Exeter: Imprint Academic, 2003.

Pascal, Blaise. *Pensées.* Trans. W. F. Trotter. London: J. M. Dent, 1931.

Pater, Walter. *Appreciations.* London: Macmillan, 1915.

———. *Marius the Epicurean.* New York: Modern Library, 1920.

Pieper, Josef. *"Divine Madness": Plato's Case against Secular Humanism.* San Francisco: Ignatius Press, 1995.

———. *Leisure the Basis of Culture.* Indianapolis: Liberty Fund, 1999.

Pitkin, Hannah F. "Inhuman Conduct and Unpolitical Theory: Michael Oakeshott's *On Human Conduct.*" *Political Theory* 4 (1976): 301–20.

Podoksik, Efraim. *In Defence of Modernity: Vision and Philosophy in Michael Oakeshott.* Exeter: Imprint Academic, 2003.

Riley, Patrick. "In Appreciation: Michael Oakeshott, Philosopher of Individuality." *Review of Politics* 54 (1992): 649–64.

Sandoz, Ellis. *The Voegelinian Revolution.* New Brunswick, NJ: Transaction Publishers, 2000.

Santayana, George. *Dominations and Powers.* New Brunswick, NJ: Transaction Publishers, 1995.

———. *Soliloquies in England and Later Soliloquies.* New York: Charles Scribner's Sons, 1922.

Segal, Jacob. "Freedom and Normalization: Poststructuralism and the Liberalism of Michael Oakeshott." *American Political Science Review* 97 (2003): 447–58.

Smith, Adam. *Inquiry into the Nature and Causes of the Wealth of Nations.* Ed. R. H. Campbell and A. S. Skinner. Indianapolis: Liberty Fund, 1982.

Sokolowski, Robert. *Moral Action: A Phenomenological Study.* Bloomington, IN: Indiana University Press, 1985.

Stephenson, Alan M. G. *The Rise and Decline of English Modernism.* London: SPCK, 1984.

Strauss, Leo. *The Political Philosophy of Hobbes: Its Basis and Genesis.* Chicago: University of Chicago Press, 1963.

Sullivan, Andrew. "Intimations Pursued: The Voice of Practice in the Conversation of Michael Oakeshott." PhD diss., Harvard University, 1990.

Tarlton, Charles D. "The Despotical Doctrine of Hobbes, Part I: The Liberalization of *Leviathan.*" *History of Political Thought* 22 (2001): 587–618.

Thompson, Martyn P. "Intimations of Poetry in Practical Life." In *The Intellectual Legacy of Michael Oakeshott,* ed. Corey Abel and Timothy Fuller. Exeter: Imprint Academic, 2005.

Tolstoy, Leo. *What Is Art?* Trans. Aylmer Maude. London: Oxford University Press, 1929.

Tregenza, Ian. *Michael Oakeshott on Hobbes.* Exeter: Imprint Academic, 2003.

Voegelin, Eric. *Anamnesis.* Notre Dame: University of Notre Dame Press, 1978.

———. *The Ecumenic Age.* Baton Rouge: Louisiana State University Press, 1974.

———. *The New Science of Politics.* Chicago: University of Chicago Press, 1987.

———. *Science, Politics and Gnosticism.* Washington, DC: Regnery, 1997.

Walsh, David. *The Growth of the Liberal Soul.* Columbia, MO: University of Missouri Press, 1997.

Weber, Max. *The Protestant Ethic and the Spirit of Capitalism.* Trans. Stephen Kalberg. Los Angeles: Roxbury Publishing, 2002.

Winch, Peter. "The Nature of Meaningful Behavior." In *The Idea of a Social Science.* New York: Humanities Press, 1958.

Wolin, Sheldon. "The Politics of Self-Disclosure." *Political Theory* 4 (1976): 321–34.

Worthington, Glenn. "Michael Oakeshott and the City of God." *Political Theory* 28 (2000): 377–98.

———. "Michael Oakeshott on Life: Waiting with Godot." *History of Political Thought* 16 (1995): 105–19.

———. "Oakeshott's Claims of Politics." *Political Studies* 45 (1997): 727–38.

———. "Poetic Experience and the Good Life in the Writings of Michael Oakeshott." *European Journal of Political Theory* 4 (2005): 57–66.

———. "The Voice of Poetry in Oakeshott's Moral Philosophy." *Review of Politics* 64 (2002): 285–310.

Index

ity, 33, 34, 45, 69, 73, 96; poetry's connection to, 8, 11–12, 13, 96, 101, 103–4, 106, 110; poetry's differences from, 101, 104, 106, 109, 110; politics of faith distinguished from, 164–65; and practice, 9, 51, 58, 72, 73, 74, 75, 82–83, 91, 92–93, 96, 101, 106, 107, 155; and presentness, 17, 30, 46, 69, 70, 71–72, 73, 74, 91, 95–96, 106, 217; and Rationalism, 162–63, 223; reasons for existence of, 93–94; and reflection, 35; as sanction for morality, 80; and self-enactment, 93, 94, 119; and self-understanding, 35, 202, 227; of spirit, 86–87, 110; theology distinguished from, 225; and Tower of Babel story, 9–10, 11, 13, 97, 219, 225; and transience of human life, 23, 94–95; Voegelin on, 190

Religion, Politics and the Moral Life (Oakeshott), 5, 9, 222

"Religion, Politics and the Moral Life" (Oakeshott), 106

"Religion and the Moral Life" (Oakeshott): and connection between religion and morality, 80–81, 83; and escape from contingency, 73

"Religion and the World" (Oakeshott): and activities as ends in themselves, 29, 70; and aesthetics, 106; and Augustinian approach to character of religion and worldliness, 17, 21, 26–27, 29, 45, 164; and Augustinian choice, 22, 73, 223; Augustinian interpretations of, 24–25; and definitions of religion and world, 30–32; and ideal types, 22, 26, 176–77; and insight, 83; and presentness, 47, 67, 69–70, 72, 73, 95–96, 159–60; and religion and poetry, 13; and religion as part of spiritual world, 106; and religious conduct, 92–93; and religious man, 154; and two cities, 30, 33, 34

Religious collectivism, 170–71, 173

Republic (Plato), 5, 22

Riley, Patrick, 4, 8–9, 21

Romanticism, 220

Rorty, Richard, 2

Rule of law, 206, 207–9, 208n35

Sandoz, Ellis, 16

Santayana, George: as influence on

Oakeshott, 6, 120, 220; and life of the spirit, 8, 217; and limits of worldly life, 224; and poetic contemplation, 4, 111; and transcendent experience, 227; and worldliness, 23

Science: and conception of self, 54; as mode of human experience, 2, 48, 49, 50, 51, 52, 112; and philosophy, 159; place of, 158; poetry distinguished from, 109; practical life contrasted with, 56

Science, Politics and Gnosticism (Voegelin), 171, 192, 197

Search for power after power: and human experience, 25, 35, 37–39; poetry as removed from, 115. *See also* Practice/practical life

Self-contradiction, 78

Self-determination: and choice, 34; and civil association, 185, 186, 188; and human freedom, 29; and moral creativity, 35

Self-disclosure, 32–33, 76, 124

Self-enactment: and civil association, 13; definition of, 118n40; and human limitations, 218; and insight, 76, 84; and moral conduct approximating art, 119, 220; morality as, 70n45; and religion, 93, 94, 119; and self-sufficiency, 118, 119

Self-examination: and Oakeshott/Augustine compared, 43, 45, 46; and Rationalism, 193; and religion, 34; and self-understanding, 24; and will, 35

Self-government, 170

Self-realization: and communities, 77; and morality, 76; and religion, 45, 93

Self-understanding: of artist, 113; definition of, 68; and human freedom, 68, 222; and insight, 84; and liberal morality, 139; Oakeshott's concern with, 43, 46; and presentness, 68–69, 71; and religion, 35, 202, 227; and self-examination, 24; and self-realization, 76; and servile morality, 127, 128, 132–33, 134

Sense of time, 55, 104

Sensuality: dangers of, 9

Servile morality: characteristics of, 127; and ideals, 132, 134, 135, 136–37, 139,